praise for *Apes to Zebras to Nosey*

"Jean's voice shines through on every page, reminding us that the Fresno Chaffee Zoo is more than just a gathering of animals. It's a living, breathing testament to the power of love, laughter, and a commitment to making the world a better place."

—Jon Dohlin, CEO and Director, Fresno Chaffee Zoo

"Jean Chaffee's history of Fresno Chaffee Zoo is more than an account of how a world-class zoo began with an orphaned bear cub. It is the skillful chronology of how the missions of zoos have changed from cages to natural habitats. Doc Chaffee focused on educating visitors who could not travel to view animals living around the world."

—Joan Newcomb, author and teacher

Dr. Paul Chaffee with young friend.

Apes to Zebras to Nosey

One Hundred Years at the Fresno Chaffee Zoo

Jean Chaffee

Editorial and production services provided by
Linden Publishing, Fresno, CA.

ISBN 979-8-218-66852-5

Printed in the United States of America
on acid-free paper.

In memory of Molly Steinsapir, Doc Chaffee's
great-granddaughter, whose love for animals and the
planet embodied his spirit. Though her time was short, her
passion will forever inspire us. This book is dedicated to
Molly, whose heart lives on in every animal we care for.

Contents

Foreword

When Jean first approached me to write the foreword for this book on the history of her life at the Fresno Chaffee Zoo, I couldn't help but smile. Jean was one of the first people I met when I joined the zoo, and her warmth and sense of humor has helped guide me on numerous occasions. She has always had a way of weaving together discussions about whatever difficulty I faced in the moment with stories about the zoo's past that were equal parts heartwarming, hilarious, and insightful.

A typical conversation with Jean can be like reading one of her books for young readers—full of whimsy and laughter. Books like *Nosey the Elephant* and *Longo and His New Shoes*, with their playful narratives and endearing characters, brought to life the "story behind the story" of zoo life. *Bubbles, Bulgy, and Babies* and *Azak Learns to Read* were similarly endearing.

Jean's professional life is rooted in education—she dedicated twenty-eight years to teaching, believing in the power of knowledge to inspire young minds. Her delight in her students and her belief in the power of connection with animals informed and shaped her writing for children. Those books have long been sold in our gift shop and are a staple in homes and classrooms, but this book in your hands is different. It's a love letter to the zoo, to her late husband, Dr. Paul "Doc" Chaffee, who did so much to shape the zoo into a modern institution, and to the people and animals who made it such a wonderful place to work and to visit.

The Fresno Chaffee Zoo, as we know it today, is a testament to the people of Fresno and their deep love for the natural world. Doc, a dedicated veterinarian who became the zoo's first director in 1965, was a man of energy and vision. He believed in the power of education, of conservation, and community, and his work shaped not only the Fresno Chaffee Zoo but the entire zoo profession, helping today's zoos become conservation organizations, places where animals are well cared for in naturalistic exhibits and where families connect with nature and with each other.

In this book, Jean takes us on a journey through the history of the Fresno Chaffee Zoo, but it's also a journey through her own life. She shares anecdotes that will make you laugh, but she also reflects on the deeper moments—the births of baby animals, the triumphs of conservation efforts, and the sadness of saying goodbye to the animals and people we care for.

Jean's voice shines through on every page, reminding us that the Fresno Chaffee Zoo is more than just a gathering of animals. It's a living, breathing testament to the power of love, laughter, and a commitment to making the world a better place. As you read this book, you'll come to understand why the zoo continues to be a source of inspiration, connection, community, and conservation for each succeeding generation of visitors.

So, sit back, relax, and let Jean Chaffee take you on a journey through time. Like a heart-to-heart chat with an old friend, it's a journey filled with joy, laughter, and a few surprises—just like life itself.

—Jon Dohlin, CEO and Director, Fresno Chaffee Zoo

Early bear cage at the zoo, 1924.

Preface

This book is lovingly dedicated to Dr. Paul Stanley Chaffee, DVM. From the day we met, my life changed forever. His eyes sparkled with a love for life. They were soft with a twinge of his sly humor—never mean or hurtful, just knock-you-off-your-chair hilarious. He lived in this world but fantasized in a larger domain. His frequent travels to Africa enhanced his dreams, which he brought home to recreate. And he was the most handsome man I knew.

Through him, I saw how vital God's creatures are, from the tiniest ant to the massive elephant. Much as I hate the snails in my yard, I accepted that they must have a purpose. I listened and learned from the one who shared his passion with me. As a teacher by profession, he clarified my purpose to teach and care about this world, viewing it through a larger lens.

After we first met, "Doc" looked at me as a potential travel partner. I had traveled through Europe, one of those twenty-day, twenty-place trips. As a former military wife, I had spent three years in Puerto Rico exploring the nearby islands. But for a California girl, the Texas panhandle life of taking cover in cellars during sandstorms and tornados was an out-of-the-book experience.

In 1986, Doc put together an Africa trip and invited me to join the group. He included my tickets with his in the other passengers' costs. I nodded my agreement, but didn't give it much consideration. When Doc pushed me to get my shots, I realized this was for real.

I found myself in Africa that July, where night was day, summer was winter, and white was black. My life exploded as new doors opened to a different world. I was enchanted by all around me—the beautiful people and the unique animals grunting, chirping, or sniffing in their natural habitat. Colorful birds soared overhead. The thrill of a kill is sometimes hard to watch until one accepts it is part of the natural order.

Our daily jeep excursions led us to observe millions of gray, snorting wildebeest, with their short, curled horns, trotting along a worn-down path to new grasslands hundreds of miles away. The zebra's black and white stripes blended into a haze, making it impossible to identify an individual, their thick black tails swishing away the ever-present biting flies. Particularly beautiful were the sleek, tan gazelles, with erect, alert ears and distinctively arched horns. Occasionally, we spotted the camouflaged lions hunched down along the edges, eyeing the weakest ones for their dinner.

But one experience from that magical trip remains embedded in my memory. One morning in Zimbabwe, we stopped on a hill that overlooked a vast rangeland. Silence enveloped us. No airplanes, no vehicles, no power lines, no roads, nothing that indicated humans had invaded the land. I looked up and thought about how close we were to touching God.

I was hooked. My adventurous spirit had been ignited and I craved more. Doc patiently pointed out each species, explaining the order of each one's migration. I inhaled his knowledge, pinching myself, knowing how fortunate I was. This man who was revered in our community was sitting next to me, sharing his decades of knowledge.

Just before a three-week excursion to Australia, I informed him I had to cancel because we were not married. And I was uncomfortable with the others covering my costs. He was the leader; I was only a guest. Although not intending to put undue pressure on him, he took the hint and we were married on July 1, 1987, one week before the tour.

There was so much to learn: mammals, reptiles, and birds from around the world, including Africa, Australia, and South America. Each trip we took brought a wealth of new experiences. My brain was stimulated to the exploding point. That first year, I hung on to this man's every word, hardly letting anyone else get close to him.

In 1988, Doc taught a docent class to guide visitors through the rainforest exhibit's enclosed walk-though. We learned it was important to keep a watchful eye for iguanas, flying birds, and the small, colorful monkeys scurrying across the paths. We became a close-knit group known as the Rainforest Rangers.

Every Saturday, sitting quietly on the rainforest exhibit's benches, I would observe the birds' life cycles, from eggs to flight, learning to spot their differences. One memory persists, reminding me why we needed to keep watch. Standing on the overlook platform, I focused on a couple holding a pillowcase, seemingly intent on capturing the magnificent, doll-sized golden lion tamarin monkey. They finally left after realizing my eye was zeroed in on them and I was not going to let them get away with their heist.

My daughter, Lynette, joined our trip to Peru, Ecuador, and the Galapagos Islands. On the islands, we encountered animals found nowhere else in the world, like aquatic iguanas and Darwin's finches, on which he based his theory of biological evolution by natural selection. South America's natural beauty was artfully captured in the people's colorful clothes and pottery. Their bazaars displayed crafts alongside hanging llama meat, with flies occasionally sneaking a bite.

Doc was colorblind, only seeing tints of yellow and brown. His basic four-door sedan was painted yellow so that he could find it. Traffic lights were tricky; Doc learned to look for the darker red or darker green lights to stop or go. One time, he alerted us in the Galapagos Islands to look for a beautiful crimson bird. "What's that red bird sitting in the tree, I asked?" He recognized it only by shape, not by color.

When we first met, I had one request: that he attend church with me. He came from a basic Christmas/Easter church background. As a scientist, he had difficulty accepting and being accepted at church, and the first chapters of Genesis were a hill too high.

Fortunately Reverend Al VomSteeg, an outgoing, forty-year-old former missionary to Brazil, immediately connected with Doc. The two often met at the zoo, where the vet was most comfortable. How I wanted to be a little mouse, listening in on their conversations as they walked and talked. Given Doc's difficulty in accepting the idea of creation in seven days, the pastor worried he might reject the entire Bible. Finally, he told Doc to turn the page; the answers would come when he met God. With that, the zoo man relaxed and his heart opened, ready to learn. In typical Doc fashion, he dug into his study with intensity, peppering me with questions about my faith. It was a great time, and we both grew in understanding. He even taught a Sunday school class on evolution!

On May 30, 1990, Paul was diagnosed with malignant melanoma. We left the doctor's office with the dreadful news to meet with the summer Africa travel group. I hid in the back room, tears flowing, as he delivered the devastating news that he could not lead the trip.

In July, the Zoo Society, Rotary Club, and the City of Fresno voted to rename the zoo after Dr. Paul Chaffee. His long-time colleagues flew in from across the country to honor and bid farewell to their dear friend, the former Association of Zoos and Aquariums (AZA) national president. He was in the hospital on the renaming day, but his doctor accompanied him so he could share in the recognition. He passed away on October 20, 1990.

Paul Chaffee gave me so much in those few years we had together. I often worried about what I had given in exchange until I realized we would be rejoined again through his newfound faith. His friends commented that the "good" man had become a "better" man.

Five years, of which six months were spent ill, were not enough time to learn everything about him. He was revered among his peers and had accomplished so much. Nationally, he implemented significant changes in zoo care through the AZA. He passed away at just sixty-two years old, plans still dancing in his head to upgrade the zoo's many remaining outdated enclosures into more natural spaces. Today, he would be proud to see how the zoo has progressed beyond his wildest dreams.

I started researching his life in 1997, taking a leave of absence from my teaching. I never returned to work, focusing on the interviewing, researching, and writing that covered the zoo's history and Doc's involvement. My friend, Lorraine LoStracco, and I spent a gratifying five years putting the stories together.

From those stories, I published seven children's books in collaboration with Ernie Hergenroeder, the books' illustrator: *Nosey the Elephant*; *Moja the Lion*; *Bubbles, Bulgy, and Babies*; *Azak Learns to Read*; *Longo's New Shoes*; *Nosey's Big Move*; and *Bosco the Wild One*.

This book spans 100 years of the Fresno Chaffee Zoo. I credit the man for whom the zoo is named, Dr. Paul Stanley Chaffee, for sharing his passion with me and many thousands of others who have enjoyed the zoo and his teachings. I hold his memory whenever I walk the zoo grounds, appreciating how he influenced my life and initiated the changes that came to fruition after his time.

Doc Chaffee and his assistant, Perry Alexander, rescue injured birds, who are released back into the wild if they can survive.

A Nutshell Timeline of the Fresno Chaffee Zoo

1880s: Frederick Roeding came to the San Joaquin Valley with a group of 8 German investors. Together they purchased 80,000 acres.

By 1903 Frederick purchased 7,000 acres. The homestead was on East Belmont, where they built a nursery. The nursery supplied hundreds of trees to create a park on the West Belmont property.

1908: The trees attracted hundreds of birds, which Roeding's son George loved. He built an aviary to educate newcomers on the bird life that surrounded them. He set aside 5 acres, as he envisioned a small zoo for the local wildlife. Sierra Light and Power brought two grizzly bear cubs abandoned in Sequoia National Park as the first animals in the zoo.

1920: Clarence Large, Superintendent of Parks, had a vision for a formal zoo. As director, he moved into the log cabin house surrounded by tall, swaying eucalyptus tress and hundreds of birds occupying the park. Local animals were common sights from his front porch. Peter Rasmusen, a forester, turned Roeding Park into a focal point of pride throughout the valley.

In the **1920s**, Mayor Z. S. Leymel loved the zoo and took home a lion cub to raise. Henry Nelson and A. A. Boyer were the first zookeepers. Sam Gilloon, with Fish and Game, set out to improve the zoo. William R. Holmes was appointed to the city board in charge of the zoo. Bears, local wild cats, hoof stock, and birds were added to the zoo and housed in log cabin-type exhibits. The collection soon grew to more than sixty animals. Unwanted pets purchased from catalogues found a welcome home at the zoo, including an undernourished monkey. An alligator stowed in a cigar box made its way from Florida to the zoo.

1922: Mr. and Mrs. A. V. Lisenby donated a grandstand for musical programs

1929: The American Association of Zoological Parks and Aquariums (AAZPA; now AZA) officially recognized the Roeding Park Zoo. The zoo collection now featured 80 mammals.

1932: the Fresno Lion's Club donated two lion cubs.

1936: The zoo grew with the addition of four lion cubs. The WPA (Works Progress Administration) built a cat barn with eight chain-link runs.

1943: The zoo's population was 6 lions, 2 cougars, 3 aoudads, 3 wolves, 6 Nilgai antelopes, 1 pronghorn antelope, 2 bison, 4 deer, 5 European red stags, 2 zebu, 1 elk, 3 Nubian ostriches, 2 bears, 3 foxes, 2 bobcats, 3 alligators, 2 peccaries, 8 monkeys, 2 coatimundis, 4 porcupines, 2 raccoons, 10 desert turtles, 8 snapping turtles and terrapins, 1 Gila monster, 2 gophers, 2 rattlesnakes, and oodles of birds. It took a lot of food. Every month the animals required one ton of rolled barley, 2 tons of alfalfa hay, 4-5 horses for meat, plus the pounds of peanuts fed by visitors.

1947: Eldon "Curley" Blocker was brought over from the San Diego Zoo and served as the Fresno Zoo's first foreman. Curley used his connections to add an elephant to the collection.

1949: The Fresno Rotary Club and the Fresno Lions Club, with assistance from the donations from thousands of school children, purchased Nosey the elephant. The *Fresno Bee* held a "Name the Elephant" contest in anticipation of the new arrival. On September 10, 1949, a colorful "49ers Days" rodeo parade introduced Nosey, the young elephant.

In the **1950s**, the Fresno Zoological Society was formed from $1200 left over from the Nosey campaign. The Zoo Society's purpose was to support the zoo by raising funds for improvements and by creating interest in the zoo. The first exhibit they built, Monkey Island, came complete with an indoor den and a water moat. The sea lion, camel, sun bear, hippopotamus, giraffe, assorted birds, and flamingo exhibits were also completed during this decade.

1957: The Roeding Park Zoo became an institutional member of the American Association of Zoological Parks and Aquariums.

1960s: Veterinarian Dr. Paul Chaffee was hired in 1963. The Zoo Society funded walk-through aviary, ape grotto, and rhinoceros exhibits. The Bronx Zoo donated three pairs of crocodiles.

1963: The zoo charged twenty-five cents for admission. The Fresno City Council adopted a Parks Admission Zoo (Trust) Fund to fund future capital improvements.

1965: Dr. Paul Chaffee was hired as the first director of the Roeding Park Zoo (while maintaining his veterinarian role). Responsibility for zoo management shifted from the Zoological Society to the Zoo Director. Dr. Chaffee added nutrition, quarantine, treatment, and education programs to meet the medical standards of zoos at the time.

1970s: The Education Coordinator oversaw the zoo's mobile school presentation service and developed other educational programs. The Curator of Education became the Director of Education. In 1971, the present docent program, Zoolynx, was initiated.

In the **mid-1970s,** the zoo grew by another one-third, creating a new bison and tule elk exhibit complex. For the 1976 bicentennial, the grizzly bear exhibit was enlarged, the sea lion exhibit renovated, and swan lake, the concession stands, and the restrooms were remodeled. The Fresno Zoo Master Plan was updated.

1978: The Park Zoo (Trust) Fund utilized revenue from the concession stand for zoo improvements.

1979: The Edward A. Kane Reptile House, built for $633,000, was recognized as the first computer-controlled reptile exhibit in the world.

1980s: The price of admission to the zoo increased. A new zoo entrance was completed, and a $100,000 Clement Renzi statue was placed in the plant area by the entrance. The Galapagos tortoise and the giraffe and antelope slanted dry moat exhibits were introduced, and improvements were made to the sea lion pool.

1980: The eight narrow lion and tiger runs were combined into two larger runs, with dirt, rocks, and water.

1981: Arbor Way was constructed to shade the south end of the zoo; the hippo display was remodeled.

1982: Nosey the elephant was moved to a modern dirt exhibit with a waterfall, pool, and interior night quarters secured by remote controlled hydraulic doors. The cost was $950,000. Two female and one male elephant joined her. It had been 33 years since she had seen another of her species.

The **mid-1980s** saw the renovation of the flamingo exhibit in 1982, the lemur island exhibit in 1983, the zoo entry walkway's lighting and landscaping in 1983, wolf woods in 1984, and the scimitar horned oryx exhibit in 1984. In 1984, Drs. Falk, long-time devoted supporters of the zoo, donated the funds to establish the Doris and Karl Falk Wildlife Education Center. This building became the backbone of the educational department at the zoo. In 1989, the Falks again donated funding for a large classroom addition to this facility, including office space for the growing Fresno Zoological Society.

The Zoo Society raised funds for zoo improvements through its membership program; managed an "adopt an animal" program; and held special events such as Breakfast with the Animals, Safari Night, Singles' Night, and Christmas at the Zoo.

1980s: The exhibits for the antelope, giraffe, camels, llamas, and zebras were remodeled, and chain link cages were removed to make room for newer exhibits. The first mixed exhibit with tule elk/kit fox. The Education Building increased by 2000 square feet.

1985–88: The name of the Roeding Park Zoo was changed to the Fresno Zoo. The Small Wonders petting zoo exhibit opened. The walk-through tropical rainforest exhibit opened.

1990: Longtime zoo director Dr. Paul S. Chaffee passed away. The Fresno Zoo was renamed the Chaffee Zoological Gardens of Fresno in his honor. It became more commonly known as the Chaffee Zoo. Also that year, Nosey the elephant's former barn was converted to a gift shop called Nosey's Treasure Trunk, and the sea lion exhibit was remodeled. The zoo entrance was moved to across from Rotary Playland and Storyland.

1991: Ralph Waterhouse was hired as the new zoo director. His previous experience included directing the renovation of two municipal zoos and holding the chairmanship of the American Zoo and Aquarium's Accreditation Commission. The zoo's budget transferred from the City of Fresno's general fund into a Zoo Enterprise Fund in anticipation of the "privatization" of the zoo. All zoo revenue went for operations. Capital improvements funding came from the Fresno Zoo Society.

1992: A new fenced area encompassed the amphitheater, the Falk Education Building, and the Zoo Society's office, creating a new special events and fund-raising location for the zoo. The zoo now encompassed 18 acres. Ross Laird's Winged Wonders Bird Show began its presentations in the amphitheater. The Zoo hired a full-time veterinarian. The former zoo nursery was converted into a small animal clinic. The zoo's administration office moved into the former Parks Division office building outside the zoo.

1993: Nosey the elephant passed away at the age of 47.

1993–94: The zoo's Education Department hired an education specialist and a natural historian. Visitors could now ride on a camel; a new giraffe barn was completed and the hoofstock exhibit expanded. The chimpanzee and grizzly bear exhibits were enlarged and improved, the concession stand remodeled, an Australian walk-through aviary was constructed, the zoo's animal commissary was remodeled, and a toucan exhibit was added to the tropical rainforest.

From **1996–2000**, the Education Center expanded to include a multimedia laboratory with computers and up-to-date audio-visual equipment. The Jungle Bungalow provided space for birthday parties in the zoo.

1996: The Zoo Master Plan was adopted. Construction began on a new hospital near the south end of the zoo that would include up-to-date equipment, a quarantine section, a sterile surgery, housing for sick animals, and a separate necropsy room.

1998–99: The Safari Trading Gift Shop and the Chaffee Memorial Zoo Hospital were completed; the concession stand was renovated, as were the dromedary camel, addax, bison, chimpanzee, and wolf woods exhibits.

During the **2000s,** The north duck pond, kookaburra, grizzly bear, and lesser spot-nosed guenon exhibits were renovated. In **2001,** the Sunda Forest area, featuring orangutan, siamang, and tiger exhibits, was opened. The African veldt giraffe, antelope, serval, fennec fox, prairie dog, leopard, keel-billed toucan, peccary, and bird-of prey exhibits were renovated. In **2002,** the wart hog and red ruffed lemur exhibits were remodeled. The food storage barn was enlarged, and a hand-wash station and a hay storage barn were added to the Small Wonders exhibit. In **2003,** the anteater, alligator, and sarus crane exhibits were renovated. Restrooms were constructed at the entrance.

2003: Director Ralph Waterhouse retired. A 10-year girl named Angel Arellano sent a picture drawing of animals to the *Fresno Bee*, expressing her support for the zoo. Her letter brought an emotional response across the country. Kids sent $1 donations in envelopes. That effort, with support from local corporation Pelco, along with years of working toward privatization, culminated in Measure Z, which appeared on the ballot in **November 2004.** The measure called for a Fresno County tax of one-tenth of one percent, or one dime out of every $100 spent, on retail transactions. Two-thirds of proceeds were to go to capital improvements for the zoo, and one-third to operations. Measure Z passed with 73 percent approval. The zoo started receiving Measure Z funds on **April 1, 2005.**

The Fresno County Zoo Authority, a public agency, oversees the financial administration of Measure Z. It's seven-member board includes six qualified electors (Fresno County voters) appointed by the Fresno County Board of Supervisors, plus the Mayor of Fresno.

January 1, 2006: The nonprofit Fresno Chaffee Zoo Corporation took over control of Chaffee Zoo from the City of Fresno. The name of the zoo changed to Fresno Chaffee Zoo.

May 2006: Lewis Greene was named interim CEO/Director. The Zoo Society disbanded.

July 2007: The zoo released a Facility Master Plan as the road map for future zoo development.

May 2009: Scott Barton was named CEO/Director of Fresno Chaffee Zoo. Scott is a Fresno native, formerly a Chaffee Zoo intern and zookeeper.

2012: Fresno Chaffee Zoo opened Sea Lion Cove.

2014: Measure Z was approved again, which enabled the zoo to provide excellent animal care, upgrade existing exhibits, establish new exhibits, and provide educational and conservation opportunities for families throughout Fresno County and to all who visit Fresno Chaffee Zoo.

2015: African Adventure opened, offering a state-of-the-art home for a pride of lions, and a large expanse housing a family herd of African elephants, cheetahs, white rhinos, and a giraffe feeding station. Columbus Zoo's Jack Hanna attended the opening. The size of the zoo grew to 39 acres.

2020: Jon Forrest Dohlin was named Zoo Director. Both a biologist and an architect by training, Dohlin previously worked for the Wildlife Conservation Society (WCS) at the Bronx Zoo as an exhibit designer and in construction management before becoming the director of the WCS New York Aquarium in 2008.

2022: Measure Z reapproved for an additional fourteen years. Ross Laird retired.

2023: Kingdoms of Asia opened.

CHAPTER 1

Frederick and George Roeding, Pioneers

Frederick Roeding (1824–1908) came from Hamburg, Germany, where he received his education in business and banking. He cast a striking figure with his straight German posture and alluring blue eyes, hinting at a profound, bold spirit. At 17, he left his home to catch a ship sailing for South America, but the lure of gold pulled him north to join the California Gold Rush. However, Frederick soon discovered that the rough life of a gold miner and brutal winters were not his calling, so he joined a financial business firm in the Bay Area.

In 1861, California merchants founded the Central Pacific Railroad Company, extending it from Sacramento into the Central Valley to expand their investment opportunities. Seven years later, Roeding joined a group of eight businessmen traveling to inspect the new area of development. They packed their outdoor work clothes and supplies for the long term, unsure of what to expect. When the newly dispatched train reached the San Joaquin River, they boarded a ferry to cross the half-mile-wide river to Herndon Landing. There, ships from Stockton delivered supplies to a barge headed for Fort Miller.

The men looked over a stretch of land and scanned the horizon as far as their eyes could see. Valley oaks and white ash were the only visible plant life; tumbleweeds blew across the windy plain.

Roeding's anticipation intensified as he skimmed the skyline. White frosting dribbled down the sides of the snowcapped mountains; it felt close enough to swipe a finger. Billowing cotton balls hung in the skies; vultures swooped through the unblemished azure sky, surveying the dry, dusty plains which abounded with coyotes and gophers. Then, finally, a location offering the perfect spot summoned them to unpack and stay. These resourceful men saw the untilled land not as dirt but as a golden domain for future growth.

The partnership purchased 80,000 acres between the San Joaquin and Kings Rivers. Roeding's portion was 7,040 acres. His holdings comprised eight parcels east of Fresno and three northwest of the new town.

In 1883, Frederick opened Fancher Creek Nursery at Belmont and Fowler to supply trees and plants for the greening of the Central Valley. His son, George (1868–1928), held no interest in attending college. Frederick made a deal with him. He would not have to attend college if the nursery turned a profit that year. It did.

The father-son team planted 3,700 trees in the Fresno area, forming a more livable space from the original desert-like plains where families could survive the hot summers. The federal government waived the import ban on foreign trees for three years to assess which trees could best survive Fresno's summers. As a result, he received 300 trees from around the world, which he planted in clusters of three. Birds flocked to this newly formed forest, chirping and singing as they flittered about, searching for the right branch to make their nest. George spent many mornings wandering in the groves, eavesdropping on their conversations. What were they talking about, he wondered. Excited to share this concert of nature, George built an aviary to display the varied species inhabiting the trees.

In 1903, workers in the nearby mountains found two fuzzy, shivering grizzly bear cubs and wondered what to do with them. Ah, they thought, the wooded park in Fresno would be perfect. George accepted them and dug a temporary pit for their safekeeping. Roeding's wooded space soon became a collection point for orphaned and unwanted critters. Although haphazard, the collection eventually evolved into a local zoo inside his park, located between Olive and Belmont and between the railroad tracks and Highway 99.

Fresno's city leaders realized that an inviting site for picnics and relaxation was essential to encourage new families to the area. Frederick was asked to donate 160 to 240 acres of green space, but first he was adamant that the city budget $3500 annually to maintain his plantings. At the time, Fresno was struggling with a recession and rejected the offer. Six years later, in 1903, Roeding agreed to donate 72 acres in exchange for an annual maintenance budget of $3000. After Frederick died in 1908, his son, George, took over the park's development, donating more land over the next twenty years. Finally, the city purchased the last 39 acres from the Roedings in 1924 for a total holding of 165 acres.

The city of Fresno hired Clarence Large as park manager in 1920. To accommodate his ability to oversee the 165 acres, he built a home for his family using logs from the park. It was small but had a kitchen, two bedrooms, and a fireplace, and sat on the edge of the property. The quaint building's porch opened to a variety of trees that changed with the seasons. The family awoke to a symphony of birds and squirrels barking over a fallen oak. On occasion, a lone mountain lion poked his head among the trees but never bothered them.

George Roeding.

Over the next century, the log cabin has been lived in by various zookeepers, and Dr. Paul Chaffee used it as his office. Later it turned into a staff room, and presently it houses the zoo's security office.

In 1922, the A. V. Lisenby family donated an amphitheater to better enjoy concerts at Roeding Park. The covered bandstand played to a crowd seated on benches that ascended six levels. The mounded dirt elevated the rows, so everyone had a perfect view. It was a beautiful way to spend an afternoon, and rolling down the mound was a kid's favorite thing to do. Sundays at the park became a summer family ritual. After attending church, families would pack picnic boxes and drive to Roeding Park. While the parents enjoyed the concerts, kids played baseball, rode bikes, or fed the animals at the zoo. In 1923, the small zoo, managed by John Meredith, included ducks, turtles, pheasants, Billy the deer, one Himalayan rabbit, Uncle Bim the ostrich, Billy the prairie dog, a porcupine, a peacock, a mother and baby monkey, mountain lions, bobcats, and seven bears.

In 1929, the American Association of Zoos and Aquariums awarded its Accreditation Certificate to Roeding Park Zoo. The zoo met the standards for animal care and living conditions, which allowed it to add endangered animals to its collections. Fresno Chaffee Zoo will soon celebrate its 100-year anniversary as an accredited zoo.

Ostrich yard at the zoo, 1924.

4

CHAPTER 2

The Big Cats of
the Early Zoo

B ig cats are historically one of the most popular attractions at any zoo. Fresno was no exception. As early as 1915, Roeding Park exhibited locally trapped North American mountain lions, bobcats, and wolves. Log barn structures functioned as their housing. The barns had chain link fencing outside to provide access to fresh air and to engage with the visitors.

When A. A. Boyer became the zoo's first superintendent in 1930, he called on his contacts to support the zoo. Fresno's Lions Club responded by donating two female lion cubs. Boyer added an additional enclosure, which required reinforced steel bar doors for the lion cubs.

Two years later, an unforgettable flamboyant character, Johnny Vaughn, passed through Fresno. Vaughn, a circus performer and lion tamer, traveled from Vancouver to Mexico as Gilmore Oil's advertising agent. His "Roar with Gilmore" created a spectacle that brought out the townspeople. He waved and tooted his horn as he drove through town in his shiny, black Mercedes. With tear-drop-shaped fenders, prominent headlights, and the convertible top down, the roadster pulled a shiny chromium-plated chariot that reflected the sun's rays onto the streets. He tipped his black top hat to the gawkers on the sides of the streets, urging them to follow him. Vaughn inched his way to the Red Lion sign at the Gilmore

Gas Station, and the crowd followed behind him like children after the Pied Piper.

When he reached his destination, the circus lion trainer stepped out of his vehicle and snapped his whip with a flourish. "Dapper Dan," as he was known, commanded attention, dressed in his full circus attire, sporting calf-high black boots, spit-polished to a mirror's reflection, with braided ribbons on each shoulder, tails, a black shirt with three black buttons to hold it all together. He was indeed one to capture attention in his flamboyant regalia.

Strutting to the chariot, Vaughn opened the doors, revealing two five-month-old male lion cubs, weighing 125 pounds each. Tawny-spotted Lion and Red Lion, with white-tipped ears and black-tipped tails, let out baby roars, winning over the ogling crowd. The cubs rolled around, pawing at each other, and stared at the crowd like seasoned entertainers. Kids of all ages lined up to meet Johnny Vaughn and his lion cubs.

Bob Daniel, Zoo Society President from 1963–64, recalls the day that Vaughn arrived in town with his famous lions. The Mercedes roadster made such an impression on the young Daniel that he eventually strove to own one for himself.

While on the road, Vaughn and the cubs spent the nights in some of the Pacific Coast's finest hotels. Driving around the Central Valley, he spotted the exclusive nine-story Hotel Fresno and booked a double suite room on the seventh floor. Taking the back stairs, he quietly led his companions to room 734. The exquisite French and Italian motifs of the wood-paneled room suited the lion tamer's elegant tastes. After removing his boots and top hat, he placed his topcoat in the closet, poured some water from the silver server, and settled on the bed for a moment of relaxation. The cubs, grateful to be out of their cage, rested nearby on the rose-colored rug. Alas, Vaughn had barely closed his eye when he heard scratching on the wood doors.

Kids being kids, or in this case, playful lion cubs, the pair managed to lock themselves into the bathroom. No matter what tasty delights he used to entice them, Vaughn could not get them to open the door. He had no alternative but to call the manager for help, who did not find the situation amusing. Once released from inside the bathroom, the manager pointed to the door and ordered them out. Grabbing his clothes and his cubs, he hastened down the back steps. The three shared the night cooped up in the chariot with nowhere else to stay.

The following day, Vaughn met Boyer at the zoo, who offered to overnight the cubs while he was in town. In appreciation, Vaughn agreed to donate the pair to Boyer on his return trip. Since the zoo already had two female cubs, this worked out perfectly. On his return four months later, Vaughn bid farewell to his pets, Red Lion and Lion, now nine months old. Boyer welcomed them into the new log cabin quarters he had prepared for them. In 1936, the zoo received a Work Project Administration grant to construct a much-needed cat barn, giving the two breeding pairs more room for their growing offspring and letting the public peek into their "private" area.

The mighty cats—especially the lions—draw large crowds to this day. Some secretly hope for a special thrill from these savage beasts as they marvel at the cats' piercing fangs and gape into their cavernous mouths. Others stand in awe of the muscular animals' commanding gait, unique feline musk, and formidable energy. And whenever the King of the Jungle releases its thunderous roar, sending delighted chills down the spectators' spines, the spirit of "Roar with Gilmore" rises again.

Over the following three years, the WPA funded eight outdoor runways, four on the north side of a connecting hallway and four on the south. The hallway was wide enough for a 1930s pickup delivery truck. For safety's sake, each side of the barn had four rows of security fencing, with a walkway for the caretakers extending from end to end. Glass doors allowed the workers to peek inside each section before unlocking the gate.

When the eight sections of the barn were completed, the exhibit featured a variety of captured cats, including leopards,

Scene from the cat barn.

cheetahs, lions, and tigers. California bobcats and mountain lions/pumas were also on display. The wild felines, identifiable by their spots, teardrop lines, stripes, or tawny manes— some with blue eyes, some with yellow or black eyes—paced their quarters while a powerful musky scent permeated the air. Their tails, raised, swaying, or drooped, hinted at their moods. Their personalities were expressed with a hiss, growl, snarl, bark, or roar. Visitors studied the differences and came to identify individual cats by their sounds and patterns. On weekends, thousands poured into the zoo to see the King of the Beasts and the other big cats face to face.

Safety for the workers was a priority. A rope pulley operated a sliding door between the animals' bedrooms and the outside. Henry Nelson, zoo caretaker, opened the doors to let the cats outside every morning. They were then closed to let the crew hose and sweep the bedrooms. In the evening, he reversed the procedure. The dividing door opened and the animals returned to their bedrooms for dinner. Once everything was secure and the doors closed, the staff exited through an outside locked gate. Despite the keepers' proximity to the big cats, there is no record of any injuries.

Nelson's uniform consisted of black pants, a long-sleeved shirt, and a tie. Although he had little background in animal care, he loved working with the animals and learned how to properly feed, train, and care for his big cats while on the job.

The middle-aged man walked the hall every day, talking to his wild beast charges. He noticed their differences and similarities, which ones responded to him and which ones ignored him. Using the tactics that worked with his domestic cats, Nelson kept a handful of treats in his large hands and passed them out to reward desired behaviors. Henry loved feeding time for the big cats. Like most keepers, he thrived on the rush of being in control of these muscular carnivores. Henry appealed to their natural predatory instincts by waving delectable bones before them as he strode up and down the walkway.

Experienced visitors planned their zoo tours around feeding schedules and headed straight for the cat barn to stake out a prime spot for viewing. The glass doors let visitors peek inside and get close enough to feel the cats' energy.

One fortuitous Sunday in 1943, Nelson opened the flap at the base of a door to toss a bone to an eagerly awaiting leopard. Unfortunately, the bone was bigger than usual. It wouldn't fit. He then tried kicking the bone through the flap but it jammed. Not wanting to disappoint the eager crowd, he carefully opened the glass door just enough to toss the bone to the other side of the enclosure. He was confident the hungry leopard would chase the bone, giving him time to slam the door shut.

Regrettably, Henry's presumption was wrong. When he opened the door, the leopard took advantage of the opportunity to escape. The sleek, powerful cat leaped upward, shattered the glass panel, and shoved past Henry's feet into the corridor. Stuck, the spotted beast found himself caught in the keepers' walkway. The seven-foot-high chain link fence separated the petrified onlookers from the equally frightened leopard. Nelson dashed to the back door and around to the visitors, instructing them to quietly slip out for help. Once he knew they were safe, he locked the outside doors, securing the leopard inside.

Superintendent Clarence Large grabbed a couple of heavy hoses and sped back to check on Nelson. By then, the confused leopard had crawled onto the top of the roof with its heavy wire overlay, where the frightened animal snarled and pawed, watching their every movement. The two men stood on opposite sides, spraying him with water. The cat tumbled off the roof onto the concrete floor. The dazed leopard escaped by crawling through the cage door. Nelson raced to slam it shut, locked it, and heaved an enormous sigh of relief. Fortunately, everyone, including the cat, escaped a tragic ending.

Shortly after his near-death experience, Nelson became the foster parent of the first lion cub born at the zoo. He proudly announced the exciting news when Gilmore and Betsy gave birth to the first of three. Unfortunately, Betsy, who had no mentoring from her mother, rejected her tiny cub after just one month. Henry wrapped the little creature in a warm blanket and took the infant Leona home. He and his wife played nursemaid and fed her powdered milk every two hours around the clock. After three months, little Leona was strong enough to survive on her own and returned to her world in the cat barn.

Although magnificent creatures can be hazardous, working with them provides immeasurable thrills. Even the most toughened keeper falls victim to those tender, soft eyes. Holding a tiny, defenseless tiger or playing with a lion cub brings unequaled ecstasy. However, the massive feet on the ends of their short legs reminds one that roughhousing is perilous.

CHAPTER 3

Curley Hits Town

World War II was over, and people were eager to start their lives anew. Downtown Fresno bustled once again. Excitement filled the air as Gottschalk's, J.C. Penney, and Roos Atkins hummed with shoppers. In the middle of this, a high-spirited personality burst into town, Curley Blocker. No one could have guessed how this one man could rally the Fresno community into a single focus.

Pulling Curley Blocker away from the San Diego Zoo in 1947 was a big achievement for the Fresno Parks Department. An experienced zookeeper, he had many contacts in the zoo world, and his colorful resume included safari game hunter, tracker, and circus animal trainer. Curley was the first experienced wild animal keeper to take over the zoo, and his personality was as colorful as his resume.

In mid-1949, Curley learned from his close relationship with San Diego Zoo director Belle Benchley that a shipment of elephants would soon leave Thailand. It would be the last chance to get an elephant for the Roeding Park Zoo from Thailand because of a recent law that halted any further shipments out of the country. As a circus trainer, he had worked with Asian elephants and loved them.

The shipment of elephants would arrive in the middle of July, giving Curley only six weeks to raise sufficient money to acquire one. According to *The Fresno Bee*, an elephant would cost $3,750 and would require minimum upkeep of 40 pounds of oat hay daily.

Curley hit the circuit of local service organizations. In June of 1949, the Fresno YMCA Men's Club agreed to lead the drive to get an elephant for the zoo. The Rotary Club and Kiwanis also put their efforts into fundraising. Soon after that, the word *elephant* seemed to fill every conversation in town.

Nosey (not yet so-named), born in 1946, was about to board a ship with twelve other young elephants headed for America. She had lived her first three years surrounded by a family of aunts and cousins. Nosey's mother belonged to a herd of working elephants, who spent their days transporting heavy loads, such as logs, from the forests. Nosey walked alongside her mother as she worked; the *mahouts* taught her simple commands and certain expectations of discipline.

The term *mahout* in Hindi means elephant keeper. The *mahout* and elephant bond, one of the oldest and most complex human-animal relationships, dates back 4,500 years. *Mahouts* owned their elephants, which would provide a livelihood for a family for generations. Deep relationships developed between *mahouts* and their elephants based on decades of cooperation, training, and trust-building. They live with their elephants twenty-four hours a day, and are responsible for their care, training, and work details. After centuries of following this tradition, the Asian elephants became domesticated, much like our horses.

For the first three to five years, most elephant calves depend on their mothers for their nutrition, hygiene, health, and security. Forced weaning disrupts a calf's natural development and can result in emotional trauma that can plague the elephant for the remainder of his or her life.

Nosey joined the line of the twelve other three-year-olds as they prepared to board the ship. These protected youngsters were about to experience separation from their nurturing herd, while being chained in the hold of a ship with no light or fresh air. An animal caretaker fed, watered, and cleaned up after the elephants during their month and a half aboard the ship.

On the voyage across the Pacific, the ship ran into a series of typhoons. One violent storm tossed the frightened calves all about the bottom of the ship. Their terrified screams filled the air, rising above the eerie sounds of the wind and rain. When the storms finally subsided and the ship pulled into Port Angeles in July, only five elephants remained. Those five were sent to the Thousand Oaks, California, Wild Animal Holding Ranch for a month of quarantine before they were released. All found homes in zoos except for the one destined for Fresno. Curley had claimed one of the elephants, but he did not yet have the $3,750 to pay for her. So Goebel and Ruhe, owners of the Wild Animal Holding Ranch, promised to hold the elephant for a few more months.

The Fresno Bee joined the urgent campaign. They printed "Support the Elephant" coupons to encourage people to become involved. Elephant fever raced throughout the Valley. Once word got out among the schoolchildren, they jumped on the fundraising wagon, becoming the driving force behind the ultimately successful effort to bring the elephant to the zoo. Youngsters all over the Valley delivered their pennies and dimes in jars. People remember, with great satisfaction, being a part of this community effort.

The Fresno Bee stepped up its coverage of elephant stories. An imaginary interview had the lonely elephant pleading with readers to hurry. Her best friends had a home, and she wanted one too. As the fund neared $3,000, Blocker contacted Lutz Ruhe and arranged to bring the elephant to Fresno. Every day, boxes and jars of money flowed in from stores and local people. With all the enthusiasm around the Valley, the promoters felt certain about bringing in the remaining $750. The children caught the vision and led the way; the adults followed. The time between the idea's origin and the elephant's arrival was less than three months!

The week before Nosey's big arrival, Mayor Gordon Dunn and the Fresno City Council added to the excitement by holding an elephant baby shower. Their gifts included two bales of hay, a bale of straw, a bucket, and a broom. In addition, major donors Harry

White and Frank and Roxie Moradian gathered several pounds of peanuts for the big Fresno welcome.

A naming contest produced such suggestions as Trumpeter, Ellafawn, Onserf (Fresno backward), Jolly, and Jumboette. After reading hundreds of suggestions, the name Nosey won the hearts of the promoters. Rosalene Swanson, 13, of East Orosi, submitted the winning name.

The city was on alert for the arrival of its very own elephant.

Young Nosey the elephant.

CHAPTER 4

Nosey Trumpets
Her Arrival

As mentioned in the previous chapter, zookeeper Curley Blocker was making arrangements and raising money to bring an elephant to Fresno. In the meanwhile, Nosey resided under the care of the trusted animal trainers who owned and managed the Thousand Oaks' Wild Animal Holding Ranch in Ventura County. This wonderful place was home to Leo the Lion of MGM Pictures fame, Mr. Ed the talking horse, Bimbo, the elephant from the television program *Circus Boy*, and Tamba, the chimpanzee from the *Tarzan* films. Nosey spent three months at the ranch, recovering after the long boat ride from Thailand. Her four surviving elephant friends had already left for other zoos, and only Nosey remained. She learned some English commands during her stay at the ranch.

The big September day that the townspeople of Fresno had waited so long for finally arrived. The hot summer days had finally faded away, but it was still warm, although with a slight chill in the air. The trees were turning red and yellow, enveloping the city with a blanket of color as their leaves floated to the ground. School had begun, and the great Fresno Fair had come to town.

Curley got up before daybreak on Saturday, September 10, 1949, and drove to Thousand Oaks' Wild Animal Holding Ranch. He delivered the remaining payment and headed for the barn to bring home his long-awaited prize. At three years old, Nosey was still just a baby, and at four feet four inches, she fit under his armpit. Happily, she appeared healthy, alert, and filled out.

He had only a short time to get to know her before they hit the road back to Fresno. Hauling his trailer over the Grapevine Mountains with a 2,400-pound load added quite an extra strain to his black 1940s Ford truck. Curley worried it would overheat and he would be stuck on the side of the road, cooling down his engine. Driving the speed limit of fifty-five miles per hour, but with one eye on his watch, they arrived in downtown Fresno with just enough time to prepare the star attraction.

People lined the streets, eagerly awaiting the start of the '49er Police Rodeo Parade. The organizers had blocked off a section for Curley to bring his truck and trailer to the parade's start. Reaching into his reserve of behavior techniques, he had to quickly build the trust between himself and his animal. The zookeeper patted her gray head and whispered in her floppy ear, easing her stress to calm her down. Sticking his hand into his pocket, Blocker pulled out his ever-ready supply of treats and prepared to back the tired youngster out of the trailer. Her agile trunk searched his pockets for more goodies.

Even with a long and arduous day already under his belt, his most significant challenge—unveiling Nosey to the excited public—still awaited the former circus trainer. Nothing in the bilingual, international traveling pachyderm equipped the youngster for her day of honor, so Curley prepared his mind for the walk of their lifetimes, taking several deep breaths. He willed the wide-eyed mammal to remain relaxed. Turning to gauge the eager crowd, Curley saw them lined up like ants along the sidewalk. His helper, cousin Fred Helzer, joined him to bookend the calf between them.

Once Curley felt she was ready, he gingerly backed the one-and-a-half-ton mammal out of the truck. He dug into his pocket and pulled out an apple to keep her occupied. Nosey moved closer to her new friend, not sure what to expect. Curley wrapped his arm around her neck, giving it a reassuring pat while speaking softly in her ear. Nosey's understanding of basic English commands gave Curley the confidence he could lead her down the parade route.

Finally ready, they turned to face the enormous crowd. The pair slowly entered the procession between groups of mounted equestrians. The new arrival stole the show, and the parade-goers shouted enthusiastically as the long-awaited superstar walked past them.

"Nosey! Nosey!"

Even her name was new to her. Overwhelmed, she kept a wary eye on the people drawn together on the sidewalks peering at her. Her ears flapped and her neck arched back as she took in the sight. She had never seen such a mass of people, much less one that shouted at her. Curley carried on a steady stream of sweet talk, rubbing her face, trunk, and back. She wore leg chains, intended to keep her stable during the parade in case she became frightened and bolted.

Blocker paused as Mayor Gordon Dunn presented Fresno's first elephant to the people. For months, the Valley towns had reached into their pockets to bring this animal to Fresno. Finally, here she was. The crowd burst out in applause. It was a thrilling moment.

Nosey hesitated, taking one step, then another step. Then, slowly, she led the way past the thousands of people who waited along the streets. Strikingly, the crowd's initial reaction turned to hushed sounds of awe as she passed by, realizing they saw, in the flesh, the reality of their efforts and dreams. Nosey perked up her head as she walked along, feeling a bit more comfortable. Her ears slowly flapped and her eyes relaxed. She raised her trunk in response, tentatively trumpeting her greeting, thrilling her admirers. It was a moment that parade attendees remembered and shared for years afterward.

But Curley and Fred Helzer had their hands full, keeping pace alongside her. Trotting, then coming to a halt, the men had to be ready for Nosey's next move. Arms stretched out to touch her and peanuts were tossed her way—it all startled the shy, scared animal.

THE FRESNO BEE

THE REPUBLICAN

FRESNO, CALIF., SUNDAY MORNING, SEPTEMBER 11, 1949

HOME AT LAST — Nosey makes herself right at home in her new quarters in the Roeding Park Zoo. A part of the large crowd that accompanied her to the park after the parade can be seen in the background.
Bee Photos.

Nosey enjoying her new home.

"Move back to the sidewalk, please. Please don't approach the animal," Curley warned.

The Asian elephant stalled and shook her head as her eyes strained forward. She panicked at the sight of prancing horses ahead of her. People were calling her name.

"Nosey! Nosey!"

It was becoming too much for her. Curley signaled the crowd to stay back and let her pass, his hand holding back the pressing crowd. He loudly announced, "Please back up! She's scared and ready to make a run for it."

At that moment, Nosey whirled around, let out a deafening trumpet, and yanked on the ropes. The two men immediately grabbed her chains to hold her back.

"Whoa, Nosey. Whoa!"

To keep the young elephant under control, Curley used his *ank*, a wooden pole about three feet long with a hook, used by the *mahouts*. The procession came to a halt to let her calm down.

After a bit, they resumed their walk, but again, about halfway through, Nosey's anxiety once more got the better of her. This time she broke loose, spinning around between Kern and Tulare in the middle of the block. The nervous youngster scampered away, with her keepers frantically chasing after her, holding on as best they could. Excited squeals rang out from the onlookers while mothers scooped their children to safety. Her owners finally regained control of their bulky runaway, but for the remainder of the parade Nosey had a special police escort.

Once Nosey's introduction to Fresno was behind her, the time came to introduce her to the zoo. Curley opened the trailer's back flap to load the young elephant, but she had other ideas. With blood-curdling screams, her eyes popping out, ears flapping angrily, she planted her feet and refused to get into the trailer. She had survived terrifying boat and trailer rides and had no intention of taking another such trip. It's not much of a fight between a one-and-a-half-ton animal and a 150-pound man.

Faced with solid female obstinacy, Curley shrugged his shoulders in defeat and, having no other option, they began the two-mile walk from downtown to the zoo on Belmont. Glancing back as they entered the underpass, it surprised him to see a long line of people following along as the second parade of the day ensued. Nosey's fans escorted her to her temporary zoo quarters, a yard and barn enclosed by cyclone fencing.

She went directly to the awaiting pile of hay and ate hungrily. The people crowding around the exhibit could not get enough of her; they were obsessed with every move she made. Then, thirsty from the long, sweltering day, Nosey ambled over to her water trough, sucking up a huge trunkful of the chilly water. Finally, she turned, and with a twinkle in her eye, she sprayed the unsuspecting audience with a surprise shower.

Thus began a long-lasting love affair between Nosey and her Valley friends.

CHAPTER 5

The Fresno Zoo Society
Gets to Work

The $1200 left over from the Nosey campaign went into a fund to improve and expand the present zoo. The city invited the citizens involved in the elephant campaign to establish a nonprofit organization to purchase animals independently from the City of Fresno.

In 1950, the Fresno Zoological Society was formed. Initial members included Alex Kleerup, the first president of the Society, Paul S. Chez, Water L. Clark, Joe Dale Sr., Sam Davidson, Carl D. Flourney, John J. Gallagher, Rau Prior, James Woodward, and Ted Shelton.

The Fresno Zoo Society set as its first task to develop a master plan for zoo development and expansion within Roeding Park (the existing zoo perimeter covered six of the park's 148 acres). The present zoo had a haphazard plan at best. They acquired animals in any number of ways: some were donated as unwanted pets, others were orphaned wild animals or smaller local animals that had been rescued. A baby alligator from Florida had arrived in a cigar box.

The Zoo Society's new board wanted to change this small-minded approach. They thought big—global-size big. With $1750 as a starter purse, their imaginations swirled. They imagined acquiring animals from Africa and Asia. After Nosey the elephant, what about a hippo, and then maybe a giraffe? The City of Fresno had limited the zoo's growth to 14 acres, which didn't dim their dreams. As the zoo's budget covered only the basics—maintenance, cost of personnel, and animal care—it would be up to the Society to develop a funding base to realize its ambitious ideas. The new board was built on the excitement of Nosey, and public support of the zoo was strong. These visionary men thought long-term. They realized they had a rare opportunity to create a zoo almost from scratch.

For the next three years, the board dedicated itself to information gathering. They wanted it done right. They went up and down the west coast, checking out the pros and cons of how other zoos operated, from animal exhibit construction to overall layout to required staffing needs. They faced big decisions, including which animals to get, how to get them, and how to care for them once they were obtained. The board set an ambitious goal to become one of the top three zoos in California!

The Lion's Club donation of a lion gave them a foundation to build on. With Nosey the elephant, they were on their way to acquiring the "Big 5" animals, which refers to the largest animals in Africa (elephants, lions, giraffes, rhinos, and hippos), sought after hunters for their wall displays.

The Zoo Society hired Kay Miles as secretary. A Fresno resident, Kay maintained a personal collection of animals, which she kept at her home on Fruit and Alluvial–outside the city limits at the time. Over the years, Kay had amassed a large file of important contacts. She knew zoo personnel, exotic animal traders, and even animal transporters by name—a gold mine of information.

The number one priority in enclosure design was for easy viewing—there were to be no bars, except for predatory animals. The board also explored the idea of using moats, which allowed for a full view while creating a safe barrier between the people and the animals. The more modern zoo facilities were using moats to achieve this effect. The exhibits for some species, such as the powerful great apes or bears, required a deep, wide moat. Spider monkeys needed only a shallow, water-filled trench to keep them confined to an island. Hoof stock, like rhinos and hippos, got by with graded slopes to a barrier wall.

Board meetings reverberated with lively debates. What should be done with the animals they had? Hoof stock and birds filled the zoo grounds. Should they keep, trade, or sell some of them? Which species should be added? The bears' antiquated exhibit had to go, although the existing cat barn with eight separate runs was deemed fit to stay (although not ideal, the weekend crowd loved it).

Beyond animal acquisitions, the other significant discussion concerned the layout of the zoo. Should it group exhibits by species, continent, or feeding requirements? Would placing all carnivores in one location simplify the storage of perishable meats? The board members grappled with the positives and negatives of these and many other questions. Their final design grouped animals by species rather than by food type.

Traditionally, zoos obtain new animals through natural increases, trades, or contributions. The nonprofit Zoo Society Foundation opened the door for donations. Each board member reached out to their community contacts for significant donations. After nearly three years, the public was ready to see the results. Finally, the time came for the exciting part: building and filling.

CHAPTER 6

Spider Monkey Island

In 1953, O. James Woodward, Zoo Society vice president, initiated the Society's ten-year plan for improving and enlarging the zoo. He stepped forward with a significant donation for a spider monkey exhibit, which kick-started a new decade of growth in the zoo. Zoo Society President Walter Clark declared, "This first exhibit will be of great interest and importance to the zoo. Its overall cost, excluding the monkeys, will be about $10,000." The design was futuristic and exciting.

Spider monkeys are classified as monkeys instead of apes because they have tails. Native to Central and South America, these small, five-pound monkeys use their tails to swing from limb to limb in the trees. They were named spider monkeys because they looked like spiders hanging upside down, their prehensile tails curled around branches, their arms and legs dangling as they swung through the trees. When threatened, they growl, emit a "barking" sound, and throw small branches to scare away predators, such as eagles and hawks. They are intelligent and have active memories. Their rainforest diet consists mainly of fruit, but they occasionally eat leaves, flowers, nuts, seeds, insects, and (surprise!) arachnids.

Keen to obtain some of these fascinating creatures for his zoo, Woodward visited zoos as far away as Seattle, talking to zoo architects and learning the pros and cons of developing a spider monkey exhibit that could both contain the little escape artists and that people would enjoy. Moats eliminated the need for chain-link fencing that blocked the public's easy viewing of the animals. The three basic moat types were wet, dry, and slanted. The wet moat design created a shallow, water-filled area surrounding a sand-filled island. The outer walls of the moat kept the monkeys in and the people out. Spider monkeys can swim, but have an innate fear of lurking snakes and crocodiles embedded in their DNA and won't take a chance entering the water.

Guests dubbed the design "The Wedding Cake" because of its shape. It had four levels of circular platforms, giving the monkeys plenty of play area. Swinging rings and trapezes, like those found in children's play areas, provided exercise for the animals and a magnet for attracting spectators. In addition, a cleverly disguised night house was hidden under a climbing apparatus, large enough for a dozen or more monkeys. Wire heating elements buried in the concrete provided warmth in winter.

The plan was for fifteen black-handed spider monkeys to come from Florida. They arrived on January 22, 1954. It appears they were not put into quarantine before going public. On January 31, 1954, Woodward oversaw the exhibit's opening. He proudly dedicated the spider monkey exhibit to the memory of Captain Raymond D. Hatfield, a Fresno-born war hero killed in Korea. The two had grown up together and attended the same school. Major General William F. Dean, a Korean War hero who spent three years in a Communist POW camp, attended the dedication. He had been released just a few months prior.

When Major General Dean opened the door to release the monkeys, nothing happened—several minutes passed before the first one poked his head out of the hole. Zookeeper Curley Blocker gathered a handful of peanuts to lure out a few more. Finally, he put on waders and crossed onto the island to shoo the other eleven out.

The moat area proved to be an advantage for the zoo; occasionally, the spider monkeys had company on their island home. Whenever a sea lion needed a "time-out" from his colony after getting into a fight, he spent time at the island. It also served as a quiet place when a sea lion became ill or needed to recover from an injury. What a sight that must have been, monkeys swinging on the rings with a sea lion sunning itself on the sand!

Keeping the agile little monkeys on the island proved to be a challenge. All remained calm when water filled the moat, but the staff did not look forward to pool-cleaning day. The water had to be drained weekly so they could clean the bottom and sides, using a dangerous powdered chlorine to remove new algae growth. This required having a second person on sentry duty with a rake to keep the quick-moving critters away from the chemicals. On pool cleaning day, the zoo accepted employee absence excuses only if one called from the ER.

Spider monkeys may be small but they are feisty. Zookeepers who worked on the exhibit learned never to turn their backs on them. They are quick and aggressive. The monkeys' arms are powerful, and their long tails make them a serious threat; they can cover a considerable distance in a split second. Moreover, their teeth are long and

Spider monkey island, circa 1953.

razor-sharp; one bite can lay open human flesh to the bone, so the men took sentry duty seriously.

From the public's point of view, they were fascinating animals. The playful primates never failed to evoke a laugh or chuckle from visitors while performing their "circus acts," as they leaped over and under the platforms onto the trapezes and back again. Guests often stood in amazement at how long the monkeys groomed each other. During his tenure at the zoo, Doc Chaffee often discussed the importance of bonding behaviors during his guided zoo tours. He would use the spider monkeys' affectionate acts to comment on the common need for all mammals, including humans, to touch and bond. Women connected to the monkey mom's affection toward its baby. The spider monkey's extended troop dynamics resemble our human family relationships of mom, dad, kids, grandparents, aunts, and cousins.

The troop of spider monkeys successfully boosted zoo attendance, as *The Fresno Bee* ran stories about the new exhibit and friends shared photos. However, the desire to provide a barrier-free exhibit occasionally had its drawbacks. Visitors sometimes took advantage of the low walls to throw food or items into the exhibit. Foreign objects, such as marbles, bottle caps, lit cigarettes, bubble gum, and food—which could cause illness or even death—were found within reach of the monkeys. The disgraceful behavior of some visitors made it necessary to add an additional low fence in order to create a two-foot-wide barrier. In addition, placing a planting bed between the bar and the exhibit wall provided a mental and visual separation that also added aesthetic appeal.

Swinging and tumbling through the monkey bars, even monkeys have accidents. One day, little Annie zigged when she should have zagged as she chased her playmate through the tiered platforms. She found herself with a broken right arm. Zoo Society board member and veterinarian Dr. Thomas Eville performed the casting on this tiny limb. Little Annie appeared relieved when it came time to remove the cast a few weeks later, as Dr. Eville gently sawed through the heavy plaster sleeve. Her new boyfriend had just arrived from San Diego, and she wanted to make a good impression. She certainly did not want to appear as a klutzy monkey!

It was bound to happen eventually. One monkey resolved to get himself off the island and into the action of the wide world beyond. Studying the situation, he realized he must first cross the dreaded moat. Although this moat was still an effective deterrent, in this case it would not stop him. Once past the moat, freedom awaited! The monkey studied the staff each week as they stepped into the moat for cleaning. It was dry during this process, but a guard stood on duty with his rake, shooing the monkeys away from the moat's edge. No one stood guard the rest of the week, but of course then the moat was full. Cross the water? Was it doable? In this monkey's mind, he *could* make it. Taking a deep breath and a short run, he leaped as far as possible. Darn, a foot short! And a big splash! With that telltale sound, keepers came running. They caught the little rascal just as he began climbing to freedom.

Doc realized this monkey now knew he could get off the island and would try again. Sure enough, an early shift worker occasionally caught a peek of the little primate wandering around the zoo. Soon it became routine. The worker would call for help, round up the adventurer, and return the escape artist to the Wedding Cake island. The wandering monkey returned peacefully, knowing he'd find his breakfast there.

The island served its purpose as a place to display the spider monkeys, and the public enjoyed watching them. But at the same time, there were concerns about the lack of shade over the cement structures during the hot Fresno summers.

One day, while sitting at his favorite table at the nearby Denny's, Doc watched the City of Fresno remove the restaurant's palm trees. Jumping up, he asked the owner if he could have the trees. He raced back to his office to call the City, requesting they deliver the trees to the zoo. With an unusually speedy response, the trees were taken to the spider monkey exhibit, where the maintenance crew promptly planted them, providing much-needed shade.

Lemurs have since replaced the spider monkeys in the exhibit. Located 250 miles off the east coast of Africa is the island of Madagascar, the world's fourth-largest island and native habitat for wild lemurs. Red ruffed lemurs and ring-tailed lemurs have both been exhibited on the island.

The remodeled spider monkey island,
now home for the zoo's lemurs.

Ring-tailed lemurs pose for the camera.

CHAPTER 7

Gracie, Bozo, and Albert, the Zoo's First Chimpanzees

Fresno went wild over its first chimpanzee. Eleven-year-old Gracie, boasting short dark hair and piercing ebony eyes, arrived on the heels of Nosey in July 1950. Zookeeper Curley Blocker had used his San Diego connection to get this great ape for Fresno Zoo. Great apes—such as chimpanzees, orangutans, and gorillas—are distinguished from lesser apes, like siamangs and gibbons, by their lack of tails and their larger size.

Chimpanzees—well known for being intelligent and sociable—are one of man's closest relatives, and like us, they have opposable thumbs. Their bodies are covered by a coat of brown or black hair, but their faces are bare except for a short white beard. Skin color is generally white except for the face, hands, and feet, which are black for sun protection.

They are found across central and west Africa, inhabiting the tropical forests and savannahs of the region. They live in large groups for security. These apes can move bipedally (upright) or walk on their knuckles, and are the most flexible of the great apes, moving easily between trees and land. Their diet includes insects, blossoms, bark, fruit, tree seeds, leaves, meat, and a wide variety of nuts. As tool users, they swab twigs in termite mounds, sliding their tongues around the insect-laden sticks for a tasty meal.

The zoo's existing collection of monkeys (primates with tails) lived in a row of basic, cement-floor cages, each about 12 by 15 feet, surrounded by chain link fencing. Each enclosure included climbing apparatus similar to that typically found in a children's playground. A small wooden night house sat at the back of each enclosure, where they ate and spent the night. Given the monkeys' close quarters, Curley was always on the lookout for cuts, bruises, or any unusual changes that might need attention.

Gracie, too, was housed in the smaller monkey cage, but these living quarters provided little space for her great ape body. Chimpanzees are tree climbers, and knuckle walkers when on the ground. Gracie's monkey cage couldn't be further from her natural home, with no trees or greenery and only a hard, cold floor. The zoo had no other options at the time, so they installed a heater to provide a modicum of comfort.

The original row of monkey cages were built four feet from the walkway, far enough to be out of the reach of zoo visitors but near enough to provide a close connection. Gracie learned that extending her hand to the visitors would result in it being filled with tasty treats. The ape behaved differently from the monkeys: she was smart, made eye contact, and entertained herself with unique facial expressions, often contorting her loose lips. Visitors bonded with Gracie and returned often to visit her, stuffing treats in their pockets. Although she seemed to enjoy human attention, she needed a mate after four years of being alone. Chimpanzees are highly social animals and live in communities of between ten and 180 individuals. A lone chimp, much like humans, can become depressed without a partner to express its emotions to.

Fortunately, Gracie received a wonderful Christmas present on December 24, 1954, when she was introduced to Bozo, a four-and-a-half foot, 120-pound, chimpanzee rescued from a circus. The Fresno Zoo Society board made national news for Fresno, boasting of its coup of gaining a breeding pair of chimpanzees. The couple hit it off immediately. Gracie and Bozo sat cross-legged, face to face for hours, peering into each other's eyes and picking out pieces of dried skin or removing parasites, ticks, or lice. Bozo would turn his backside to her or lie down, and Gracie would patiently pick out the irritating bugs; then she shifted around and he returned the favor. This bonding behavior is like human mothers combing their children's hair. Occasionally, they took a breather to tickle, scream, and race around the cage. Bozo's years with vaudeville circuses taught him how to entertain his fans.

The zoo's concession sold popcorn for the animals. They encouraged this feeding to provide diversion from boredom for the caged creatures and as a supplement to the zoo's food budget. Bozo, a master at begging for his share, rewarded the public with his antics. Chimpanzees use body movements, hooting, panting, and screaming to express their emotions. But playful loose lips can switch like lightning to display razor sharp teeth, signaling an aggressive disposition.

Wild animals in human care tend to mature sooner than their counterparts in the wilderness. Bozo, eight years old, and Gracie, eleven, were approaching adulthood. Their breeding went unnoticed, and baby Albert's arrival surprised the staff. He was born one year after Bozo joined Gracie. The zoo had no choice but to provide the chimpanzee family with more room.

Bozo, Gracie, and Albert received larger quarters, extending the popular monkey row. Spacious and better equipped, the new space had a swing, ladders, and bars to provide the chimps with exercise beyond just extending their arms for begging. To ease the stress of moving, zookeeper Curley Blocker's wife shared his love of the zoo and ran the concession stand. She soothed them with her tasty orange sodas.

Sammy, a white-faced, dark-bodied capuchin "organ grinder" monkey, was moved into the vacated original chimp quarters. These rainforest natives are known for their intelligence; in fact, they are considered one of the cleverest animals in the world. Just eight pounds, with soft, expressive eyes and a long tail, Sammy examined his new quarters from top to bottom. He turned to his chimpanzee neighbors and introduced himself with fiercely fanged snarls.

On January 3, 1957, Albert celebrated his first birthday in his new home. Mrs. Blocker whipped up a special cake for the event. She decorated it with plastic horses, cowboys, fence rails, bits of chocolate candy wrapped in gold foil, plus other candied items resembling carrots in the frosting. A single candle signified his birthday year. Curley's wife paraded the cake around the six-acre zoo, inviting visitors to the birthday party. Before offering it to the chimpanzee family, she removed the plastic items, then slid the cake through the cage wire openings. But Albert's protective mother refused to let him get close to the goodies.

Bozo, with his curious nature, ambled over to inspect it. He picked up a piece of the wrapped candy and turned it around, examining all sides. Carefully slipping it into his mouth, his face twisted with a disgusted look. The paper wrap sailed to the floor. Smacking his lips, he picked off each of the candies with his thumb and finger, eating them with delight.

Meanwhile, outside their cage, the public gathered to share in the festivities. All the fuss upset little Albert. Gracie sulked and covered her face whenever a camera aimed her way. Albert tucked his head under her arm, peering out for brief glimpses. Bozo filled his mouth with water and, taking aim, shocked the two closest women with a cold New Year's shower.

Meanwhile, Sammy, the capuchin, screamed for attention like a spoiled child. He demanded his share of the cake! Reaching through the fence, he snagged a piece and greedily shoved it into his mouth. Mrs. Blocker let every other animal close by share in the merriment. The geese, gibbons, ducks, and even the pelican with the injured wing tasted the cake. Only the honored birthday family refused to partake in the festivities.

When Albert reached his third birthday, he entered the US Air Force National Air and Space Academy program in Colorado as a lab animal. In exchange, the zoo received a one-year-old female,

Tahlulu. The offspring of a lab chimp, she no longer needed to nurse, but still needed the comfort and security of a mother. Gracie, true to her name, adopted her. Like a good parent, she let Tahlulu ride on her back. Gracie groomed and played with her, giving the new little one plenty of attention. Bozo also accepted her as part of his troop.

One chilly January morning in 1961, while doing their rounds, zookeepers found Gracie on the cold concrete floor. She had died during the night with no warning or telltale signs of symptoms. Gracie's devoted public had a hard time taking in the sad news. The zoo supporters all well remembered when she first arrived ten years earlier, and had followed her life's events since. Gracie's timid and quiet nature endeared her to the public. The memories of her gently adopting Tahlulu as a scared one-year-old youngster remained as her legacy.

The staff took advantage of the Association of Zoos and Aquarium conferences, where they learned how to enhance the habitats of their animals to better meet their needs. They added to the enclosures balancing ropes, tree limb highways, and observation perches for movement. Zookeepers worked behind the scenes, training the chimpanzees to respond to commands of body parts. They rotated pet store enrichment toys, climbing rings, and treat dispensers that stimulated thinking and influenced the primates' temperaments.

CHAPTER 8

Ichabod and Ila, Baby Gorillas

Following the arrival of Nosey in 1949, the community came together with strong support for the zoo. Funds flowed into the newly organized Fresno Zoo Society. 1953, the Zoo Society launched its ambitious 10-n-10 Master Plan. Kay Miles, Society secretary, used her worldwide connections to acquire ten major animals within ten years. Construction boomed. Trucks began arriving with hippos, giraffes, rhinos, sea lions, polar bears, flamingos, and monkeys. The one missing animal was the gorilla.

Lowland gorillas typically live in Africa's tropical rainforests and wet lowland forests, their habitats ranging up to 4,000 feet. The male gorilla can weigh up to 450 pounds and stand four to five-and-a-half feet tall. As he ages, his black back hairs turn gray, earning him the title of "Silverback." He is legendary for his chest-beating, high-pitched barks, and throwing objects to prove his virility and protect his troop. Gorillas are quiet, shy, nonaggressive animals; their only predators are humans and leopards, which the male scares away.

And so it was with Ichabod and Ila, two six-month-old lowland gorillas from Cameroon, Africa. As adults, they would come to resemble their human relatives, with wide skulls, pronounced brow ridges, flat noses, small ears, and round jaws. The scientific name is easy to remember: *Gorilla gorilla*.

The Zoo Society paid African trackers $5,000 for each gorilla. It took six months of searching before they were able to locate two youngsters meeting the requirements of the Zoo Society. They put the names Ila and Ichabod on the crates and loaded them on the plane for their new home across the ocean. In the Zoo Society's rush to fill the zoo with major animals, they ran out of time to prepare a proper place for the toddlers to live. Arriving on September 11, 1960, the gorilla youngsters had no place at the zoo to rest or adjust from their long journey. A local veterinarian was called in to check Ila and Ichabod. He was appalled that the zoo had not planned for their arrival. He insisted they needed to find a sheltered location for the young gorillas until were at least one year old.

Ila, the female, weighed 20 pounds, while Ichabod, the more fragile one, was just 17 pounds. Ila stayed close to Ichabod to comfort and protect him. They clung to each other for security after being removed from their mothers, communicating with each other using up to twenty-five complicated sounds and gestures. Still a baby herself, Ila hovered over her frail companion, stepping in for the missing adults.

Kay Miles, Zoo Society secretary, located a family willing to provide a nurturing home for the interim. At first glance, caring for a couple of ape babies sounds like fun, but there are limits to hand-raising them. Just as with human babies, the responsibility for adopting two six-month-old toddler apes was full-time and exhausting. The young apes required a lot of cuddling and attention to overcome the fears and stresses they suffered from the traumatic changes they had endured.

Gorilla mothers typically nurse their infants for about two and a half years in the wild. The pair were too young for teeth, so they survived on soft baby food. Hand-raising them meant bottle feedings every several hours, 24/7. In addition, the baby gorillas wore diapers, which were inconvenient to deal with in the early 1960s, before the appearance of disposables. However, having raised children of their own, the parents were prepared for the sleepless nights and worked as a team, alternating their shifts.

Most ape youngsters can sit up and walk by the age of four months, but Ila and Ichabod's traumatic early life had hindered their growth. The couple looked for ways to strengthen their hand and foot grips. The little ones hung onto the adults' clothes when walking around the house, much like they would hang on their mother. Little Ila held onto a swinging rope to build up her muscles.

A short ladder let them climb up and down, using both their hands and feet. The foster parents loved playing with their charges, as long as they were floor bound. However, it got wild as the toddlers grew stronger and began to explore their surroundings. Ila led the way as the older, stronger female, but Ichabod copied everything his big "sister" showed him.

Visitors were no longer invited to see the cute little apes, as the rooms were littered with toys, kitchen pans, and feathers torn from the pillows. Swinging from the drapes, leaping from chair to chair, the little "monkey" apes saw their world as a toy and everything as fair game, destroying everything in sight. As they grew stronger, the two swung and climbed on anything in their sphere, damaged the house and, most likely, the nerves of their host family, who were happy when the time came to return their charges to the zoo.

The day finally arrived when the pair had to leave their secure surroundings and return to Roeding Park Zoo. The foster parents understandably had mixed emotions as they said good-bye to the nine-month-olds and their lives returned to normal; however, their stories entertained guests for years.

Sadly, Ichabod's health regressed until he died, ten months after he arrived in Fresno. Doc Chaffee, the on-call vet, watched over little Ila as she suffered from depression with the loss of her companion. Doc ran numerous tests while he fed her bitter medicine. He tried various things to cheer her up to ease her loneliness. In desperation, he brought Tahlulu, the three-year-old chimpanzee, over to play with Ila. The two girls hit it off instantly. They played for hours, rolling, tumbling, and chasing each other around the exhibit.

Doc delighted in Ila's improved disposition, until Tahlulu had to return to the Oakland Zoo. He tried everything to rebuild Ila's strength. Upon finding her lifeless body early on August 31, 1962, he felt like lightning had struck him in the heart.

The two tragic gorilla losses overwhelmed and frustrated him. The early years of his tenure at the zoo also saw tragic losses of other major animals, such as a stillborn hippo, followed by a fatally injured newborn hippo. In addition, the zoo had lost four black rhinos and several tiger babies. He knew the losses were preventable with proper care and facilities, yet none of the staff were trained in animal husbandry.

Doc holding a baby gorilla.

Doc resolved to make changes. This determination signaled a turning point in his career. In 1963, Doc closed his private veterinary business and went to work full-time at the zoo. The zoo provided a new outlet for his enormous curiosity. Needing a place to treat the smaller animals, he cleaned out a storage area behind the food preparation commissary that had access to water and electricity. He set up an examining table and added small cages for his recovering patients. The veterinarian laid out his medical tools and officially opened the small but efficient medical clinic he would use for the next thirty years.

Engrossed in his quest to improve conditions for the animals, he buried himself in his old textbooks. He contacted other zoo vets across the nation and instigated an invaluable networking system to gather all the knowledge he could. Given the scant existing research on many exotic animals, Doc learned through trial and error, and through the exchange of information with others in his profession. He had inherited incomplete record-keeping, which led to repeated mistakes.

In 1965, the City of Fresno added Zoo Director to Doc's title. Now he had the authority to make changes. His number one priority was training the staff. Doc instituted basic improvements, such as keeping accurate health records, and providing heat lamps during the cold winters and shaded areas for protection during Fresno's hot summers. He provided clean drinking water to the animals. His next priority was to build a nursery to offer motherless primates the extra care they demanded. He stated that he would not authorize the arrival of additional young primates until he had a functioning nursery and trained nursery aides.

However, these changes created tensions between himself and a few Zoo Board members. After a decade of developing the zoo through the Zoo Society, Secretary Kay Miles fought losing her authority. For a man who hated confrontations, Chaffee became fodder for the local media. But he didn't budge. Tensions between the two rose for eight months until the City Council stepped in as referee and had to officially recognized him, again, as the "Director in Charge." For most, it was a welcome transformation. Despite their differences, Doc respected Kay's achievements and appointed her as Education Director to train docents to work with the public. She developed the position and created a cadre of well-trained docents.

Doc went on to develop animal protocols based on prevention, healthy diets, and natural exhibits, all with an educational message for the guests.

CHAPTER 9

The Formative Years of Dr. Paul S. Chaffee

Paul Stanley Chaffee, born on January 27, 1928, grew up along the banks of the St. Clair River, Lake Huron, where ships navigated the waters day and night. His three-story brick home sat within a stone's throw from the river. The young boy developed a fondness for birds, studying them as he walked along the waterside. He even set up a clinic in his garage to care for the injured ones he found.

A close family, they shared their day around the dinner table, supporting each other. The children were five years apart: Jacquelyn, Walter (Buzz), and Paul (Stanley), the youngest.

Mother never relented on her exhortations to follow the Golden Rule: "Do unto others as you would have them do unto you." The young boy planted her words in his heart. The virtues of honesty, responsibility, and truthfulness were the family expectations that he strove to honor.

Early on in life, he showed his leadership ability. At age 9, Stanley represented his elementary school's safety patrol at the national conference in Washington, D.C. The principal wrote to his parents stating, "Any honors that come to Stanley are none too good in our opinion. We rate him as an ideal child who will wear the honor with modesty and get, educationally, all he can out of the trip."

In terms of personality, he took after his outgoing mother, who loved to host parties. Quite the dashing young man, his picture showed up in the newspapers with pretty dates for school dances. Popular with both girls and the guys, it was Peggy LeFrance who caught his eye as a bouncy, blond classmate. She cheered in her short skirt and pompoms at his football games, giving him an extra shout out when he caught the ball.

Following graduation, money was tight, so he enlisted in the army, where he henceforth became known as Private Paul. He aspired to become a surgeon, but his grades were barely above average. However, his army aptitude test qualified him for the medical corps, which allowed him to serve his country on Hawaii's warm, sunny beaches. Private Paul worked with guard dogs and learned the basic skills of a medical technician. Returning home, he entered junior college, where he became involved in the Veterinary Medicine Council, eventually serving as its president.

In 1949, Peggy and Paul Chaffee married in Peggy's house, but regrettably, she got measles and they had to forgo the honeymoon. As newlyweds, they attended Michigan State. Peggy majored in nursing while the Paul pursued his veterinary goals. Along with brother Walt and his wife, they lived in the married student barracks, aptly named Fertility Row, where the clotheslines were filled with diapers blowing in the wind. The new father spent his evenings with a baby draped over his shoulder and a book in his hand. The four of them shared many happy times with their growing families. These were treasured memories, when the brothers expounded on their philosophies of life and goals. The sounds of happy laughter always permeated their gatherings.

Despite the family pressures, Paul qualified for a scholarship based on his academic standing, character, personality, and participation in extracurricular campus activities. He graduated with honors from Michigan State, class of 1953, as a Doctor of Veterinary Medicine.

The new vet detested his first job, working with the carcasses of animals in a Chicago pet clinic. The beckoning warm weather of the Pacific seaboard drew them to move near his brother in California. He scoured the veterinary ads on the West Coast, and in 1954, "Doc" answered an advertisement for quality control in a meat processing plant in Fresno, California. During the interim year waiting for his license to clear, the work he did there tested his ethics and honesty on a daily basis. If he saw signs of bacteria on hanging meat, he marked it with a black X, signifying it was unfit for selling. Then he prepared for threats or a bottle of Scotch on his desk as a bribe. For a man used to being well-liked and popular, it was difficult being seen as an enemy. It was years before he could touch, much less eat, a piece of meat.

The Fresno newcomer encouraged his parents to move by enticing his father to assist in managing the soon-to-open pet clinic and his mother to help with the children. By then, he and Peggy had three boys, David, Dan, and Dick, and a daughter, Denise, who was born in Fresno.

Doc joined Dr. Griffenhagen's practice. The older vet purchased an abandoned bar and moved the building to an empty lot on Fresno Street and McKinley for Doc to eventually set up his private practice. Father and son worked together, renovating the bar into a functioning pet clinic. Those days were among the happiest for the pair.

In 1957, the day arrived when Dr. Chaffee hung out his shingle and proudly opened his McKinley Pet Hospital. Doc quickly gained respect in the community for his ability to set broken and damaged bones, especially with birds. With "Paps" as his assistant, his reputation soared as stories spread about how he overnighted in the clinic, caring for someone's beloved pet.

Ray Appleton, a KMJ radio talk show host, shared a remembrance from the mid-sixties, the dawn of the space age when rats traveled into space. "Every young kid, including myself, had a pet white rat. It was a lousy dark winter, and my mom and I lived in a cold, drafty apartment just a few blocks from the pet hospital. My rat, Wikki, got sick, and I bugged my Mom to do something. Finally, in total frustration, she picked up the phone and called the vet hospital.

"Doc says, 'Bring him down.' So my mom bundles me up, and we jump into her 1948 Studebaker. We get to the office and find him pacing up and down, wringing his hands, looking into a small box. The box held six wiggly black and brown boxer pups, scrunched together, born prematurely. He was spending the night fussing over the pups. He turns to us and says, 'Well, I don't know what I can do with the pups right now, so give me your rat.'

"We go home, and I am sure my rat's dead. My mom warns me the rat's dead. A couple of days later, I go back. I find Doc Chaffee still there, looking rather haggard, and see six healthy pups and one healthy rat cured of pneumonia."

In the mid-sixties, Doc went through a troubling period. In 1961, when "Paps" died, Paul sunk into a depression. His best friends, Dr. Wilfred Pimentel and Marie, his wife, spent many evenings with him. Wil reminisced about those days: "Doc was impressive in disguising his difficulties, never showing any signs of problems, and was always cheerful. You could sense the tension, and we knew the stress, but he was always pleasant. It was the business end of the practice that he hated. He was lousy at asking people to pay for his services. He couldn't turn down treating any animal that needed care just because the client said they had no money."

Peggy kept reminding him that he had four children to feed and clothe. When Dr. Herb Piper filled in for him, he tried diligently to collect payments, but the clients would say, "Oh, Doc doesn't collect right away. I'll send it in when I have the extra money." Sadly, the conflict over money eventually ended his marriage.

Although Doc made good money as a pet veterinarian, he complained that it didn't satisfy him and he aspired to a greater purpose. Sometimes he wondered who needed the most care, the pet or the pet's owner.

Dr. Griffenhagen was the on-call vet for the Roeding Park Zoo and often took Doc along to assist him. In 1961, Griffenhagen retired and turned the zoo gig over to him. Now, instead of dogs, cats, and rats, Paul had tigers, hawks, and snakes. He was in heaven. He dug into his books, scouring the pages for ways to deal with their needs. He soon discovered a common denominator. It was their dire, unsuitable living conditions that was causing most of their illnesses.

"Doc bloomed when he got into the zoo," commented Marie Pimentel. "From the beginning, he had a vision for the zoo, which was his legacy. He loved the animals; he loved the environment and loved the people. He loved everything about the zoo, and it showed in the responses from people around him."

Dr. Piper added, "He was a good vet in whatever he did. Our bird training consisted of a few chickens for six weeks. As a child, his unique abilities with birds helped him work with the zoo population. He didn't hesitate to call on other vets searching for the right approach."

Marie Pimentel had vivid memories of going to the zoo when animals were needlessly dying, some of their food came from the concession stand, and they lived in cramped, boring cages with cement floors. Marie was especially sensitive to the surroundings, being married to a veterinarian. At the time, Curley Blocker was the zookeeper in charge. Curley's circus background and on-the-ground zoo experience did not provide the scientific knowledge he needed to provide high-quality animal care. Doc's heart anguished whenever Curley used a whip to beat Nosey into submission.

The newly hired veterinarian started by cleaning up the haphazard records. They were found in piles or drawers or were simply nonexistent. Doc started from scratch by compiling meticulous health records on every animal he treated. The mortality rate for the zoo animals was unacceptable. To learn the causes of death, he performed postmortem tests on each one. From the test results, he created a database for revising nutritional requirements and treatments from which he could work.

Based on analysis of records he compiled from October 1962 to October 1963, most of the deaths were caused by the stress of change. He enforced the quarantine policy for all new arrivals to prevent the spread of disease and to set aside a quiet, secure area to give them time to adjust. Each animal now received all their necessary shots, as well as an enhanced diet. Doc watched with satisfaction as the survival rate climbed.

The inadequate condition of the exhibits was another prominent cause of health problems. Simply adding heat lamps and shaded areas made an immediate improvement in the animals' comfort. Doc held training sessions for the animal caretakers. He taught

Doc treating a tapir.

them about nutrition, diseases, and reproduction. Just their change in attitude from receiving this knowledge enhanced the program. They felt part of a team that was concerned about the welfare of their charges. "The added knowledge encouraged the keepers to take an active interest in feeding and to appreciate the importance of a good keeper-animal relationship," said Chaffee.

Doc's newly instituted policies resulted in such significant changes that on October 22, 1964, Fresno's Parks and Recreation Commission adopted a resolution commending him on his outstanding technical skill and professional leadership in the operation of the Roeding Park Zoo. It was the first such resolution adopted by the Commission.

On February 10, 1965, Paul Chaffee was officially named the zoo's Director/Veterinarian. The $945-a-month position represented a cut in income but a new lease on his life. As Director, he now had the authority to institute major changes. He knew he risked stepping on toes and incurring resistance from long-time employees. Still, his priority was the well-being of his clients, who could not speak for themselves.

CHAPTER 10

The Living Symbol

During the 1950s, the Fresno Shriners wanted their organization's mascot to represent them in parades. Ray Prior, a Shriner and original Zoo Society Board member, prepared a proposal that the Shriners would pay for a camel, including transportation costs, if the zoo would house it and train it for their use in parades. The Zoo Society had a ten-year plan to expand its collection of major animals from around the world, and the camel fit right into their design.

In 1870, the Shriners Organization was formed to serve and help build a better world. A polio epidemic swept across the United States, and it became apparent that many children were going without the appropriate care. In 1922, the group began construction on the first Shriners Hospital in Shreveport, Louisiana, turning away no one. In Fresno, the Shrine is known for its colorful parades and distinctive red fez (hat).

Donations poured in from 2000-plus Shriner members up and down the Valley for the camel. Ray Prior held the title of Chief Camel Herder, but up until now, it had been a hollow title. The time had arrived for them to educate themselves about this bizarre, aloof animal. A camel? A desert animal from Australia? Would it be tame or feral? Camels were first introduced into Australia in the 1840s to explore the inland territory, which was a hot, barren desert. Soon, Australia had the largest population of unmanaged feral dromedary camels on the planet. Unfortunately, the more than one million camels on the continent caused an environmental disaster. Australia needed to reduce its population and willingly gave the camels away.

There are two major species of camels: the one-hump dromedary, like those in Australia, and the rare two-humped Bactrian found in the Gobi Desert. The hump is a fat reservoir for energy; concentrating body fat in one place decreases the heat effect it would have if distributed throughout the body. Camels can go for ten days without drinking water. In addition, for protection, camels have three sets of eyelids and two rows of eyelashes to keep blowing desert sand out of their eyes. Their thick lips let them forage for thorny plants other animals cannot eat. The dromedary has rough chest and knee pads that protect it from the hot sand when kneeling. Even their small, round poop contains a minimal amount of water.

Australian handlers loaded a dozen or more young camels onto the boat and tied them down in the cargo hold. An animal handler fed, watered, and cleaned them during the journey. A camel in the wild stays with its mother for three to five years, but these young calves, barely weaned, had a stressful time making the long trip across the Pacific Ocean, alone and scared.

Excitement grew as Zookeeper Curley Blocker alerted the Shriners that the shipment would soon arrive from Brisbane. Curley's experience as a circus trainer qualified him to halter break and train the camel for parade use.

The caravan of dromedaries went to Lutz Ruhe's Wild Animal Holding Ranch in Thousand Oaks for a month of quarantine. At quarantine's end, Curley drove down to select one with a calm temperament, willing to obey his trainer's commands. He checked the coat and teeth for unhealthy signs, and was observant for any indications of aggression, which would not be acceptable. He checked their huge feet, which allowed them to walk over the soft desert sand that would bog down anything with wheels. "Camels go where cars can't," was the camel aficionado's motto. Finally, he found a camel which suited him. He boarded it onto the truck and headed for Fresno.

On Friday, the thirteenth of November, 1953, Curley introduced this new addition to the Roeding Park Zoo. At 450 pounds and six feet tall, the new camel immediately established her dominance through a combination of strength and stubbornness. Scared and tired, she laid back her ears, planted her feet, and refused to exit the trailer. Curley needed to draw deep into his history of getting what he wanted from animals: he coaxed, offered food, pulled, and whispered sweet things in her ear. Nothing.

The young female camel also knew how to get what she wanted. She reached over, appearing to take a bite out of Curley's head. Instead, she nipped him with her long lips, telling him, "Don't mess with me. I'm not in a good mood." Eventually, she succumbed to his special treats as he lured her out of the trailer.

Nosey the elephant had reveled in being the Zoo's celebrity and thrived on the public's adoration, but Friday the thirteenth was a bleak day for her. She did not like being upstaged by this curly-haired, hump-backed, aloof creature. The "Queen" trumpeted her unhappiness, pacing up and down to win back the attention of her fans. Today, however, they came to greet her new neighbor, the camel.

Meanwhile, the chimpanzee, Gracie, watched with great curiosity, her hoots echoing throughout the zoo, which set off all the monkeys and created a sense of pandemonium. In turn, the birds in the flight cage fluttered in excitement, while the lion sniffed the air for a potential lunch tidbit and roared his approval. Even the docile hoofstock had to check out the new resident.

The Shriners put out a call to the children to participate in their "Name the Camel" contest. Hundreds of entries for the naming contest came in by mail, including Ms. Hairy, Nipper, and Hump Along. But it was one suggestion, Miss Tehrana, that truly caught the eyes of the Shriners. The reason was: "She's a lady member of the Temple, and her family could be from Egypt."

Nearly 700 children attended the christening event for the composed Miss Tehrana. To the children's delight, she made a big to-do about pulling Curley's hat off his head, sticking her soft furry muzzle into his face, and kissing his cheek. After several months under his training regimen, she had settled into gentle compliance, knowing a big treat would follow each time she leaned over to plant a "smooch" on his bald head. One could feel the air of momentary anxiety whenever she placed her mouth on his head, followed by the chuckles and sighs of relief once it became apparent that a kiss had been planted.

The public loved Miss Tehrana, and she made the perfect living symbol for the Shriners. Five years later, the Shriners decided to locate a mate for her; she needed some company, and the prospect of acquiring an offspring led to further donations. Members who donated $1 or more received a membership card in the Shriners' Camel Rustlers Club. It did not take long to raise the needed $1500.

Animal traders located a male camel from North Africa. He traveled by boat to Germany, where he was loaded onto a ship to cross the Atlantic. After spending several weeks in the hold, the

The camel barn, 1953.

camel and his ship landed in New York City. Next, the male camel climbed onto a truck built to hold large exotic animals and traveled across the country, arriving in Fresno for a month of quarantine.

The Shriners planned a gala June "wedding." This event, a solemn affair, came complete with an accordion rendition of the "Wedding March." The camels' aloofness gave an air of royalty that caught the guests' imagination. Curley Blocker stood by the bride's side as Nobel Ray Prior brought in the shy groom-to-be. Stopping at the "chapel gate," Ray waited until the male saw the beautiful Miss Tehrana. Had she known what was coming, she might have combed her messy hair, but she nevertheless joined in with great anticipation. In a brief ceremony, Potentate Dr. Ginsberg spread his hands in a benediction and then introduced the pair as Mr. and Mrs. Tehran. Their two offspring, Temple and Clyde, remained at the zoo.

In the early 2000s, the zoo replaced Swan Pond with a camel yard and built a platform to offer popular camel rides. Many fantasized themselves as Omar Sharif in *Lawrence of Arabia*, atop a camel wearing flowing tunics.

Nosey and Miss Tehrana, two good friends.

CHAPTER 11

The Gentle Giants

The word *giraffe* comes from an old Arabic word *xirapba*, which means "the one that walks very fast." The giraffe's extended legs lend to its long walking steps, letting him run up to nearly thirty-five miles per hour. Lions don't mess with adult giraffes because a good kick with its dinnerplate-size hoof could send the big cat's head rolling. Nature's gardener manicures the trees into a flat top with his seven-foot neck, accessing food sources beyond the reach of other herbivores. While these trees have long thorns, giraffes use their 22-inch tongues and prehensile lips to reach around the needles to avoid injury. Even the end of his tongue is purple to protect it from sunburn. These silent savannah inhabitants blend in so well that only their eyes and ears over the tips of the trees give them away.

In the 1950s, Heinz Ruhe, a long-time trusted African animal trader, transported eighteen immature, wild-caught giraffes to his ranch in Kenya. Between ships, planes, and quarantine time, it was nearly a six month journey from Africa to supply Fresno with its giraffes.

Over the years, Chaffee Zoo exhibited two giraffe species that share similar habitats in Africa. The Masai giraffe's irregular patterns look like fallen leaves on a painted surface, while the reticulated giraffe has regular patterns featuring a bright chestnut color and white spaces like puzzle pieces.

The first female giraffe was a two-year-old Masai named Skyla, who arrived in 1966. Visitors clamored to the zoo to see this new exotic animal that stood over the trees. Her gentle demeanor and soft eyes mesmerized them as they watched this mammal gracefully glide across her exhibit space. Soon, a second female, Fresnella, joined Skyla. Now all that was missing was a male to join them.

Later that same year, the zoo received two Masai males. Longo's trip to Fresno from Africa took him through New York and Texas. Snorkle's origin is unknown. Four-years-old Longo was in good health but exhibited a slight limp, which continued to worsen until he could barely walk.

Snorkle passed away in 1961 without siring any offspring, so any potential giraffe offspring now hinged on Longo. Dr. Paul Chaffee, who at the time was still operating his local veterinarian practice, was invited to check Longo's painful leg. This impaired African male's wild genes made him a highly valued specimen for breeding. Hope ran high as Longo had both females from which to choose, but he needed to stand on his back legs to breed with the females, which he could not do in his current condition.

Doc developed a plan to build up Longo's legs to give him that required strength. He trimmed Longo's hooves every six months, but the giraffe's difficulty with walking did not improve; instead, it worsened. He walked like an old army veteran at seven years old, clearly in pain. Doc treated him with penicillin for infections, but it was not enough. Frustrated, he contacted zoo vets nationwide concerning giraffe hoof problems but received little information.

Doc speculated if he could adjust Longo's hoof angle, the muscles in his legs might develop strength, much like a human's legs. He contacted a local farrier (horseshoer), who agreed to fashion two custom shoes to attach like a horseshoe to Longo's back hooves.

Doc anesthetized Longo with a tranquilizing dart. Once he was asleep, the keepers tied ropes around his long neck and legs to keep the powerful animal down and prevent his kicking. It took nine keepers to hold the rope ends: two on his long neck, two on his body, two on each front leg, two on each back leg, and one on his head. It was a risky procedure because even in his sleep, Longo was so strong that when he twitched his head or feet, he sent the holder flying. It was all they could do to keep him still.

Meanwhile, the farrier measured Longo's back hooves to shape his customized horseshoes. Then the farrier nailed the shoes

Sharing a treat.

in place to the bottom of Longo's hooves. The metal shoes added a one-inch bar lift on the back, giving the hooves a wedged shape. It was intended to ease the tendon strain and prevent crippling.

Once Longo began to stir, the staff gathered around to watch his reaction to the new device on his hoof. Awakening from his anesthesia, he moved like a newborn calf, wobbling and shaking. He awkwardly rose to his knees, sensing something was amiss with his back legs. Longo lifted his now-weighted hoof, edging it under him. Then, pulling both back legs underneath his body and lifting his front legs, ever so slowly, he rose to his feet. The 17-foot tall mammal shuffled like a little girl in her mother's high heels. After kicking and shaking his hoofs, he finally accepted the added weight.

The farrier made daily visits to his unusual client. Within a few days, the male started to walk with a straighter gait. It became apparent that their creative plan showed promise. Longo wore his orthopedic shoes for thirty-three days. His unique hoofwear worked, and soon Skyla became pregnant. Unfortunately, the calf was stillborn. Now that Longo could stand and breed with Skyla, the watch for any romantic connections became a craze among the staff. Doc continued the hoof maintenance program on Longo's legs, eager for another successful breeding. Alas, Longo died before the zookeepers observed any further romantic overtures.

On August 13, 1971, Skyla surprised the arriving staff with a six-foot tall, 150-pound calf. Female giraffes carry their calves for fifteen months, with few indicators of pregnancy until the last week, when the swollen nipples give it away. The miraculous process of a giraffe giving birth is something to watch. First, the newborn inches out, its head resting on its front legs until it slowly drops six feet to the ground. It lands on its back, which essentially quick-starts its breathing. Next, it stretches and pulls its neck to break through the birthing sac. Most newborns can stand and wobble within an hour, searching for Mom's milk. In the wild, this is a vulnerable time, as predators are drawn to the smell of the birthing fluids and sacs, so the ability to move is critical for survival.

The staff agreed on the female's appropriate name, Patience. It had been thirteen years since the last live, healthy giraffe had been born at the zoo, and she was a welcome addition.

Doc now looked for a new, suitable mate for Skyla and her daughter, Patience. The Utah Hogle Zoo had a healthy male giraffe named Vagabond, so Doc went to Utah to check him over, ensuring he was fit. Lutz Ruhe, his trusted transporter, built a special crate to allow Vagabond's head to see over the top while traveling. Next, he rigged the flatbed to ride lower to the ground. Ruhe made a trial run, checking out underpasses and detours for the trip from Salt Lake City to Fresno. Some tunnels he skimmed through by a mere four inches.

However, when the time came to load Vagabond, he refused to step inside the crate. It is impossible to tranquilize a giraffe while traveling because they have nowhere to lie down. After three days, Ruhe finally went home and waited for a phone call. Three weeks later, Vagabond decided to get into the crate, at last ready for the long, twenty-four-hour trip, creeping along at thirty miles an hour.

Unloading the giraffe required a section of the exhibit's fence to be removed and rollers and winches manipulated until, inch by

A giraffe mugging for the camera.

inch, the massive crate was finally settled on the ground and Vagabond released. The two females were kept in the barn until the new male was unloaded. With the crate opened, Vagabond made a slightly wobbly debut. He was allowed to rest alone overnight and was introduced to his harem the next morning.

Staff and zoo visitors gathered at the exhibit to observe the debut of the long-awaited male. The onlookers held their breath as they awaited the introductions, hoping for a positive greeting. A spontaneous round of applause burst aloud when it became obvious that it was love at first sight.

Skyla and Vagabond were a famous couple that parented eight calves. Skyla died in 1991, and Vagabond then paired with Patience, adding to the Masai species.

CHAPTER 12

Bubbles, Bulgy, and Babies

"A baby hippo is coming! A baby hippo is coming!" Crowds of excited visitors hurried to the zoo to see the one-year-old youngster. The female had already traveled the world during her first year. Taken from her mother in Africa, she traveled across the Atlantic to New York. Then, the hippo calf rode across the country to her new home in Fresno, where she was to live for the next half-century. To create excitement, the Zoo Society sponsored a naming contest; the young hippo received the name Bubbles.

The Zoo Society scrambled to construct the exhibit, which featured a pool with a ten-foot cement deck wrapped around it. A six-foot wall separated the pool from the keeper's walkway. For added safety, a chain-link railing circled the exhibit to keep the visitors at a safe distance but close enough to feed the massive mammal. Anticipating a mate for Bubbles, a two-bedroom barn with secure steel doors was built to keep the semi-aquatic animals safe at night. The crew finished construction just before the 300-pound aquatic female arrived on October 16, 1956.

Eighteen months later, on Valentine's Day, 1958, a year-old male companion, Bulgy, was introduced to his potential bride. Rubbing against each other, the two youngsters enjoyed lying side by side in the pool or chasing each other around the water. Their enormous heads, tiny wiggly ears, and bulging eyes made for an odd-looking couple. Huge nostrils snorted bubbles underwater, and when they opened their mouths, one could see deep into their cavernous throats.

Keepers grew attached to the pair, daily bringing them special apples and carrots as a midday snack. The hippos' small molar teeth are perfectly designed for grinding plant food, and the male's two long, lower tusks are deadly instruments to protect their territory.

The Zoo Society had visions of baby hippos swimming in their pool. Little did they know what they were asking! Most female hippos become sexually mature around the age of five to seven. The Zoo Society's dream came true when Bubbles became pregnant. This birth held significance, plus a splash of terror, for the young Doc Chaffee. His mentor, Dr. Griffenhagen, had left Doc in charge while he was out of the country.

Doc worried about Bubbles' young age of five years, the unfamiliar habitat, and the lack of supporting females, which she would have had in the wild. His experiences as a small animal vet hardly prepared him for a now-2,000-pound pregnant female hippo. Nightmares invaded his sleep, with visions of an unsteady newborn falling into the pool and drowning in front of the public. As Bubbles' eighth month of pregnancy approached, Doc drained the pool to eliminate any chance of drowning.

The zoo staff looked forward to the birth with great excitement, constantly checking on Bubbles' progress. To make it more interesting, they placed bets on the day of birth and the sex of the newborn. Every quiver of Bubbles' monstrous tummy led to rampant rumors. People hung around the emptied pool, hoping to be among the privileged few to witness a historic moment.

After all the careful preparations, Doc received a frantic call in the middle of the night. He hurried out to find a dire situation. Sadly, his worries about Bubbles' immaturity had been realized: the calf arrived stillborn.

Stimulated by the scent of the strong hormones, Bulgy got excited and tried to breed with Bubbles immediately after giving birth. In the process, he knocked her down, injuring her.

Determined to understand more about hippo births, Doc called zoo vets nationwide. He discovered that hippos are naturally born in the water and then pop up like a cork, returning underwater to nurse. This knowledge eased Doc's worry about a newborn drowning, so he had the pool refilled.

The two enormous hippos apparently found each other quite appealing, because Bubbles soon became pregnant again. Eight months later, the keeper, making his early morning rounds, came upon a proud Bubbles and her healthy newborn male standing beside the pool. He gave a quick visual check and radioed the news to Doc. As word spread, the July crowds gathered at the exhibit, edging themselves forward, Kodaks ready to snap prized photos. With a wide-smiling mouth, bouncy cheeks, and large eyes reflecting specks of water, the brand-new infant toddled about for his "Celebrity of the Day" pictures.

Unfortunately, all the excitement surrounding her enclosure stressed the protective mother, so the concerned staff tried to move the reluctant onlookers back while they roped off the site to keep Bubbles calm. A Zoo Society board member quietly slipped past the ropes and stood near the front of the exhibit. Despite the staff's

Bulgy and Bubbles enjoying a day by the pool.

efforts, Bubbles was distraught with the public pressing forward and making noise. Her maternal instincts thrust in, and she did her best to get her infant away from the crowd. She tried to push him out of the pool toward the night house. The helpless newborn, his short stubby legs unable to master the steps, knuckled under as Bubbles pushed. Anxious, she accidentally pushed too hard, injuring the calf. A team of zookeepers finally enticed Bubbles away from the newborn long enough to rescue it. Tragically, it died two days later.

Doc took drastic measures before the next birth, installing bars down the middle of the exhibit through the pool to separate the adults. Planning for the future, he also built separate quarters, with a nursery pool, away from the public eye for the mother and newborn to bond.

Early on June 25, 1964, zookeepers discovered a healthy mother and female calf swimming in the pool. Baby number three debuted at 100 pounds. After two disastrous births, the third time proved to be the charm for Bubbles. She treated her newborn like fragile glass, gently but firmly, and touched the public's heart with her demonstrations of tenderness. This time, the calf managed to climb out of the pool alone. She wobbled like a drunken sailor on the slippery cement area, taking several minutes to get her legs moving in the same direction.

Doc had to see for himself that newborn hippos are safe in the water. Having missed the pop-up birth, he set up a chair alongside the pool to watch the underwater nursing. At 2:00 that afternoon, Bubbles slowly rolled over in the shallow end on her side. The baby then ducked below the surface and nursed. The calf closed its nose and ears to block out water when it dove. Doc's eyes filled with wonder and awe as he marveled at this miracle of nature.

Bubbles proved to be a great mom, never leaving her infant's side, even refusing to get out of the pool long enough to feed herself. The keepers tied carrots to a long pole that stretched across the water to where she lay, thus ensuring she got enough nourishment to sustain herself.

Bulgy reacted casually toward his offspring. The newborn calf glided through the bars for brief visits with her dad. The keepers watched carefully, but the male was a relaxed dad.

With the completion of the behind-the-scenes nursery pool and quarters, the time came to move the mother and daughter to their private quarters. Bubbles refused to go, ignoring even the enticements of food. Giving in to the stubborn, obstinate female, Doc moved the male into the separate nursery pool, giving mother and child access to the entire exhibit. Distracted by food, Bulgy chomped along the line of cantaloupe slices straight to his new home.

Bubbles and Bulgy produced fourteen more healthy calves, making them one of the most productive pairs in the United States. Doc enjoyed an excellent problem: finding zoos wanting to add a hippo to their collection. Bubbles died on January 31, 2002, at age 46, weighing 4,000 pounds.

The results of the necropsy (animal autopsy) caught Doc by surprise. It revealed that Bubbles had sustained a broken pelvis when Bulgy tried to breed following the first birth. Doc had observed her limp, but getting an X-ray was impossible. Plus, the injury did not seem to be a problem in her small enclosure. The necropsy revealed, however, that she had suffered through her many pregnancies and deliveries with this undetected handicap. The small space of the exhibit did not allow Bubbles room to get away from Bulgy. In many species, the males, stimulated by the increased hormones following birth, are ready to mate, which is apparently what drove Bulgy into his state of agitation.

The public loved Bubbles and Bulgy; they hand-fed the pair lettuce and tossed food pellets into their gaping mouths. Every day, Doc made his rounds, checking on his "family." He had relationships with all the animals in his care. As he approached the hippo pool, Bubbles and Bulgy strolled to the edge and opened their four-foot mouths, ready for their daily jaw rubbing.

The mighty hippo mouth, ready for a treat.

But Doc realized that even hippos deserved a treat. Since their diet consisted primarily of dry hay, and the addition of greens was a nutritionally sound practice. In 1969, he contacted Hydroculture, Inc. of Phoenix, which loaned the zoo a hydroponic unit on a trial basis. The unit consisted of rotating shelves that held the seed and water-filled trays the grass grew in. It stood in a temperature-controlled 8-by-10-foot aluminum shed behind the hippo exhibit.

At the time, a ton of hay cost $60, while a ton of grass cost only $36, almost half the price. The operation was simple: Put the seed in the tray and place the tray on the rotating rack. Leave it alone, and seven days later take out the tray filled with 12-inch-high grass. By constantly replenishing the seed, you could have a never-ending supply of fresh grass. The unit could grow 360 pounds of grass every day!

Bubbles and Bulgy liked this addition to their diet; the wet grass was more like the grasses in their native Africa. The fact that this grass was grown inside a portable container did not matter to them. In the afternoons, their mouths opened in wide anticipation upon seeing the keeper carrying a tray of grass on his shoulder. Each day they happily chomped through their ration of fresh grass. Zoo visitors crowded around the exhibit to watch the big clumps of grass being tossed to the hippos.

Unfortunately, this system did have drawbacks; the pumps and hoses needed frequent service, and minor variations in humidity and temperature caused mold on the grass. Plus, the unit itself cost a whopping $5,000. After considering all the pros and cons, Dr. Chaffee decided against purchasing the unit for the zoo. He instead supplemented the hippos' hay diet with alfalfa cubes, which they ate with just as much relish.

Bulgy died on November 10, 2005. He was 49 years old and weighed 6,000 pounds. The zoo demolished the exhibit soon after he died. Sometime earlier, the National Association of Zoos and Aquariums had deemed it unacceptable but permitted Bulgy to stay until he died rather than upset him with a new environment in his old age. The visitors loved Bulgy and Bubbles and felt a close connection to them.

CHAPTER 13

Rajah and Sheba, the Feisty Tigers

The Bengal tiger is one of six living subspecies of tiger. It is found in India, Bangladesh, Nepal, and Bhutan, with some living on the edges of populated areas. Bengal tigers are formidable creatures. Most individuals are just under ten feet long and weigh around 550 pounds. They sport reddish-orange fur with black stripes and white underbellies. A shape like a black sprig of bamboo lies in the middle of their forehead, and most have white spots behind their ears and white-tipped tails that they use for communicating with others in their group. A tail in the air means they are not on a hunt.

In 1953, two feisty seven-month-old Bengal tigers from the wilderness near Calcutta, India, arrived at the Fresno Zoo. They came like they left India, aggressive, snarling, and scratching at everything in sight. Placed in the cat barn, the striped-coated Rajah and Sheba joined the zoo family by spitting on their neighbor, the elder lion Cap. They then growled their wrath at Leona's two lion cubs on the other side of the barrier. All this didn't bode well for promoting friendly relations in the cat barn. The public flocked to the zoo for a close-up view of these 60-pound belligerent carnivores. Rajah and Sheba always succeeded in putting on a good show.

As cats are prone to do, Rajah and Sheba soon began breeding and altogether produced seven litters. In 1962, Sheba gave birth to her first set of twin daughters. Not knowing what to do with these tiny nuisances, Sheba killed them. Her next three litters she also killed or ignored.

Doc decided to use a different approach with Sheba's fourth litter of newborns. He removed the pair into a portable incubator, to which he added a heating pad and a supply of the formula Esbilac, and then headed home. He greeted his family with two fragile one-and-a-half-pound cubs in hand. His family, usually nonchalant over having animal patients around the house, hovered over these "wild" day-old kittens. The three Chaffee boys became instant celebrities among their schoolmates.

The euphoria faded quickly as the cub's delicate situation required feeding them every two hours around the clock. Doc's wife, a Valley Children's Hospital nurse, cared for the remaining cub after one died. Peggy and the cub shared a birthday, so Doc honored his wife by naming the cub Peggy Lou. "It was touch and go with the survivor for several days. We only barely pulled her through," said Doc at the time. "But tender loving care, careful attention to sterilizing every contact she had, and baby food did the trick. Today, Peggy Lou is a happy, healthy, and contented pussy-cat—I mean tiger." The cub loved her morning hugs as the kids left for school, thriving on the special attention.

After gaining some strength, Peggy Lou became a full member of the Chaffee household, which included Boots, the house cat. Each morning, Doc bathed the growing cub, put drops in her eyes, and gave her vitamins. Peggy learned to wear gloves while giving the cub a bottle; her growing claws had already left a scratch.

Doc's parents had moved to Fresno from Michigan to help out the family and Doc's pet clinic. His father stayed at the pet clinic when Doc had to make his zoo rounds. He had neglected to warn his mother about this furry addition to the family that needed special care. It didn't surprise his mother, though, since her son had collected all manner of wildlife growing up on the shores of Lake Huron—although Mother had drawn the line one day when she nearly washed a snake hidden in his pants pocket. Even so, she never dreamed she would serve as a surrogate mother to a tiger.

Every night, the cub enjoyed the bath-licking from Boots, who adopted Peggy Lou as her own. As Peggy Lou grew more robust, the three boys took turns roughhousing and playing "cat and mouse" with her. The young tiger sensed their four-year-old sister was unlike her brothers, never baring her claws when playing with Denise. Little Ms. Peggy sometimes climbed into the children's toy box and tossed everything onto the floor. When no one noticed, the curious feline would slip into a closet and emerge with shoes and slippers to chew. The family's most cherished keepsake became a mangled and clawed slipper.

The doorbell frequently rang with friends and neighbors bringing gifts and hoping for a peek at the wild one. "The lucky ones got to don gloves and feed her a bottle of milk. The gloves protect hands from the claws of a greedy kitten," said the elder Peggy.

Finally, after nearly four months of happy living among humans, Peggy Lou had to return to the zoo. The Chaffees sent along her heating blanket and toys to comfort the little royal Bengal feline. She was taken to a holding area to give her time to adjust to her new environment. Even the seasoned keepers relished the opportunity to romp with this hand-raised young tiger. Each day, they stopped by to visit and play, until it became too risky as Peggy Lou grew. After a month, she was transferred to the adult cat barn, adjusting to life as a full-grown tiger. She was placed in the run next to her parents; Rajah chuffed his welcome while Sheba ignored her.

Will the four-month-old remember the Chaffees? visitors wondered. *The Bee* responded, "Her tameness will disappear soon after she returns to the zoo. At that time, she will be on solid foods, including raw meat, and her natural, wild instincts will predominate. Doc will continue to see her daily, but there will be bars between them for safety."

Sheba's due date for the next litter was mid-November 1963. Knowing her track record for killing her newborn cubs, Doc set up

Sheba with her babies.

an every-two-hour watch to keep an eye on her. At that time, the zoo had no fence enclosing it, so the park's police officers took turns checking on Sheba during their rounds. The police perked up with the new responsibility, as it provided a nice break from their boring night duty.

No private area was available in the cat barn to shield Sheba and the new litter from onlookers. Excited crowds made her nervous, and nervous tiger mothers tended to destroy their babies. After the litter was delivered, Doc got the call. He dashed to the zoo and bundled up the three cubs and once again headed home. The healthy hand-raised cubs eventually joined the circus, and Sheba went to another zoo in 1967.

At one time, Peggy Lou and her father, Rajah, had to share a space. Doc assumed it was safe, as the young female was only two years old. But Peggy Lou became pregnant. Inbreeding can lead to genetic disorders, but it didn't seem to bother this pair. Peggy Lou and Rajah successfully parented three more litters, which yielded nine surviving, healthy cubs. Peggy Lou died in 1969; Rajah lived for another two years.

Soon after the death of Peggy Lou, Doc located a second pair of Bengal tigers. Confusion exists because the next set of tigers carried the names of Rajah #2 and Peggy #2. They arrived together in February 1970 at four months of age. Knowing that tigers, unlike most cats, love water, Doc got busy and built a small pool in their enclosure before they arrived. Fresno has sweltering summers, with temperatures often rising above 100 degrees. The new pair enjoyed taking a daily dip and, in warm weather, submerged themselves up to their shoulders to better cool off. Rajah, Rajah #2, and Peggy #2 were often seen frolicking together in the water.

At four and a half years old, Peggy #2 and Rajah #2 began having babies, and then more and more babies. Once they got the hang of it, they never quit. Doc considered a vasectomy for Rajah #2 after litter number three, and was still thinking about it after litter number 9.

Rajah #2 and Peggy #2 spent sixteen years living together. They slept together in the same night house, even though they each had their own space. Even the keepers were impressed with the level of devotion they had for each other. They ate side by side, unusual even among household pets, much less wild animals. The only separations happened when a new litter of cubs arrived. When this happened, Rajah #2 would hover on the other side of the barrier and yowl for his mate. His emotional outcry was impressive in that tigers are nomadic in the wild. They only come together for breeding and then go their separate ways. Male tigers rarely see their offspring.

When Peggy #2 died in January 1986, Rajah #2's response astounded zookeepers and visitors alike. Tigers have a "moaning" cry used in the wild to communicate over distances. After Peggy's death, Rajah cried daily. This moaning cry flooded the zoo, sending chills down the spines of those who heard it. He continued this cry every day for two years until he died.

There are genes from the pair's twenty-three of twenty-five surviving cubs throughout zoos in the US and China.

CHAPTER 14

Suma and Sumac

Zookeeper Curley Blocker used his San Diego contacts to arrange for the purchase of two wild-caught orangutans, one of each sex. The orangutans are great apes native to the rainforests of Borneo and Sumatra. Their name is derived from the Malay words *orang*, meaning "person," and *hutan*, meaning "forest"—thus "Man of the Forest."

It takes time to track these animals in the thick Indonesian rainforests; fearful of tigers, they rarely come to the ground. They drink water captured in large bamboo and banana leaves during the daily rain and obtain their food from the trees.

The native people shared the islands with the "orange man" for millennia. The apes use their long, sparse, orange or reddish fur like an umbrella for protection from the heavy rains. The male's thicker long hair resembles dreadlocks. The dominant adult male develops distinctive cheek pads, or flanges, only a mother could love, which are capable of making long calls that attract females and intimidate rivals.

Two teenage orangutans arrived separately at the Roeding Park Zoo in 1959; they came straight out of the forests of Sumatra. The primate enclosure had three sections: chimpanzees, orangutans, and gorillas. It had a cement base for easy cleaning and bedrooms behind the scenes, where the apes received training and were separated, fed, and checked for injuries.

The information is scarce related to the capture of these animals. Suma (female) and Sumac (male), named for their homeland, hit it off from the beginning. Females mature at about ten years old, so Suma, born in 1950, was near breeding age. Sumac, born in 1953, was several years from reaching maturity.

Suma and Sumac spent time getting to know each other as they sat and stared across the enclosure. But soon the obvious affection between the pair tugged at the public's heart. Sumac, double the size of Suma, enveloped her in his long arms. They loved to cuddle. Sitting face to face, they gazed at each other, touching lips gently. This close relationship between orangutans is rare in the wild. Males typically seek out a female only when he senses she is ready to breed. After mating with her, he returns to the forest. Their local environment cannot accommodate two large apes together, so they live solitary lives, unlike their chimpanzee and gorilla counterparts. Zoologists found Suma and Sumac's intimate behavior out of the ordinary and spent years studying them with great interest.

The healthy birth of little Rosie in 1961 caught the zookeepers by surprise. And of course the zoo-loving public went crazy in love with her. This rare in-captivity birth brought national attention to the zoo. Predicting how wild-caught animals will react in a captive situation is complicated. At times, the unnatural living conditions in a zoo will distress them, and they lose the desire to breed. Nonetheless, Suma and Sumac successfully produced offspring.

Doc Chaffee spent every spare moment researching the available literature on primates. Adult male orangutans weigh about 165 pounds and stand five feet, while females reach 82 pounds. Their solid and long arms carry them as they brachiate (swing) through the branches; the short legs with long curved fingers and toes help them wrap around tree limbs. They have thirty-two teeth, capable of cracking, crushing, and chewing fibrous food. These "red people of the forest" are omnivores, eating leaves, fruits, bird eggs, and rats.

Orangutans are highly creative: They use sticks or rocks as tools to rip open the outside covering of seed pods to get to the delicacies they love, and they push long sticks deep into ant holes to reach the nourishing ants. Zookeepers learned the hard way to check for

Orangutan on climbing apparatus.

loosened bolts and screws. These adept apes will quietly unscrew a nut on their cage until the door falls into their hands. They have astonishing patience, keeping at a task until it is complete.

Orangutans, the largest arboreal mammal, are very well adapted to life in the trees. They are a food source for tigers, wild dogs, and crocodiles, so they sleep high in the trees to escape predators. However, the white cement of the Fresno Zoo's exhibit in no way resembled Suma and Sumac's familiar green trees habitat in the Sumatran rainforests.

In the wild, the female raises the offspring by herself for eight to ten years, teaching youngsters all the skills necessary to survive alone in the rainforest. In this case, however, the male Sumac helped with caring for his new baby. He never showed hostility toward her, and was very patient with their active little daughter, spending many an afternoon as a jungle gym for little Rosie to climb on. A young orangutan builds strength by gripping the long hair of their parent as they swing through the trees. Sumac played an essential role in her development, letting his daughter develop her strength by gripping his dreadlocks.

In 1965, little brother Roger came along. According to *The Fresno Bee*, Roger's daytime birth brought delight to the "jillions of kids" who witnessed it. Suma and baby Roger spent a few quiet weeks behind the scenes alone. They needed some bonding time after the excitement of Roger being born in full public view. When Roger turned one year old, he left the zoo in exchange for another young male, Itu. Itu came to Fresno as a future mate for Rosie. He was a Bornean native and still immature at six years old. Rosie and her new friend set up housekeeping next door, but they were not together long. Any offspring would have been rejected for further breeding because of its mixed Bornean and Sumatran genes.

The Roeding Park Zoo had no choice but to send their juveniles to other facilities, the orangutans having filled out their allotted space. Young Denny, the third offspring, born in 1967, went to Monroe Zoo in Los Angeles for $4,000. As a point of reference, $4,000 equaled the price of a Cadillac in 1968. Rosie and Itu went to different zoos for $4,000. Most of the $12,000 the zoo received for the three apes helped to buy new animals, while some went into the nursery building fund. A fourth offspring, Azak, was the only one to remain at the zoo.

Suma and Sumac had six offspring, twenty-one grandchildren, and seven great-grandchildren. Their Sumatran genetics, when not mixed with Bornean orangutans, were prized. Fresno was fortunate to receive the pair; today, the countries of Sumatra and Borneo have banned the further exportation of orangutans. Orangutans are considered critically endangered, primarily due to poaching and to habitat destruction caused by the planting of palm oil trees. Suma and Sumac's many offspring have greatly aided the preservation of the species.

CHAPTER 15

Tahlulu, Midge, and Andy

In 1961, at one year old, Tahlulu the chimpanzee lost her adoptive parents, Gracie and Bozo. After Gracie died, Bozo went to another zoo. The Zoo Society contacted other zoos, looking to find a companion for Tahlulu. On Valentine's Day, 1961, Midge arrived as a companion for Tahlulu. The documents were sketchy then, and Midge's history is unclear. She came as a toddler through a well-known Dutch animal dealer. Her capacity to trust humans suggests she had positive human encounters in her past.

At just eight months old, Midge still needed the care essential for an infant. Separated from her mother at an early age, she had flown in the hold of an airplane across an ocean. Loading onto another plane, she crossed the continent to San Francisco Airport and was taken by a car driven by zookeeper Curley Blocker to Fresno. All the ordeals and changes understandably made her nervous and fearful. She needed comfort and security to feel safe again. Her long, human-like fingers clung to Curley and his wife as they spent endless hours with Midge cuddled in their nurturing arms. Chimpanzee mothers never put down their infants during the first several months. After that, the baby rides on the mother or stays within arm's length until they reach four or five years old. At the Locker home, Midge used the window curtains as her swing to strengthen her arms.

A third chimpanzee, Andy, two-and-a-half years old, arrived in late December 1964. The trio, Tahlulu, Andy, and Midge, required more space than the series of cages provided. Under Doc Chaffee's new leadership, the Zoo Society rushed plans for a new exhibit, to be called Ape Grotto, to offer more expansive and healthier quarters. The design called for three outdoor cement sections to exhibit the primate species: chimpanzees, gorillas, and orangutans. The modern exhibit's deep, dry moat gave visitors an unobstructed view; it almost felt like sharing the same space.

Behind the outside wall, the apes' night quarters were an improvement. Each of the night quarters divided into smaller bedrooms. Central heat and the air conditioning blew through the open space to kept them comfortable in the Valley's frosty winters and sizzling summers. Keepers checked them every day for any recent cuts or other injuries, inspected the chimps' droppings, and closely monitored the amount of food they ate.

The three amigos became zoo favorites with visitors. Comfortable with their keepers, they related to the humans outside the exhibit. The threesome chased, screamed, and ran after each other with arms flying. They made funny faces, keeping the visitors in stitches over their antics. Fresnans followed their stories in The Fresno Bee, which featured articles detailing the chimps' histories and inspired the community to appreciate them even more.

Tahlulu, the gymnast of the three, found she could jump to the top of the roof and look at the outside world. Multiple requests went to the city council to add a board along the roof to block her access, but these request went unheeded. When she turned five years old, her Houdini escapades came more often. Her fans loved it. They came loaded down with picnic treats, secretly hoping for one of her infamous visits.

On the other hand, the zoo did not welcome her notoriety. On one notable occasion, hearing picnickers in the nearby amphitheater, Tahlulu could not resist the temptation of a friendly visit. With a single leap to the exhibit's rooftop, she had an unobscured view. Walking along the top, she spotted an activity that interested her and off she went to check out the action. Once there, she plopped down in the middle of flabbergasted picnickers and helped herself to their tasty morsels. The picnickers' screams sent her to another table for fried chicken and a friendlier reception. Black-and-white Kodak photos of this rare and unforgettable occasion verified the stories to friends and family, who were shocked or envious. Finally, a frazzled zookeeper lured the breakout queen home with the enticement of a tasty popsicle. After several such escapes, the staff kept handy a stash of popsicles to bring the wanderer back. Eventually, the city council approved an addition to the roofline to keep her from anymore getaways.

For some reason, chimps are sometimes kept as pets. However, they are the most unpredictable of all the great apes in the wild. Captive or pet chimpanzees attack people far more often than their wild kin because they can lose their fear of people altogether. Chimpanzees typically direct their aggressive and sometimes predatory behavior toward children. During attacks, chimps target a person's face, hands, feet, and genitals. This is why Tahlulu's persistence in getting out created too much risk for the zoo. In 1966, she was transferred to a new zoo that featured a more secure exhibit space. Andy left in 1970.

CHAPTER 16

The Bleak Black Rhinos

Kay Miles, Zoo Society secretary, was a huge asset to the growth of the zoo from the Society's formation in 1950. With a pencil stuck in her blond hair, glasses atop her head, and a phone attached to her right ear, she focused, absorbing the crackling words from distant continents. The map over her desk, littered with pins stuck in countries around the world, hinted at her profound knowledge of the animal traders' domains. Kay was in her element, making phone calls to the most remote areas and bargaining with exotic animal dealers.

The Zoo Society aimed to acquire ten major animals in ten years. They now had four of Africa's big five: an elephant, lions, giraffes, and hippos. The last holdout was the rhinoceros. In 1962, Kay hit pay dirt when she contracted with trackers Heinz Ruhe and Louis Goebel from Thousand Oaks, California. They set out for South Africa and returned with not one rhino, but two. Getting a prized breeding pair of southern black rhinos in the collection would improve the zoo's status in the eyes of the Association of Zoos and Aquariums.

Two major rhino species are found in Africa: southern white and southern black. They have very different temperaments. The white rhinos are calm and live in social groups. Technically, they are not white but gray; their name came from the Dutch word *wiet-lipped* (meaning wide), which sounded like white, and it stuck. The most notable difference is that black rhinos have a hooked upper lip, while white rhinos have a square lip. Both species have very poor eyesight, so they rely on sounds picked up by their ever-shifting ears and on their excellent sense of smell.

The black rhino stands four to five feet and weighs 1,800 to 3,100 pounds. Their average life span is 35 to 50 years. The critically endangered black rhinos are browsers, with prehensile lips that wrap around stems, pulling leaves to their mouths. They are generally solitary and antisocial, and do not maintain long-term social bonds. Far more shy, secretive, and aggressive than the white rhino, the grayish black rhino can be challenging to track and spot.

Populations of black rhinos declined dramatically in the twentieth century at the hands of European hunters and settlers. From 1960 to 1995, black rhino numbers dropped by 96 percent, from around 65,000 to fewer than 2,500. The Chinese hunted them for their horns, which were used as an aphrodisiac that promised virility. However, the horns, which are not bony but combine hair and keratin (fingernails), provide no unique qualities—although that has not slowed the poachers. The Zoo Society's plan highlighted endangered species such as rhinos to educate and draw attention to the urgency to protect them.

In the summer of 1962, Heinz Ruhe and Louis Goebel traveled to South Africa and hired safari trackers to take them deep into the bush to locate two perfect black rhino specimens, a male and a female. Once found and tranquilized, the pair were loaded into two crates built specifically for their size and put on a truck. The traders drove several hundred miles to a port and loaded the crates onto a boat headed to Germany. From there, they caught a ship across the Atlantic, passed through the Panama Canal, and finally docked in Long Beach, California. The arduous trip took a toll on the animals, and they arrived tired, hungry, and stressed.

By December 1962, the Zoo Society had received word the rhinos were on their way. Unfortunately, work on their exhibit had just begun, and it would be months before completion, forcing Kay to find a temporary home for the pair. She contacted the San Francisco Zoo, but they declined to assist, having no space for two four-year-old adult rhinos. Fortunately, Ruhe and Goebel agreed to hold the animals at their Thousand Oaks ranch.

In August 1963, eight months later, with the exhibit at last completed, Kay Miles arranged for their delivery. Meanwhile, Doc Chaffee combed through the sparse research, looking for anything on black rhinos and finding little of substance.

When news broke of "Romeo and Juliet's" pending arrival, the public came out by scores to greet the pair. The driver backed his large, flatbed truck up to the rhino fence, where the unloading team took over. One man stood on the truck bed, gently talking to the animals, reassuring them that all was safe and secure. The crates were windowless to reduce the likelihood of them getting spooked.

The heavy crane lowered a thick chain, which was wrapped around each of the substantial wooden crates, and then a large hook was attached to the top of the container. Once confident that the boxes were secure, the crane operator slowly lifted them one by one off the truck, careful not to let the crates swing in the air. He eased the prized cargo down onto the ground. When no noise emanated from the crates, a worker crept on top of each crate and lifted the doors, allowing the black-horned mammals to step into their new lives.

Black plated, with rough covering, Juliet gingerly tested one foot on the ground, looked around, sniffed the Fresno air, and calmly stepped out amid the cheers. Then, the 3,000-pound Romeo decisively strode out of his crate, ears rotating in the air, listening for danger, and headed straight to the spread of fresh hay, ignoring the commotion.

The new facility's design eliminated the bars that typically surrounded zoo pens. Instead, a sloped, dry moat created a safety zone to keep the rhinos in but did not interfere with a perfect view. A small pool gave the rhinos a refreshing place to cool off in Fresno's scorching summers. The large night house in the rear quarters comfortably held the two massive rhinos.

After exploring their new area and stretching their legs from the trip, the pair bedded down together on the hay-strewn dirt floor; the staff felt confident they would settle in quietly after several months together at the Thousand Oaks ranch. Everyone left for the night, satisfied that they had accomplished their mission.

Keepers headed to the barn early the following day to check on the new arrivals. They first spotted a dent in the fence where Romeo had rammed it during the night. Something felt wrong; their hearts quickened and an uneasiness permeated the air. To their alarm, they spotted the severely injured Juliet lying on the ground, not moving. It appeared Romeo had rammed his mate. The men immediately called Doc Chaffee, who threw on his clothes, grabbed his medical bag, and rushed to the zoo. Heartsick by the gravity of the injuries, he knew he couldn't save her. She died within a few days from internal injuries.

Six months later, the Society found a second female, Geranium, for the lone Romeo. To prepare for her arrival, Doc installed a set of bars to separate the pair at night. However, when the two-year-old Geranium stepped out of the crate into the exhibit, she spotted Romeo and immediately charged him, ramming her horn in his side, striking him where the skin folds at his back leg. Fortunately, the injury did not hurt him, but, as luck would have it, Romeo got overly excited during their first night together and attempted to reach his new mate. The male's elongated 300-pound head became jammed between the newly installed bars separating their bedrooms, and he couldn't disentangle his horn. He had twisted his body into a pretzel, trying to wrench himself loose.

The next day, the keepers found him in misery, entwined and unable to move. Once again, Doc received an early morning call. Despite all efforts to release Romeo, they could not free him and had to cut the bars from around his head. Sadly, he died several days later, leaving Geranium and the zoo staff devastated.

To locate another male for Geranium, the Zoo Society contacted Gunner Wolfgang, a South African hunter. Wolfgang and his team stalked an African herd for weeks, attempting to dart one. Their challenge was that the rhino's tough, prehistoric-like hide kept resisting the darts. It was so problematic that the determined hunter traveled 400 miles back home for more darts. Finally, one of the shafts stuck into the black rhino's horny hide, and he slowly crumpled into a calm, deep sleep. His days of wandering the bush had ended.

Wolfgang crated the huge male and traveled with him on a freighter to the US, then by truck from Louisiana to Fresno. The massive animal, dubbed Geoffrey by Dr. Chaffee, stormed around when he stepped out from his small, uncomfortable crate, stomping his displeasure to the welcoming crowd.

Sadly, in December 1965, just four months later, he died from an infection he had picked up in his native Africa. During the necropsy, Doc found bottle caps embedded in the rhino's feet. Deplorably, in those days, visitors were (and still are) notorious for throwing items into zoo exhibits, creating hazardous conditions for the animals.

The eight-year-old Geranium died in December 1970 from emphysema. Doc, who by then was the full-time Zoo Director, determined that the days of maintaining wild black rhinos had ended, and any further rhinos would be the white species.

Accredited zoos today work closely with international groups to protect and save critically endangered black rhinos through education and financial support. The AZA and individual zoos support protective work in the field. Today, black rhinos can be found in only nine zoos. The San Diego Zoo boasts eighteen black rhinos in their Wild Animal Park.

According to the African Rhino Specialist Group of the IUCN's Species Survival Commission, the population of black rhinos has grown by 12 percent in recent years, from approximately 5,495 individuals in 2017 to more than 6,000 in 2023.

South Africa, Namibia, Zimbabwe, and Kenya realize that safari tourism is a lucrative income and have turned former poachers into paid protectors. The comeback of the critically endangered black rhino is today's success story.

CHAPTER 17

The Nursery Becomes a Reality

The Fresno McKinley Pet Clinic veterinarian, Doctor Paul Chaffee, mourned whenever he lost a client's beloved animal. He hovered over each one, giving them his best care, even staying the night when needed. His reputation as an excellent and caring veterinarian spread throughout Fresno. Decades later, people have fond memories of him as their pet veterinarian.

From 1961–64, Doc assisted Dr. Griffenhagen (his landlord) in the veterinarian care of the Fresno Zoo animals, splitting his time between the two facilities. Griffenhagen had confidence in Doc, leaving him in complete charge whenever he went on vacation.

During his years as a part-time zoo staff member, Doc improved basic elements that helped the general health of the animals. He installed heat lamps and updated the water and waste removal systems. Still, too many of the young offspring died from overexposure to the cold. With the limited exhibit space, certain vulnerable animals were at the mercy of aggressive males. But it was the loss of the zoo's young gorillas that particularly disturbed Doc. The childlike apes resembled his own babies, and he took it personally.

In 1965, when Fresno City appointed Doc full-time Director, constructing a nursery topped his agenda. The building was located close to the primate section in the northern part of the zoo. Doc included a small office for himself so he could be close to the fragile animals as needed.

The design provided the ability to control various environmental factors to ensure the animals' comfort. Part of the facility included a kitchen with built-in sterilizers, a stove, a refrigerator, and a locked cupboard for keeping medications. Food storage bins provided optimum conditions for diet preparation. There was also a storage closet with a washer and dryer. An egg incubator was added for ostrich and emu eggs, which benefited from being rotated slowly. Multiple baby alligators were also hatched in an incubator.

To handle full-time medical needs, Doc went through Fresno State College's science department to find help. There was no money in the budget to hire a medical technician full-time, so he recruited female biology students to staff the medical facility. Their responsibility would be to care for the youngsters, giving the same attention they would get from their mothers: feeding, grooming, and nurturing. Food was measured and weighed. Everything was sterilized. Before entering the room, all staff walked through a box to disinfect their shoes. The nursery aides were given clean white medical gowns to wear daily. Some of the girls worked as volunteers while others received $1.65 an hour. Because they were students, the staffing schedule revolved around their class schedules so that not all of them were on duty at the same time.

Doc recognized that animal babies were a strong attraction to the public and took advantage of their interest. He always had an eye toward increasing attendance in the zoo. The nursery was built in the middle of the zoo's six acres so that visitors could find it easily.

Each occupant in the nursery had its own separate quarters. There were five smaller cubicles, and a larger one for young apes was nearest to the kitchen. With the public in mind, Doc had glass windows installed at each enclosure. Visitors tiptoed by the individual stalls so they wouldn't disturb those inside while hoping for a glimpse. "No Tapping on the Window" signs encouraged visitors to follow the rules and not frighten the little ones. *Ohhs* and *Ahhs* were commonly heard from captivated guests. Zoo fans had their favorite babies and returned frequently to follow their progress. The staff celebrated when a nursery baby graduated into an exhibit to reunite with his family.

Doc added a small petting area next to the building to hold the hardier small mammals, such as the Barbary sheep lambs and the young elk. The area was open to the public, but in a short time, he came to hate the petting zoo so much that he had it converted into an exercise yard to build up the animals' muscle strength. He couldn't stand to see the young animals mistreated by the visitors, and he felt that it sent the wrong message. His belief was we should respect wild animals not as captive pets but as magnificent wild creatures.

One of the earlier attendants was Sally Smith, who worked at the zoo for nearly thirteen years. Sally claims she had the best job in the world—working with animal babies. She clearly remembers the day that her life took a sharp focus on what she wanted to do when she grew up. Sally recounts her first meeting with Dr. Chaffee.

"I met Dr. Chaffee when I was eight years old. He was our family vet, and I was working on my animal card badge for Girl Scouts. My mom called for an appointment for me to interview him. Much to my amazement, he cleared the entire afternoon for my friend and me. He acted as if we were the only people in the world. That afternoon, he answered all our tedious questions and taught us how to listen to a heartbeat and take our pulse. From then on, I worshiped him and wanted to be just like him.

"I took classes in high school preparing to work at the zoo. When I was 15, I talked to Doc about volunteering for the summer. They had no programs for young teens then, but he set me up with a local vet. Then I heard the zoo hired college biology students to work in the nursery. I pestered him until I got the call in August of 1968."

Because Doc had no secretary, the aides helped as his office assistants. From his side office, he could hear everything in the nursery. It gave the students confidence, knowing he could be at their side whenever they needed help.

"He taught us everything we needed to know," shared Sally. "We learned how to do everything legal for a medical technician, from injections to using the dart gun. I am very fortunate to have had the best teacher in the world standing beside me every step of the way."

Doc often treated local native birds with broken bones and wings because no other animal rehab center was available. Once Fish and Game discovered his willingness to care for them, they sent hundreds of injured birds to the nursery. Doc had an unusual knack for orthopedics and he could set just about anything. One special bird was a wounded golden eagle, and Doc was able to pin and wire its damaged wing back together.

Ether was the only anesthetic available at the time; it was used in veterinary medicine whenever it was necessary to operate on an injured animal. No guide existed for treating and anesthetizing exotic animals. After the birds recovered from surgery, they had to be taught how to hunt again. A six-foot-long wire enclosure was added for birds to practice flying in. After they became self-sufficient to hunt independently, they were released back into the wild. Occasionally, when a bird couldn't be released due to its injuries, it went on exhibit or was used in the zoo's mobile program for educational talks.

Doc thought out each move so as not to cause injury to the animal or the keepers. Part of his documentation on every treatment included his observations of their behaviors as well. As a part of his daily rounds, he studied each animal and came to know them through their personalities. Watching him, Sally was mesmerized by the way he handled animals. His gentleness was so natural that they trusted him even after treatment.

Doc was a pioneer, along with Dr. Murray Fowler at UC Davis, for putting together protocols for treating exotics and helping to develop it into a specialty. He never hesitated to call others in the field for help. He encouraged other zoo vets to send him reports on anything special they had done recently. He then retyped those reports, made copies on the mimeograph machine, and transmitted them to all the AZA zoo vets. That was the origin of the AZA's *Zoo Veterinarian Journal*, published from his office.

Sally reflected on the impact Doc had on her life. "Everything I have done since I was eight years old was because of Doc. Nearly all my philosophies about the Earth came from him. His view about our role as stewards of the environment and his respect for wildlife is one that I have adopted by watching the way he treated them. He was passionate about his beliefs; how he lived them out made them real to me. Today, I am a licensed, trained animal practitioner, and I am sure he would approve. What a wonderful person he was."

Several of the original nursery attendants continued to work at the zoo as full-time zookeepers. It was an entry point for women to enter a field dominated by men. Doc hired Mary Swanson as the first female zookeeper in the state of California. She worked with carnivores, especially lions. Sally Smith and Kim Cook worked with Nosey the elephant. Kim retired after nearly forty-five years with elephants, including the massive African elephants. Linda Cover worked with the birds before transferring to another zoo, then returned as the zoo's registrar.

Because so many animals coming to the zoo were separated from their mothers at a young age, they had no role models for when they became parents, and thus ignored or abandoned their own offspring. Every effort is made today to encourage mothers and offspring to remain together.

People continue to share special memories about walking past the nursery. Many, being parents with their own children, readily related to the animal babies. It touched their hearts in a way that caused many to see animals as creatures much like humans, that care, nurture, and bond with their offspring. These people often went on to became ardent supporters of animals found in the wild.

CHAPTER 18

Baby Animal Nursery (by Paul Chaffee)

from Director Paul Chaffee's desk, June, 1971

Since its construction in 1965, the Baby Animal Nursery has been a most successful operation. Hundreds of baby animals, many of them rare species, have been hand reared in the Nursery by attendants trained in the specialized care of wild animal infants. Thus the nursery has been responsible for saving the lives of many baby animals that would not otherwise have survived under more "natural" conditions with their parents.

There are several reasons why baby animals must be hand reared, especially in captivity. Often babies are born during the cold season of the year to animals that originate from tropical environments. Even if the living quarters are properly heated, the young animals may become chilled when they go outside with their mothers. Occasionally, small baby animals may be injured by larger adult animals in an exhibit with whom it is difficult to compete for territory. There are other behavioral problems which may account for lack of proper mother-infant relationships. Some species of primates, for example, are highly socialized animals and learn proper infant care techniques from other members of the social group by observation. Some females, born in captivity or raised as infants in a laboratory or zoo, are deprived of some social experiences they may have learned in the wild.

Our female Hama-
dryas baboon has
exhibited abnormal
mother-infant behav-
ior on the three occa-
sions that she has had
babies. In each case, she
had no difficulty with
the actual birth, but
appeared to lack any
idea of what to do with
the newborn infant.
She would pull the
baby about the exhibit
by a leg, or pick the
baby up by a leg, allow-
ing it to dangle upside
down, frightened and
screaming; as a result,
her babies are removed
immediately following
birth for hand rearing.

Mary Swanson, the Fresno Zoo's first
female zookeeper, started out in the baby
animal nursery.

Our chimpanzee colony consists of one male and two adult
females. In August, 1970, the female, Pampy, gave birth to a fine
little baby, which she cared for in excellent fashion with no signs of
aggression on the part of the other female. Three months later, the
other female, Tiki, forcibly kidnapped Pampy's baby and a violent
struggle ensued. The baby chimp, Brucie, had to be removed for his
own safety and is currently residing in the Zoo Nursery.

Care of infant wild animals has become a specialized part of
zookeeping. Our nursery attendants are college students, usually
young women majoring in biology or wildlife management, who
must prepare many unusual formulas, keep the animals and quarters impeccably clean, attend to the behavioral-psychological needs

of the babies, and often take young ones home for endless hours of night feedings.

In addition to its role in conserving valuable wildlife, the Nursery has also become one of the most popular zoo exhibits. As of the writing, the Nursery is home for Brucie the chimpanzee, a two-year-old baby orangutan called Azak (short for the American Association of Zookeepers), a one-year-old baboon named Belinda, and Belinda's newborn brother, Joshua.

Zoo Attendance for May, 1971

Paid Admission	24,541
Free Admissions	
Children not on tours	19,252
Guided Tours	13,888
Adult escorts	2,690
Total	50,371

Zoo director Paul "Doc" Chaffee
in his office.

CHAPTER 19

Two Seasick Rhinos and a Zoo Director

African safari hunters in their jeeps, camouflaged pants, shirts, and stun guns had captured five black rhinos for the Fresno Zoo between 1963 and 1971. Each outing took weeks and sometimes months, as it was not easy to find the elusive, horned gray mammals. The trips cost tens of thousands of dollars for shipping, permits, and quarantine. Four of the captured rhinos died within days of their arrival and the fifth survived but was sold to another zoo. Not ready to give up, the Zoo Society asked Doc Chaffee to research the differences between the black and white rhinos, thinking maybe they'd have more luck with the latter.

The southern white rhinoceros is one of the largest and heaviest land animals in the world. It has an immense body and large head, a short neck, and a broad chest. White rhino females travel in groups, called "crashes," while the females of the black species are more solitary. The white has a calmer demeanor, enabling it to adjust to the confines of a zoo. A unique feature of this animal is its two horn-like growths, one behind the other on its thick snout. These are made of solid keratin and hair. However, it's their limited vision that makes them dangerous. With 8,000-pound short, squatty bodies, they will blindly charge, destroying whatever is in front of them, possibly including a jeep full of photo-snapping visitors.

The white rhino's wide mouth is ideal for grazing, whereas the black rhino's narrow prehensile lips are designed to wrap around branches and leaves. Most southern white rhinos are found in just four countries: South Africa, Namibia, Zimbabwe, and Kenya.

In 1971, after the devastating losses of the black rhinos, Doc applied to escort a pair of white rhinos safely across the Atlantic Ocean. The Zoo Society agreed to pay $15,000 for the acquisition, including the vet's expenses from the Netherlands to Fresno.

The captured pair was quarantined for thirty days in South Africa, then crated and put aboard a ship headed for Rotterdam, the connection point for international trade, where Doc met them.

Piling through mountains of red tape and travel requirements was the sacrifice for entering the United States with his two rhinos. Once he finished the paperwork, he learned about the longshoremen strike along the California west coast. His original route had the freighter going through the Panama Canal to California, a much shorter trip than going overland. Now he had to locate a freighter going to the East Coast that would accept his rhinos. There was no time to waste with two large mammals forced to remain in crates. Fortunately, he quickly located a freighter willing to take him and his cargo to New York. Finding a qualified New York exotic animal trucker across the international wire lines was a bigger challenge. But at last, one agreed to meet him at the port and be ready to roll across the country. Then Doc crossed his fingers that nothing else would go wrong.

Doc and his rhinos shoved off for the long trip across the Atlantic Ocean. During the voyage, Doc strolled up to the steering compartment and talked ships with the crew. His own St. Clair River experiences as a child made for an instant relationship with the crew, who gave him free access to any part of the boat.

The four-ton rhinos occupied a specially designed crate that fit snugly in the ship's hold. Doc was the rhinos' sole caretaker and had to make multiple trips a day down the stairs to care for his animals. With his vulnerability toward sea, air, and height sickness, he struggled to control his queasy stomach every time he stepped down into the overly warm and smelly hold. He kept his bucket close at hand.

The rhinos had their own bouts with seasickness. According to Doc, "You have not lived until you have to clean up after two rhinos suffering from diarrhea." The male was good-natured, but the female had a mean temper. Sometimes when he reached his rake inside the crate to remove the mess, she turned to kick him, worsening the clean-up process.

The rhinos had learned to eat dry alfalfa cubes and drink from a bucket before leaving Africa, which reduced the amount of waste. Occasionally, they revolted against the pellets. The vet chewed them first, making them more palpable. He did most of his work in dimmed light, worried that suddenly turning on the lights might startle them. Squeezed into their tight space, any sudden moves could easily frighten them into a precarious position in the crates.

Using an oil can, he squirted an ointment on their joints to keep them limber. The freighter crew laughed as they watched him "oil the armored creatures." Doc added a new line to his resume as "Rhino masseuse." As the animals were cooped up in their tight crates for weeks, Doc attentively massaged their stiff muscles, giving them some well-deserved relief. The hours he spent with the pair created a lasting bond.

The dock strike spread to the East Coast while they were crossing the ocean, forcing them to remain anchored offshore for several more days. All three were ready for solid ground when the freighter finally tied up in New Jersey. The trucker found them quickly, as they were the only African rhinos aboard the ship. After settling the final paperwork, the two men loaded the truck and started out for the 3000-mile cross-country trip. Forty miles an hour was their limit, given their hefty and precious load. Each night, he and the driver looked forward to the reactions as they registered at a motel. "We would like a room for two men and a place to park our rhinos." "Pardon me?"

Having started his trip from California in August, Doc had not packed for East Coast September rain or freezing weather. Wearing all his shirts, he pulled on a hooded jacket and climbed on top of the truck twice a day. Pulling back the tarp, he fed and watered the rhinos, raked out the manure, and cleaned the truck bed.

At long last, the Highway 99 Belmont sign pointing to the Fresno Zoo indicated their travels were finally ended. The travel-weary southern white rhinos had been in their crates for six weeks: three weeks on the ship and three weeks in the truck. A welcoming crowd had collected at the gate to wave their hellos as they followed the tired travelers to the prepared exhibit. A hushed silence fell over the assemblage as the truck backed into the landing ramp. The crane carefully lifted the sheet-covered crate onto the ground and a keeper crawled on top to unlock the cage door. As the door lifted, Doc expected an explosion from the cantankerous female. Instead, both rhinos exited slowly on their wobbly legs.

The massive white rhino.

Weak and stiff after spending so long in one standing position, they calmly looked around. Getting a whiff of fresh air, they sauntered to the nearby pile of green hay and dug in.

One rhino developed a dreadful case of diarrhea soon after their arrival. Doc tried everything to solve the situation. He experimented with different diets and medications. He called other zoo vets for information. After several months of observing their every move, two-inch-long flies were spotted crawling in the manure. These alien-looking insects appeared to be straight out of a movie. Researching this peculiar fly, it was discovered that African stomach botflies (*Gyrostigma pavasii*) lay their larvae on a rhino's huge flat lips. The larvae then attach themselves to hay when swallowed and lie dormant in the animal's stomach. The process of infestation had begun months earlier before the animals left Africa. The distressing diarrhea continued for months.

Trying every combination of feed, Doc at last found success with same alfalfa cubes they had chewed across the ocean. From then on, he did not deviate from their diets. He never wanted to endure another round of rhinoceros diarrhea. It was heartwarming to observe the bond that had developed during those long weeks of traveling continue on once the animals were in their new home. Whenever Doc made his twice-daily rounds of the zoo, he greeted the rhinos with their special head scratching.

Mudder and Fodder were always a unique attraction at the zoo. Unfortunately, they never produced any young. Rhinos need the atmosphere of a larger herd to be successful breeders. In 1992, the pair went to San Diego Wild Animal Park, where Fodder sired several offspring of this highly endangered species, and Mudder became a mother several times. With the opening of the Chaffee Zoo's Africa Adventure exhibit, a pair of southern white rhinos were added. They are a beloved pair to observe with their biannual offspring, which offer much entertainment.

CHAPTER 20

Bones in the Moat

It started as a typical day for the keepers. Dressed in their khaki pants, shirts, and hats, they moved through the zoo in the cool of the morning, scanning for anything unusual. Nothing appeared abnormal. The lion's roar woke up nearby Olive Street neighbors. Monkeys hooted, the eagle screeched, and Nosey trumpeted her welcome. The keepers worked their way down the rows of cages, hosing, sweeping, cleaning, and scooping poop before the gates opened and the visitors came streaming in. A pair of beaten-up shoes lay next to the concession stand. "Did they belong to anyone?" the keeper asked. No one spoke up, so the shoes were set aside until someone claimed them.

The city jail often sent the overnight drunks and other minor offenders out on work details. The previous day, a group from the jail had worked in the zoo and the park, cleaning up the usual debris from picnickers and zoo-goers. Maybe one of the crew had left their shoes? But who would forget them? That was like going without your pants.

The three bear grottos were closest to the entrance and the concession stand; grizzly bears were among the first to greet visitors as they entered the zoo, the brown bear second. The playful yet menacing polar bears lived in the third grotto, closest to the commissary gate. Polar bears hold a unique fascination, coming from the Arctic region. The bears' white fur blended into their native cold snow and ice surroundings, adaptations that seemed out of place in Fresno's hot summers. The hollow hairs acted as solar heaters, keeping them warm; their fur-covered paws with nonretractable claws enabled traveling over snow and ice. A third eyelid protected their eyes when swimming underwater hunting for seals.

The commissary, or kitchen, sat in the middle of the nine-acre zoo grounds. It had a large walk-in refrigerator, a long prep table, and a double sink where the zoo's kitchen staff prepared individual pans based on each animal's dietary needs. When delivering food supplies, a truck would turn at the polar bears' wall and pass through the unlocked gate to the commissary.

Ice and Berg were a playful pair that enjoyed their eight-foot pool year-round. Feeding time for the polar bears became a popular event for guests. The keepers tossed fish into the pool twice a day, so the bears had to dive for their meals, much like they would in the wild. Public feeding demonstrations were performed for three reasons: to reduce the number of items thrown into the exhibits, to demonstrate the animals' natural eating habits, and to provide enrichment for the captive creatures.

That day in 1966, as a keeper rounded the end of the polar bear exhibit toward the kitchen to get a food tray, he spotted red blood on the polar bears' cement floor. He assumed a peacock had inadvertently flown over the end wall and landed in the exhibit. If so, it had quickly become a breakfast treat. The zookeeper continued his duties, making a mental note to tell the supervisor.

As a second keeper passed the exhibit, he heard unusual sounds coming from the bottom of the deep, dry moat; it caught his attention. Grr . . . gnash . . . grr. The 25-foot-deep moat which separated the carnivorous bears from the public allowed guests to observe the bears without the obstruction of a fence. As the employee looked over the wall into the moat, he spotted the polar bears hovering over what appeared to be a dummy. He stared at the form, trying to understand what he saw. The more he stared, the more he realized a human body lay in the moat.

"Come quick! There's a man in with the polar bears," he yelled.

The stunned workers stared in disbelief at the grotesque sight. The intact figure had no clothes. The bears' claws had ripped the clothing off to get at the meat, tearing at the body. Instinct had taken over these zoo-raised polar bears as they relished their first live meal. The man had no shoes on his feet. The limbs appeared in one piece, except for some loss of flesh from the thighs. Ice and Berg hovered over the body, playing with it, their tongues licking the meat while growling at each other. Chilled icicles trickled down the observers' backs as they watched the white furry clumps systematically pick at the body.

As soon as Doc got the word, he rushed to the exhibit. On his way to the scene, questions raced through his mind: Who is this? How did he get in here? The staff wondered if it could be a City Parks employee—someone they knew. Doc issued a directive: "Close the public entrances until the police arrive and can evaluate the situation."

The next issue caused more angst. Doc had to decide what to do with two 600-pound carnivores. Some experts consider polar bears the most dangerous carnivore on earth, even more so than lions. Polar bears will kill for sport, not just for food, making them unpredictable. Doc called everyone together to get staff input on retrieving the remains from the bottom of the moat. One suggested using the meat hook in the zoo's kitchen to snag the body. But first, they had to get the bears to climb out so the men could work without interference. Only on rare occasions did the bears find themselves at the bottom of the moat, needing to haul themselves out. A ladder was attached to the side wall for people to exit.

Getting the bears out of the moat proved more manageable than they expected. As a rule, food works as an effective lure for zoo animals. But the keepers worried that the white-furred carnivores would ignore their regular food since they had already dined on fresh meat.

On the back side of the exhibit, a ladder led to a roof overhang. From there, a keeper tossed nibbles into the exhibit while observing the bears' behavior. At the scent and sound of their regular food, with full stomachs dragging, the greedy bears managed to heave themselves out of the moat, up the side wall, and over to their next course. The keeper continued to toss tidbits while the rescue team worked to reel in the body. Even these experienced keepers underestimated the capacity of the bears' appetites.

The rest of the staff quickly went to work once the bears were safely away from the carcass. Attaching the meat hook to the end of a long rope, the best fisherman in the group got the job of casting the hook near the body. After several tries, it landed just past the corpse. Then, slowly dragging the hook toward the dead man, it snagged the remains enough to reel it out of the pit. It was a gory sight: a dead man at the end of a hook with parts of his body exposed where the bears had chewed at it.

The shreds of clothing, still reeking of alcohol, had a plastic tag bearing the name Carl Martin. The police pieced together the most likely scenario. Martin, a man of many aliases, had come to Roeding Park to serve his one-day jail punishment for drunkenness. Although a regular drunk tank occupant, he apparently didn't remember that his sentence concluded at the end of his workday. Martin hid out in the park to avoid the ride back downtown. With no police security to check things, he had the park to himself.

Familiar with the zoo from past visits, Martin clambered over the menagerie's outside fence, searching for food and a warm place to sleep. He probably was headed to the kitchen but made an unfortunate wrong turn. Instead of climbing over the commissary gate, the intruder climbed over the adjacent exhibit's wall into the polar bears' lair. The authorities determined that he fell to the bottom of the moat and died from the fall. The gruesome experience left those who were involved shaken. One keeper retained vivid memories of this event when interviewed decades later.

Doc Chaffee had requested security support for many years because of vandalism in the off-hours. However, his frustration over the issue of security continued, because even after the unfortunate death, the city council, once again, refused to authorize the budget item to hire a guard.

The tragic event is the Fresno Zoo's only incident of an animal killing someone. Fortunately, the city did not demand the zoo destroy the bears, concluding that the intruder had died by his own means.

A polar bear cavorting with a keg.

CHAPTER 21

Nosey's Body Language

Doc Chaffee's gentle handling with his McKinley Pet Hospital's patients brought him respect as his reputation spread. Animals responded to his calm, quiet way of establishing trust. As previously mentioned, Chaffee was known to spend the night in his clinic to watch over beloved animals, even including a sick pet rat. During his hours at the zoo, Doc observed how zookeepers handled the animals in their care. Zookeeper Curley Blocker's circus background meant he trained by using whips to make the animals obey out of fear. Doc once watched in horror as Curley grabbed a primate by his head, pulling him out of the cage. Despite her size, Nosey got much the same rough treatment.

Phil Robinson, Doc's pet clinic aide, accompanied him to the zoo as a trusted assistant and animal handler. Phil watched everything his boss did and modeled himself after him. Chaffee encouraged Phil to approach the animals in a much more caring and gentle way.

Nosey would occasionally throw fits of frustration. She'd stomp around on her concrete floor, swaying her trunk and bellowing loud enough that all could hear. As soon as he heard the disturbance, Phil went straight to her enclosure to check it out. As soon as she stopped for a breather, he quietly walked up and began rubbing on her chest, and Nosey relaxed, to Phil's amazement. A deep reverberation emanated from what felt like her whole body, making low sound waves. In his research, Phil found that elephants emit that deep sound whenever they communicate with friends. He regarded that among his highest compliments.

Nosey's original pen, where she lived from 1949 to 1982.

From 1968–1997, Sally Smith worked in the zoo nursery through a part-time Fresno State work-study program for biology majors. She became skilled at handling newborn or orphaned animals. As a student, she added extra hours by filling in open shifts to become familiar with the rest of the zoo's inhabitants, including Nosey the elephant. After a one-year absence, Sally returned to find Nosey in a neglected state. For six months after her primary keeper, Curley, retired, no one had worked with her. She got the essential feeding and cleaning she required, but nothing more—no baths or special attention.

Sally shared her concerns with Doc. After years of living on concrete, Nosey's cracked toenails and ugly callouses showed the neglect. She reeked, adding humiliation to the situation.

Training is essential for primary elephant health care, along with giving injections and checking the ears, teeth, feet, and any cuts. Anesthesia would be dangerous for such a heavy animal, and it is best to treat them while they're awake, so it was necessary they learn to comply with commands.

After being assigned to hoofstock, including the pachyderm, Sally researched Asian elephant animal care, although there were very few animal science references in the libraries at that time. She attended elephant conferences to keep abreast of the modern methods of care.

Sally observed Nosey when she cleaned her pen, suspecting that Nosey knew more than she was showing. In Thailand, mahouts (trainers) lived with their elephants 24/7 and prepared the offspring to follow in their mother's footsteps, doing the heavy lifting jobs. Sally remembered Curley initially walking Nosey around the zoo, but that practice didn't last long as Nosey grew bigger and stronger. What did the 30-year-old adult remember, if anything, of those early years? The years of standing around in a concrete box with no stimulation probably erased her early memories.

Paul Barkman's name came up frequently as a knowledgeable elephant trainer from Marine World/Africa USA, near Vallejo. Meeting him at an elephant conference, Sally urged the "elephant whisperer" to visit the zoo. Barkman surprised her by readily accepting the opportunity to visit Fresno. A chance meeting with Doc years before had made a lasting impression.

Barkman shared his memories of that day: "I remember when another keeper and I delivered animals from the Sacramento Zoo to San Diego and Los Angeles. We were driving back on Highway 99 when we got to the Fresno sign. Back in 1973 or '74, it was called the Roeding Park Zoo. We decided to pull off the freeway, take a break, and walk around the grounds. We ran into the foreman, and as we talked, another gentleman with a beard walked up and joined us. He spoke as if he belonged there but wore regular clothes instead of a uniform. It took a while to discover that this man ran the zoo. Now, I had never met a director who treated us as equals. We spent about an hour having coffee and talking. His impression never left me, and I hoped to meet him again."

Doc also remembered Barkman from that first meeting and knew of his reputation. He and Barkman connected right away, not only by their common name, Paul, but by a common philosophy of respecting the animals. They bonded through their hearts.

Both men stood out within their zoo circles as having something extraordinary, something unique, that few had. Unlike many elephant keepers who came from the circus world and trained to instill fear, this man revealed a gentler side.

When the 5'10", average build, Paul Barkman arrived in Fresno he started his day by getting to know Nosey. Dressed in khaki pants and short-sleeved shirt, Barkman possessed the ability to look into a pachyderm's eyes and read them, and he caught something special about this elephant. What knowledge did Nosey have to follow directions? He found a two-foot diameter, 12-inch high tub to set her feet on while he trimmed the jagged nails. He decided to quietly test her. Lo and behold, she readily responded to Barkman's cues when he placed his ank, or stick, in the right places. She complied by doing different stances on the tub. Nosey lifted one front leg and the opposite back leg at the same time. At one point, Paul climbed on her bent leg and sat as she lifted him. The giant mammal's quick responses surprised and delighted Paul, especially considering Nosey had been alone all her adult life. He confirmed the rumor that an elephant never forgets.

Barkman gave no hint of his discovery. Soon enough, Doc came over to watch the progress. Quietly, Barkman began to put Nosey through her stances as she performed what looked like a dance. Within fifteen minutes, she had gone through twenty positions. Doc watched spellbound as this pair put on a show, his mind racing through a maze of thoughts. Barkman met every criterion Doc needed to lead his expanded elephant section.

He invited Barkman to his office and began sharing his plans for Nosey and his dream to establish a breeding group of elephants. He needed a man like Barkman with experience and knowledge of dealing with male elephants, a man he could trust implicitly to carry out his wishes, a man who could oversee the expanded elephant program. Doc reeled him in like a prized tuna, slow and easy. Doc could see Paul Barkman's mind whirling with excitement as the director continued to share his dream.

Barkman evaluated the situation. He had known of Doc Chaffee's reputation for being a great boss. He recalled when the American Assoc of Zoos and Aquariums turned to Doc for help facilitating the elephant keepers' rebellion against a new hands-off elephant care policy. It was a hot issue, and Doc managed to calm them down to reach an agreement. Barkman jumped at the offer to return as the zoo's elephant program manager when the new enclosure was ready. He looked forward to working with Doc Chaffee.

Barkman included a training session for zookeepers Sally and Danny Abundis for follow-up after he left. He taught the two zookeepers how to use an ank as a cue for different behaviors. He taught them how to lift Nosey's feet on a stool to work on her nails. He gave them training tips to prepare Nosey for a move into a new exhibit. Furthermore, Nosey seemed to like the new mental challenge of following directions. It gave her needed exercise and prepared her for future moving when she would have to follow directions.

Sally later drove to Marine World USA to observe Barkman handle his elephants. "I got a lot of ideas and ways to train the elephants watching Barkman; he trained his elephants very well.

Zookeepers Paul Barkman and Sally Smith file Nosey's feet.

Indeed, he was the elephant whisperer," she said. "I watched him treat his elephants only with gentleness." She looked forward to the time Barkman would bring his training methods to Fresno.

Wistfully, Sally reflected on her time as a zookeeper: "Nosey was a smart 'ole girl. I miss her dearly."

CHAPTER 22

The Cheetah's Day of Fame

The palaces of the ancient Egyptian pharaohs featured cheetah statues overlooking the entrance. According to ancient Egyptian lore, the cheetah was a significant animal in early times. They were often seen in mosaic art with the high priests dating back to 1700 BC. Cheetahs are a rare breed of wild feline in that they can be trained. Egyptian paintings often showed cheetahs sitting at the feet of the queen as her guardians. The sleek felines' arrogant, regal appearance, with their small round heads held high in the air, imitated the queen herself. Families kept cheetahs as house pets; they were valuable for pest control for snakes and other vermin. They were also associated with several Egyptian gods over the centuries.

The cheetah is known for its golden-yellow, black-spotted fur, which blends into the African savannah. They are the smallest of the African felines, but also the fastest, capable of reaching up to 70 miles per hour. They weigh between 74 to 110 pounds, making them vulnerable to the larger African lions and leopards. Their sleek, aerodynamic body is made for speed: They have a flexible spine for quick turns, and their long tail acts as a rudder, swinging back and forth. Their deep chest aids heavy breathing, although they can only sprint at top speed for less than a minute. Novice zoo visitors sometimes confuse the cheetah with the leopard because of their similar spots. However, the cheetah's distinctive black "tear marks" that run from his eyes past his nostril sets him apart

Tommy, a young adult cheetah, came to Fresno from the Miami, Florida, Rare Bird Farm on March 23, 1963. He was purchased for $1300. At first, Tommy resided in the animal nursery, where Doc Chaffee had his office. To Doc, the former cat and dog vet, Tommy was just a big kitty cat. The cheetah lay down by Doc's feet, and they quickly became comfortable in each other's company. Doc could feel the cat's tenderness. However, it was Tommy's intelligence that amazed him.

Tommy's tabby-like purring sounds often led visitors to assume that Doc had a pet cat, and they were surprised to learn it was the spotted, streamlined cheetah lying near his desk that was releasing the soft purrs. The nursery attendants often caught Doc scratching Tommy. "Just bonding," Doc explained.

Doc's first breakthrough with this wild feline came during his veterinary preventive medicine practice. If one can train an animal to assist in its treatment, it can eliminate the need for a sedative, thus reducing a major risk factor. Tommy voluntarily opened his mouth when Doc checked his teeth for periodontal problems, displaying none of the usual hostile resistance. With that encouragement, Doc slipped into the feline's quarters at every opportunity. Before long, he had a toothbrush in the cheetah's mouth.

In 1972, after Tommy died, a second male cheetah replaced him. Duma, Swahili for cheetah, was another amenable cat that became Doc's deskmate. Doc again developed a gentle relationship with this graceful animal. Gaining his confidence, Doc rubbed his flanks, easing his way up until he could touch his head. Soon, a collar was slipped around Duma's neck. Encouraged, Doc added a few steps each day on a leash until they were able to take short walks. First, they walked around the tiny indoor clinic. Then boldly, Doc opened the door and led Duma around the nursery's walled outside space; the cat never attempted to escape. So the next day, they walked outside the clinic's space, where Duma discovered stimulating new smells and sounds. Each day, it was a few more steps forward.

A master at devising ways to advertise the zoo, Doc enticed the press's cameras to include an animal or two in their photo shoots. Waiting for the right moment to spring his surprise, he continued to prep the lustrous, photogenic feline. On an early fall day in 1974, the John Robert Powers Modeling School requested a photo shoot in the zoo. "Of course," responded Doc. This event had the makings of a perfect advertising moment. What could be better than a beautiful female and an aristocratic feline?

The girls came out on a bright November day; the autumn chill permeated the air. Doc had scoped out the zoo and suggested the Barbary sheep exhibit at the south end. The massive, craggy, sloped boulders simulated the sheep's native environment. The Barbary's impressive, curved horns added a regal image overlooking the visitors. The modeling school agreed that it would make a perfect backdrop for the girls.

As they set up, Doc slipped into Duma's enclosure. Putting on the leash and stepping outside the fenced nursery space, he returned, parading the sleek cat. He visualized the cheetah sitting on a craggy ledge: tawny body blending into the rocks, black spots sparkling in the sun, his long legs matching those of the models.

The cheetah behaved beautifully, stretching and purring in the sun, turning his head in that haughty manner that mirrored the models. His big chest thrust out, emphasizing his strength. The climax came when Duma turned his tear-lined face toward the cameras, stopping hearts.

When the girls had finished shooting for the day, the photographers began to load up their equipment. Doc took the leash to escort the cheetah back to his enclosure, but the cheetah had very different thoughts. Having had a taste of basking in the sun and looking at the lovely girls, he balked. He braked and refused to move; they tried pulling and bribing him. They tried everything, but still, the cheetah remained firm. They couldn't lift or pull him; he was too strong. Finally, one of the keepers got a bright idea to put a garbage container over Duma's head. But the garbage canister changed nothing. They needed something underneath to raise him off the ground to move him.

The coward boards! A coward board is a large plank of wood keepers used as a shield. Two keepers go in together if a nonaggressive animal is awake when it is time to clean its exhibit. One uses the board to maintain a barrier from the animal while the second keeper rakes the yard. They located the board and, very carefully, managed to slip it under the cheetah's legs and the garbage can. With one man in front, one in the back, and one guarding the can, the noble feline finished the day with an undignified escort back to his enclosure.

A cheetah's life is complicated. This smallest feline on the African plain competes with leopards, lions, wild dogs, and hyenas, needing to outrun and outsmart all of those more powerful predators. Cheetahs hunt during the day to avoid the nocturnal hunters, but they must keep moving, not settling for one primary territory. The females are the sole charge of their offspring, which usually number two to four, and they constantly need to move them to a safer hiding place.

Today, the elegant cheetahs are in trouble. Habitat loss, human-wildlife conflict, and poaching have lowered the cheetah population to 8,000 as of 2024. Wilderness conservation efforts and captive breeding programs work together to halt the cheetah's race toward extinction.

Breeding cheetahs is a tricky science. Fresno Chaffee Zoo is a proud partner with other zoos to protect the species from extinction. After many decades, Fresno Chaffee Zoo was approved by the AZA to exhibit a pair of female cheetahs as part of its African Adventure venue.

Male cheetahs produce better quality sperm when they are away from the public eye and in a group with other males. Researchers have observed wild male cheetahs often living with their brothers. On the other hand, female cheetahs are more successful at breeding when they transfer away from their home facility. Fresno Zoo is a favored holding facility for two female cheetahs. When the call comes for their services, the females are "on call" to relocate to a breeding facility. When one leaves, another female replaces it.

At the Fresno Chaffee Zoo, the cheetahs have ample space to run or climb trees, but frequently lounge near the large viewing window, which disguises heating and cooling pads to encourage them to stay near the visitors. They create amusement by tracking young children or staring at other animals in the African Adventures exhibit.

Doc Chaffee inspecting a cheetah.

CHAPTER 23

"Please Don't Feed the Animals"

"Please don't feed the animals," pleaded Dr. Chaffee. He had recently performed a necropsy on a favorite primate and scooped out twenty pounds of nickels and pennies from inside its stomach. Normally, Doc was long on patience and slow to anger, but this incident pushed him into action.

Prior to the 1970s, few zoos had developed specialized diets to fit an animal's natural food habits. Roeding Park personnel assigned to tend the zoo animals received little to no animal care training. Little thought went into their diets beyond bones and meat for carnivores, carrots and lettuce for herbivores, and a mix for all the others.

To solve two problems, the public was encouraged to bring edible items to feed the animals. Besides supplementing the zoo's food budget, this outside source of food provided enrichment and variety to the animals' daily routines. Guests brought bread, bananas, and lunch items from home, and popcorn was available for purchase at the concession stand. The young black bear had learned to bang the bell over his head, knowing a flurry of popcorn would come his way

Nosey the elephant suffered the most from this free-for-all approach to feeding. The massive animal's typical diet was hay and grains, plus an apple or carrot treat. But on Saturdays, well-meaning fans brought baskets full of fresh lawn clippings, which she gobbled up. Later, her abdomen would bloat with gas, and she would sway and swing her trunk to ease the pain. She endured long nights of moaning and groaning from her stomachaches.

Visitors frequently tossed unsuitable items into the enclosures to pique the animals' curiosity and hopefully produce a "Kodak moment." Such items included cigarettes, pennies, bubble gum, Coke lids, lipstick, and much more. This litter kept the keepers busy with cleanup chores. And all the while, Doc ground his teeth. For Doc, every lost animal felt like losing a child, and the things visitors were tossing into the enclosures, whether edible or not, were causing more problems than they were solving.

There was a pattern among zoo veterinarians not to share information to preserve a hierarchy of importance. However, Doc's primary interest was in keeping his flock healthy. Always one to develop relationships and create networks, he forged ahead and reached out to gather information from his peers.

The concerned vet spent hours on phone calls comparing observations. He took copious notes while treating sick cases in the zoo clinic, looking for common threads for the ailments he encountered. Teeth rotted and fell out. The tiger's pelvic bone cracked when giving birth due to calcium deficiency. Animals died short of their life expectancy. Tossing a bone or raw meat to a carnivore did not seem to provide the needed nutrients.

Discarded trash and food in animal exhibits was
once an all-too-common sight.

In the early 1970s, Doc initiated a new policy. Going against tradition for the average American zoo visitor, Doc risked his reputation for the sake of the creatures. He asked the public *not* to give food to the animals. He knew the guests would not be happy, and his staff thought he had gone "bananas," but he needed to halt the trend of feeding inappropriate food to the animals.

"NO FEEDING" signs were posted to remind visitors of the new program, but to no avail. Doc conferred with zoo vets around the country, who agreed to follow suit. The TV stations, radio, and newspapers carried his message to the public, explaining the health hazards. Doc looked the camera in the eye and asked, "Is it worth putting the animal's health at risk?" One handful of peanuts could not hurt a monkey, thinks one visitor, but so do 4,000 other visitors tossing peanuts on a busy Sunday. The animals gained weight from eating human food; the heavier they became, the less active they were, and the more difficult it became for them to work off the excess poundage.

Feeding the animals was a complicated business! The zoo commissary prepared seventy special diets for 560 assorted critters. The Reptile House raised hundreds of mice to feed the reptiles. The zoo's feed budget included seventy-five tons of cubed hay and 1,500 pounds of fish for the year. Fruits, vegetables, and meat rounded out the list. Mealworm larvae plus dried and frozen crickets from Louisiana fed the birds and monkeys. Horsemeat for the carnivores was changed from chunk style to ground, making it easier to blend in necessary minerals and vitamins. The flamingos received fish spiked with carotene juice to maintain their glowing bright pink. Grocery stores often donated their overripe fruits and vegetables. Interestingly, the larger the animal, the easier the diet to satisfy them. Nosey the elephant, for example, lived on coarse hay and grain, while the hippos loved their diet of lettuce, watermelons, and fresh vegetables. The lizards and birds were more picky, eating hand-raised worms and specialty beetles. The zoo's entire food bill ran about $38,000 in 1967.

In 1970, six zookeepers attended a "chef school" to learn the latest on animal nutrition, and the animals appreciated this effort. For example, take some finely chopped tomatoes and horsemeat, mix in some mashed egg yolks, stir it with infant formula and milk, top it with vitamins, and you have a happy anteater. "Yummy, good!" sniffed the long-nosed anteater as his long, sticky tongue slurped his delicious milkshake. It was a perfect ant or termite substitute for animals with no teeth.

The nursery babies had the most critical diets. The nursery made every effort to keep the mother and baby together. This was crucial because the mother's rich milk carried nutrients and lots of fat for fast growth, essential for survival in the wild. A substitute was needed when a mother could not or would not nurse her infant. Many newborns were allergic to cow's milk, so Doc again reached out to his zoo vet contacts for the best replacements, since time was critical.

"In the zoo, food is brought to them, a rather dull situation for the animals, whose instinct is to hunt," said Doc Chaffee. "After that, they spend the rest of the day in boredom. They stare at visitors who stare back at them, waiting for action." Doc created special daily feeding events to educate the crowd. The keepers incorporated feeding the animals as part of their daily zoo talks, while giving the audience a rare peek at the animals dining on their natural diets.

The zoo's two sea lions, harbor seal, and two polar bears received a daily diet of frozen fish. Then, in January of 1972, the zoo rolled out a new and exciting routine. At the 10:00 a.m. feeding, keepers tossed a few live carp into the grotto pool, and the hunt was on!

Doc narrated the action: "Immediately, the polar bear dives into the water, catches the pound-and-a-half carp, climbs out of the water, puts the fish down with his paw on it, shakes the water from its fur, and then he eats it." The harbor seal took to the hunt naturally, but the sea lions were confused. "Perhaps they have been away too long from their native habitat, the ocean. They must relearn what a live fish is all about," explained Doc. "The sea lions swim after the fish and play with them, but so far, they don't know they are supposed to eat them. Maybe when we put the seal in with them, it will teach them what to do."

The Chaffee Zoo was the first such facility in the nation, if not the world, to institute a live fish feeding program. Dr. Chaffee had worried the public might be squeamish watching the seals eat live fish. Instead, the crowd loved it, and the experimental program continued for several years.

As previously mentioned, the zoo received an experimental hydroponics unit, which was set up near the hippos' exhibit. The hydroponics unit was a large steel case with shelves holding several rows of trays. Barley seeds, soaked in water for a few days, grew to a three-inch clump, perfect for a hippo treat. Visitors lined up to watch the hippos' gigantic mouths open as the keeper plopped in sections of grass. The zoo enjoyed the use of the hydroponics unit for several years.

The "Thanks, But No Thanks" no feeding policy has now been in effect for fifty years, with limited abuses. In the earlier days, the Fresno Zoo intentionally set the animals' living quarters close to the viewers to foster an eyeball-to-eyeball personal connection. Using a human's arm length and the animal's arm length worked to figure out the right amount of spacing—except when it came to the orangutan exhibit. There, a glass wall allows the eyeball-to-eyeball connection while eliminating the begging arms.

Doc Chaffee was a visionary. He thought outside the box and did not let the past influence his thinking. He wanted the public to appreciate how each species was created to survive in their native habitat. Yes, it is an artificial representation of their life, but one must see and learn before one can care.

Doc Chaffee was admired among his peers for his willingness to break tradition to find better ways to better serve both the animals and the public. In 1980, he was elected president of the national AZA organization, which was an honor, considering Fresno is one of the smaller zoos in the country.

CHAPTER 24

Freddie and Nina Arrive

Much had changed in the five years since the tragic losses of the young gorillas, Ila and Ichabod. Doc Chaffee, now Director/Vet of the zoo, finished building the promised nursery and had everything in place to care for nursery-age apes. His detailed preparations convinced the Zoo Society to allot $7,000 to purchase a pair of lowland gorillas, and he proceeded with the final arrangements.

Freddie and Nina were born in 1964 in Cameroon, in western Africa's lowland forests, most likely the abandoned offspring of poached parents. After their rescue, they went to a game farm in Holland, where they lived for two years. The dealer, Franz Van der Brink, had a good reputation for animal care, and he gently prepared the animals for the long flight to California. They were three years old when they arrived in Fresno on January 28, 1967.

Doc had thought through every minor aspect of Freddie and Nina's lives at the zoo and planned for any circumstance. Then, once the deal was set for the young gorillas to arrive, he enacted his plans. He recruited five female Fresno State biology students as aides to cover the day shift, working around their school schedules. Then he hired a male attendant to cover the night shift, so that there was twenty-four-hour care for the youngsters. Doc felt optimistic as he, his wife, Peggy, and keeper Perry Alexander, drove to the San Francisco airport.

Doc prearranged with the airport to set up a clinic in the airline office for an on-the-spot health check. Their names on the crates helped to identify the two gorilla travelers. Taking them to a back room, the vet set the crates on a table and opened them individually. Freddie peeked out of his opened gate and slowly lifted his foot onto the table. He looked at the unfamiliar sights and sniffed the air. Doc touched his arm and gave a reassuring pat, whispering in his ear. Peggy, a Valley Children's Hospital nurse, laid down a towel and set out the instruments. Doc dug into his pocket for his ever-ready treats and let Freddie get comfortable. Temperature, blood pressure, upper respiratory system, eyes, throat, abdomen, and teeth all checked out. Next, the more timid Nina accepted her treats and laid on the table for her checkup.

With an initial clean bill of health, the Chaffees crammed into the backseat of their car, holding their two new charges, while Perry drove them back to Fresno. Freddie weighed 40 pounds and Nina 29, about the same as four- and three-year-old children. Nina rode most of the way home on Peggy's lap. Both youngsters were happy to be out of their crates; Freddie thumped his chest while Nina pulled Peggy's hair. It made for an exciting trip down Highway 99. Of course, the delighted looks they received from other travelers made the proud "parents" even more delighted to show off their new tots. Doc lifted Freddie to the window and helped him wave to those gawking passersby.

The college attendants anxiously awaited their arrival, practicing the steps of caring for their first nursery babies. The area had to be germ-free, so they washed and disinfected the walls until not even the hardiest bug could survive. The five biology students, Doc, and the night attendant were the only persons allowed into the quarters. Each one who entered the nursery walked through a disinfectant footbath and then disinfected themselves carefully before putting on a clean gown. In addition, they washed down the floor and walls of the nursery with a sterilizer several times a day.

When, at last, the travelers reached Fresno, they went straight to the new nursery. The excited college students ran out to meet the car when it arrived. Two tired, haggled adults in crumpled clothes, hair in disarray and with bloodshot eyes, emerged. The primates clung in living terror, looking over their shoulders at the outstretched arms of the nursery aides waiting to embrace them.

Freddie and Nina looked much like human children, with flat faces, small ears, open nostrils, and piercing black eyes. They appeared to be frowning because of their ridged brow, but they are known as the "Gentle Giants." The black gorillas walk on all fours by curling their front fingers under, called knuckle-walking. Mountain gorillas live high in the montane forests and have thicker fur. Most zoos have lowland gorillas, but both lowland and mountain gorillas are endangered. Gorillas and chimpanzees each share 93 percent of their DNA with their human cousins.

Doc loved to go to work; his office was positioned as a side room of the always active nursery building. As a result, he accomplished little of significance during those first weeks after Freddie and Nina arrived. During the day, the pair had an hour of free time to explore the nursery, and being very active and curious, they took advantage of their freedom. The college aides often found the two playful imps fooling around in the vet's office, jumping off the walls, his desk, or racing around the room, which he thoroughly loved. The sounds of his happy chuckling echoed throughout the nursery. Doc gave them a quick checkup each morning to ensure that nothing surprised him. These animals were masters at hiding ailments, so he wanted to see a problem before it became a crisis.

Doc planned the care and feeding of the two gorillas primarily by watching them closely, as little literature was available. As the scientist, he kept meticulous notes for sharing and exchanging with other zoo veterinarians. The attendants kept busy caring for the pair. Once a day, they received an oil rub for their skin and hair. They ate five times a day, their diet consisting of celery and fruits, boiled breast of chicken, milk, raw egg, honey, baby food, plus a generous dose of vitamins. At night, the male nursery attendant slept near their quarters. He got up every half hour to check on them. He often found the two cuddling, with their arms wrapped around each other.

Freddie, the stable, serious one, protected Nina, the delicate, excitable one. Nina depended on Freddie for security and protection, but occasionally she displayed a streak of independence by teasing him. She liked to sneak up, pull his hair, then race off screaming as an enticement to play chase. Doc felt a deep sense of satisfaction watching the pair grow up, and their development delighted everyone.

Freddie and Nina became instant hits for zoo visitors. The steady stream of curious watchers beat a path before the nursery windows. The gorillas' many admirers enjoyed following the growth of the two playful moppets. Freddie loved to hit on the glass of his nursery windows, taunting his fans. He continued to grow stronger until, one day, he broke the glass, and Doc had to face the reality that this 80-pound primate needed to graduate out of the nursery. In March 1968, the two left the security of the aides for their permanent home in the ape grotto.

The outdoor primate keeper, Bruce, became enamored with his young charges, as their open affection toward each other melted his heart. He found ways to sneak in special treats and playthings to please them. Bruce felt no fear with the friendly gorillas as he cleaned their area. Freddie would drape his big arm around his keeper, displaying his obvious fondness. This friendship extended to the adoring public, who responded with a long-lasting love affair.

The two apes were vulnerable to Fresno's cold weather, and caught colds and pneumonia easily. After Doc added heaters in their quarters, they were less susceptible to those infections. But a bigger problem faced the keepers: the gorillas attracted a lot of attention for the zoo, but unfortunately the visitors persisted in throwing litter into the exhibits. Fear of the apes ingesting the tossed pennies, balloons, popsicle sticks, plastic bags, and cigarettes kept the keepers on their toes, retrieving the items before Freddie or Nina got them.

When Nina died in 1974, the community mourned her loss. She had not produced any offspring, so the Association of Zoos and Aquariums pushed to find a mate for the now adult Fred. Big Fred had all the markings of a perfect specimen to produce offspring needed to preserve the endangered species.

Fred the gorilla.

CHAPTER 25

Tales of Tails and No Tails

Baboons, aka hamadryas monkeys, had a long history with the Roeding Park Zoo, residing there from 1946 to 1992. Unlike apes with no tails, they have long tails and long faces. Their narrow, deep-set eyes are set in a wave of blond fur on a blushing face. A distinguishing feature of Old-World (African and Asian) monkeys is the tunnel-like nostril at the end of the nose, giving a peek into the brain. But most unforgettable is their hairless red and blue bulbous rump.

The first hamadryas baboon came to the zoo in 1946, where he lived until sent to a UCLA lab in 1960. A one-year-old baboon, Eleanor, replaced him in 1964; her mate, George, followed her four years later. Being hand-raised, Eleanor had no idea what it took to be a good mother. She gave birth in 1970 and acted confused about what fell from her bottom onto the ground. She walked away and did not try to touch it. The keepers rescued the newborn and rushed it to the nursery, but the infant did not survive.

Eleanor continued to be confused for the subsequent four births. After one birth, she realized something had fallen from her bottom and turned around to check it out. Picking the thing up by the tail or the leg, she swung it like a rag doll but quickly lost interest. The zookeepers kept watch, hoping for a motherly moment of recognition, but it was not to be. They finally rescued the newborn, whisking it away to safety in the nursery.

Then, in 1974, Eleanor welcomed Precocious, her sixth baby, which, for some reason, she cared for properly. Tenderly nursing the infant, she cradled it in her arms all day. As she grew, Precocious entertained the guests with her wild antics and facial expressions, turning around to show off her colorful bottom. One day, while swinging around in her enclosure, the active youngster got her arm stuck in the chain-link fence. In her attempt to free herself, she broke it. Doc gently eased her broken limb out and took the injured baboon to the nursery, where he wrapped her arm in a cast.

While recuperating in the nursery, she became acquainted with Geoffrey, the eighteen-month-old orangutan. The somber Geoffrey missed his playmate Kalanyo, the chimp, who returned to the San Francisco Zoo after nine months of keeping Geoffrey company. Humans had not previously handled Precocious; at first, she found them frightening. Finally, nursery aide Sally Smith introduced herself to the baboon. With Sally's patience and liberal use of treats, Precocious finally relaxed, letting Sally pick her up. Before long, she found herself comfortable in other attendants' arms. It looked like Precocious might be the answer to their search for a friend for Geoffrey, and they introduced the two youngsters.

The young, blond baboon and reddish-orange orangutan communicated using their native behaviors, speaking two different languages, which resulted in some funny moments. Precocious made all the gestures any well-trained baboon used, but Geoffrey did not understand what she wanted. She presented her rear in greeting, and he grabbed her tail. He clung to her hair as good orangutan babies do to their mothers. She tried grooming him, and his blood-curdling scream echoed across the zoo. Unlike his mother, she responded with a bite, and Geoffrey fled across the room. Eventually, they learned to work through the difficulties of cross-species gestures and ignored the conflicts. After a few months, they reached an understanding, and the barriers melted between them. If Precocious went outside in the play yard and Geoffrey did not, he threw a tantrum until he was allowed to join his friend. Precocious kept Geoffrey company until her arm healed and she returned to the baboon enclosure to live with her family.

Soon after, the time arrived for Geoffrey to become familiar with his own species. He needed to understand orangutan language and behaviors, recognize his position in a group, and submit to older orangutans. He moved out of the nursery and in with the big apes.

The ape enclosure had individual bedrooms, where the keepers spent time training and checking for cuts or scratches. During an introduction period, the newcomer was placed next to another enclosure to allow for a safe space to become comfortable. A keeper kept watch in case there was a need to intervene. The other older apes were curious, as they reached through the bars to touch this newcomer. Geoffrey, now two, Kifli, age three, and Azak, age six, were in another room, where they could see each other. The trio communicated with their whoops and grunts.

Geoffrey's next step was to join Azak and Kifli in the open grotto. Much thought and discussion went into this introduction. All three had experienced human contact, so the keepers felt safe entering their close quarters. First, zookeeper Bruce entered the exhibit to supervise. Azak, not known for her congeniality or sweet personality, presented the biggest variable. How would she react to Geoffrey on her turf? Everyone's eyes and ears went on alert. Once Bruce gave the OK, the nursery attendants, Linda and Sally, patted Geoffrey on the head, whispered in his ear, and then ventured forward. The young male clutched to the safety of Sally as they entered the unfamiliar ground. Azak, the ornery orange female, slowly lumbered over for a sniff. Curious, she touched Geoffrey, tugged a little on his arm, and then calmly sat down. This successful meeting had a short but sweet outcome.

Finally, it was time to wean Geoffrey from the security of his keeper. It required two people to physically release his death grips while screeching at the top of his lungs. Once on the ground, he chased the keepers in fear and fury. Their arms represented safety.

These temper tantrums finally got Kifli's attention. When Geoffrey got too close to the keepers, Kifli intervened by stepping between them; he thought Geoffrey needed to grow up. During his daily visits, Geoffrey began the process of assimilation. He learned to climb, pull himself out of the moat, and hold his own against the rough-and-tumble Kifli. When Kifli got too boisterous with the younger one, Azak intervened to separate them.

All went well until Azak went into estrus.

Azak wrote the book on PMS. Poor Geoffrey got the worst of it as the smallest and youngest. Kifli, frustrated, picked on Geoffrey also. After being bitten on the rump by Azak, Geoffrey moved back to the nursery, where he gobbled down his food and then slept for two days. As for poor Kifli, there was no respite for him; he had to endure the tempestuous Azak. Whenever he got caught by himself or in a vulnerable situation, he came out as the loser. Kifli spent several weeks in the hospital after one beating. Eventually, Geoffrey returned after Azak made it through her "time of the month."

Doc took every opportunity to advertise his zoo by taking a well-trained animal with him to engagements. He took Geoffrey, boa constrictors, or birds to Rotary meetings, earning him the designation of "Most Popular" Rotary president. Doc received calls for Geoffrey's attendance at special events. Geoffrey's charm tugged at the purse strings, never failing to bring in more funds.

When Geoffrey turned six and a half years old, he left his zoo family for a Florida zoo. The primate staff gave Geoffrey a farewell party as they said goodbye. Even knowing this was best for Geoffrey, they felt sad to lose him.

Kifli left Fresno for Colorado Springs in 1987. Azak remained at the zoo, where it was hoped she would breed and carry on the genes of her wild-caught parents, Suma and Sumac. She moved into the new ape enclosure, where she could swing on ropes and walk on grass with her friends. She never produced an offspring but enjoyed the company of being with the other orangutans.

CHAPTER 26

Azak Learns to Read

D oc joined the national American Association of Zoos, Parks, and Aquariums (AAZPA) as a way to network. In 1969, there were no AAZPA groups at the state-level, so he took the initiative to form a California group of zookeepers (AAZK) by inviting them to Fresno.

The zoo director's reputation for unique and entertaining events was well known, whether in his home, at Rotary meetings, or the zoo. He sent invitations to all the California zoo directors to attend the first California Zookeepers' conference on April 11, 1969, in Fresno. Two hundred zookeepers registered to attend. In the 1960s, zookeepers had little specialty training beyond high school biology, and this was a first-time visit to another zoo for many. They arrived wearing their zoo staff uniforms and sporting various hats, making for a colorful troupe. He spruced up his 12-acre zoo to welcome the 200 visitors and planned the weekend carefully to account for every minute.

In his khaki shorts, matching short-sleeve shirt, and safari hat, he greeted each of them with a name tag, schedule for the day, and gift bag. Doc's staff led morning tours, sharing information on animals, enclosures, diets, and training. The visitors peppered the guides with questions, leading to a valuable and beneficial dialog between zoo personnel as they compared their zoo with other facilities.

Few zoos at that time had primates because they required advanced care due to their natural intelligence. Excited, the conference-goers gathered around the three-sectioned primate exhibit featuring chimpanzees, gorillas, and orangutans.

The exhibit featuring orangutans Suma and Sumac was quite popular. The male orangutan, Sumac, with long, reddish-orange hair, tangled dreadlocks, and flared cheek pouches, studied the crowd with his deep-set black eyes. Fingernails crowned his four long fingers and small thumb, which in his native habitat enabled him to swing through the trees, avoiding the ground where the tigers hunted. His cement jungle in Fresno had only an umbrella-shaded metal table to sit on to observe his surroundings. The more delicate female, with smooth orange hair and a narrow face, sat beside her mate.

Doc kept to his scheduled plan until he heard a voice call out, "Come here. Look! Are those little eyes peeking out from under the ape's arm? Oh, my, is that a baby orangutan I'm looking at?" the voice yelled excitedly.

Doc joined the rush to investigate the excitement. Looking closely, he spotted the newly born orangutan infant. Caught by surprise, he did a quick assessment of Suma's fourth baby, and both mother and child appeared to be healthy. Since her previous three youngsters had been transferred to other zoos, this one was a welcome addition. No one could blame Doc Chaffee for strutting like a peacock; acting like the proud father, he lapped up the praises of his peers.

The birth of a rare Sumatran orangutan made the national news. It was only natural she was named Azak from the American Association of Zookeepers conference in Fresno, connecting her forever to that 1969 event. Suma and Sumac, proven parents, raised Azak for two years until she moved into the nursery when Suma became pregnant again.

Azak met Brucie, an orphaned nine-month-old chimpanzee, in the nursery. Every day, Susan, a nursery aide, devoted several hours to working with them, patiently coaxing Azak to trust her with little treats and kind words. Azak studied the confident Brucie as he rode astride Susan's hip. Finally, imitating her friend, she reached out her arms for Susan to pick her up, and then they glided around the nursery, letting the little orange youngster get used to her big human friend.

There was never a dull moment in the facility. It often looked like a nursery school, except these youngsters climbed the walls, leaped across the room, and chased each other with wild abandon. Visitors streamed past the windows, hoping to spot some monkey antics. The nursery aides introduced a few preschool activities and discovered that the pair loved to finger-paint. Soon, the phone rang off the hook with people asking for their works of art. The zoo sold the duo's paintings to lucky zoo-goers, who cherished their prizes.

Charlene, a nursery aide, observed several differences between Brucie, the chimpanzee, and Azak, the orangutan. Brucie stared, mimicking any new behavior; however, Azak used reasoning to figure things out. Charlene could almost see her wheels turning; Azak was highly intelligent and fun to watch. Jumping up on the sink, she stacked and washed her dishes. Given a key, she learned how to stick her arms through the bars and turn her hand to unlock the door to her space. Once free, she raced to jump onto Doc's lap in his office, conveniently located in the nursery.

Doc believed in education. He developed a Zoo Mobile program where he took animals to the classrooms. He usually took Brucie instead of Azak, because the young orangutan, being a tree climber, crawled out of reach in one class. Surprised, Doc immediately raced to lock the classroom door. Getting her down entailed a game of chase until she surrendered and returned to the floor—lesson learned; no more school events for Azak.

As they grew more secure, Brucie and Azak were released into the adult ape grotto, where the public gathered to watch. One of Azak's favorite games was chasing Brucie around the area, both screaming at the top of their lungs, while laughter from the crowd burst through the air as parents were reminded of their children's similar antics.

1974, when Azak was three years old, Gary Shapiro came into her life. With the approval of Doc Chaffee, Gary worked with her for his Fresno State master's thesis on the nonverbal communication of orangutans. At that time, most primate research focused on chimpanzees because they were social animals like humans. Gary conducted the first in-depth, one-on-one research with orangutans.

A baby orangutan in the nursery.

The solitary male orangutan's primary vocalization was long calls to communicate his status and location. These calls informed females that he was in the area and warned away any lesser males. In addition to the long call, they display various other vocalizations, from middle-range calls and grumbles to kiss squeaks and raspberry sounds.

Every day for twenty-one months, Gary sat cross-legged in Azak's enclosure, enduring the cold cement and the hot summer days. She eagerly awaited him and then leaped onto his lap for her welcoming hug as they developed a unique, long-lasting bond that went beyond the typical teacher-student relationship.

Gary taught her how to communicate using magnetic letters as symbols. Placing them on a whiteboard, they played a variation of Scrabble; each of the colored plastic letters stood for a different noun or verb. Azak learned to separate the letters by color and shape and match the picture. But just like any energetic three-year-old human child, she had limited attention. She would suddenly erupt with energy, racing and screaming around her schoolroom. With great satisfaction, Gary watched as Azak began using her letters to form sentences requesting a banana, or to have her hair brushed, or to demand a big hug.

Still a juvenile, Azak wanted full attention from her human friend, hopping onto his lap for a kiss or a hug, and as with most children, she quickly learned all about rewards and treats. When her cup of juice became empty, she would send it sailing across the enclosure. Gary nodded to her, and then she would retrieve it and, with cup back in hand, sit patiently waiting for her reward. She beamed when he praised her, but if he scolded her, she slinked off to a corner, turning her back to him and pouting, sometimes for hours.

One day, Gary gave the young primate some orange juice. She immediately requested more, but Gary had not taught her the symbols for the word "orange juice." Curious about what she might produce, the teacher sat back and waited. Azak expectantly looked at Gary, but when he did not react, she became frustrated; he pointed again to the letters, indicating he wanted her to use them to communicate. He took careful note of each of Azak's moves to better identify her reasoning ability: her glances toward him, hoping for a clue, how she studied her letters, how she put them together.

Gary was thrilled when Azak handed him the symbols for orange and water. He rewarded her with a glass of orange juice. He recognized this feat as a significant step in his research. His work with Azak proved that an orangutan could connect symbols to objects or actions, demonstrating her ability to reason. The "Orange Woman" had figured out that orange juice and water were in the same category as liquids. "Pretty smart for a so-called 'dumb animal,'" he observed.

Azak spent her whole life at the Fresno Zoo. After twenty years away, Gary returned to the Fresno Zoo as a regional zoo docent conference speaker. He called out Azak's name from across the enclosure. She strolled closer to look at who called out her name and appeared to recognize him. She then turned her back to him. He acknowledged that was her normal response when she had felt ignored.

AZA leaders placed great hopes on Azak's future. She carried the genes of Suma and Sumac, natives of the beautiful Sumatran forests, and held the future of a pure bloodline for an endangered species. She met with several potential boyfriends but rejected them, sometimes violently, and thus she never had any offspring to continue her genes. Maybe she dreamed Gary would come back for her.

Because of his work with Azak, Gary continued collaborating with orangutan researchers in the wilds of Borneo and Sumatra. He became the national president of the Orangutan Foundation International, educating the locals about the importance of protecting their rainforests and native wildlife. I had the privilege of joining him in Sumatra to see orangutans in the wild.

Azak lived long enough to enjoy the zoo's new and improved orangutan exhibit, with a new set of companions, swinging lianas, and trees to climb. Her muscles had atrophied after years of flatland living, and she had to develop new muscles for swinging. The public loved seeing her have a chance to act like a happy primate.

CHAPTER 27

Azak Meets Busar

In the early 1980s, Doc upgraded the three-sectioned ape exhibit built in the 1950s that held gorillas, chimpanzees, and orangutans. By then, the gorillas had either died or been transferred to other zoos, leaving only two ape species. The chimpanzees were down to two animals. The cement floor was gutted and replaced with dirt, and a divider was removed to double the space for the orangutans. In 1998, the zoo began a two-year construction project on an orangutan exhibit filled with trees, grass, and rope lines for swinging. It was a drastic improvement over the small exhibits and treeless area where they had spent three decades.

The zoo made one more attempt to find a mate for Azak. They hoped to locate a newcomer and complete his quarantine and introduction phase before the move into the new habitat.

Busar, a 16-year-old male, arrived two years before the opening of the new orangutan habitat. A shy, anxious orangutan with deep-set dark eyes, large cheeks (flanges), and shaggy auburn dreadlocks, he came from the Yerkes Primate Research facility in Atlanta, Georgia, where he had been separated from other primates and had little freedom. Following a month of quarantine in his new home, the keepers set up a meeting between Busar and Azak. The night rooms let the animals observe each other while separated into safe spaces. Unfortunately, Azak did not put her best foot forward; instead, she greeted Busar with a hostile, full-mouth glare.

The old orangutan exhibit had an umbrella table that provided shade and a place to sit but little else. The zookeepers let Busar outside by himself to explore the space. He found the cardboard box left for him to play with and explore. What did he do? He put the box over his head and sat in a corner for three days.

In the beginning, each animal was let out into this area separately to become comfortable before letting the other one out. The staff's hope for positive interactions between the two orangutans evaporated; their contact came as scratches and bites. Busar did nothing. He spent his time sitting in a corner, hands covering his face. If the keepers put a box out for stimulation, it sat on his head. He refused to go inside when he was outside and refused to interact with Azak when she went out. If Azak noticed Busar outside, she turned around and went back in. All attempts to put them together led to failure.

In a directed learning program, the zoo's goal is not to provide entertainment. The purpose is to reduce the stress on an animal by having them participate in a preventative program. The staff devoted an hour each day developing a rapport with each orangutan. First, they were introduced to their body parts. While working with one, the other waited in anticipation for his or her turn.

Azak and Busar turned their ears to the keeper when told "ear." Then their ears were cleaned. They presented their arms for poking to simulate injections. They showed their teeth for teeth brushing time. On command they pointed to their stomachs, feet, elbows, eyes, and even turned around to show off their backsides.

The tension between the two seemed to slowly ease. Yet still, when the two went out together, one returned with evidence of a dispute. Busar no longer backed away, and the female now received her share of bruises and cuts.

July 26, 2000, marked a monumental day in the life of Azak, as the new exhibit was finally completed and she moved in. After thirty-one years, she felt dirt and grass under her feet and had water to splash about in during the sizzling hot days. Those who loved

Azak shared her delight in exploring the wonders of the newly open space.

Azak needed to strengthen her muscles. Typically, this would happen while clinging to Mom for the first year of her life. She lost that connection at two years old when she moved to the nursery. By playing in their new environment, she, Busar, and Sumac slowly regained the necessary muscle strength in their hands and arms. Soon, they were swinging from rope to rope and climbing from top to bottom. Although most apes get water from plant diets, the design included a pool. Azak investigated it on day one, getting down on her knees to take a drink. That was the first and last time she went near the water. For orangutans in the wild, dangerous snakes or Sumatran tigers were not worth the risk of coming to the ground for water. That instinct was still strong in Azak and her companions.

At last, she could be a regular ape, but the new setting frightened the shy Busar. He spent the first days sitting on the smooth surface of a flattened, giant eucalyptus branch. He covered his head with a box. For three days, he left his safety position only in the dark when the owls were out. That's when he slipped down, grabbed a banana plant, and slunk back up to the refuge of the branches.

The war continued when both were outside together, usually ending in battle scars. The keepers finally let Busar stay out during the afternoon while Azak enjoyed the peaceful morning shift, unperturbed by the loathsome Busar.

The apes had toys like soft animals for entertainment, comfort, or learning tools. Some toys were "indoor" toys, and the more natural items were outdoor toys. One day, against the rules, Azak decided to take her indoor toy outside. She slithered down the wired-enclosed tunnel to the gate leading to the outside. She kept her back to the keepers. Recognizing Azak's antics, a keeper called out, "What do you have, Azak?" She kept on as though not hearing, quietly edging to the opening while clutching her toy doll. When the gate opened, she rushed out and proudly flashed her prize.

Busar and Azak filled their days creating ways to wreak havoc in each other's lives. With Busar outside, Azak managed to sneak into his space and leave a juicy little gift on the floor. Busar looked at her as if to say, "What's a guy to do?" For Valentine's Day, the staff decorated the ceiling with cards and hearts. Oh boy, this gift could not be true! Azak sneaked a bamboo stalk in from the outside. Next day, with Busar outside, she took the stalk and gleefully poked a hole into every Valentine card, one by one.

The arrival of two female orangutans from Florida changed Busar and Azak's relationship. These two, Sara and Seibu, had been together for about twenty years. Sara, twenty years older than Seibu, fostered Seibu when her mother could not care for her. The introductions between Sara, Seibu, Azak, and Busar took place in their night enclosures, where they could safely see and hear each other. The keepers kept a watchful eye on the four, trying to detect which pairs would be more compatible, considering the unique personalities of Busar and Azak.

Seibu warmed up to Busar, leaving Sara with Azak. Busar turned into a loving, attentive companion. He was often seen with his long arms contently wrapped around Seibu. No sight is sweeter than to watch two orangutans, sitting face to face, tenderly kissing with their long lips touching.

With the initiation of Sara into Azak's life, she blossomed into a happier ape, finally having the company of a girlfriend. Azak continued to amaze with her level of intelligence. One day, she decided to give her new best friend, Sara, a drink of water. She broke off a bamboo branch and carried it to the water faucet, just inches outside the wired enclosure. She reached her fingers through the wire and tapped on the faucet for a slow water drip. Then she lifted the bamboo branch to the faucet and leveled it enough for the water to run down. She waved Sara over for a drink of water. How did she know what to do? Mind-boggling is the only description that applies. Within days, staff blocked the faucet.

Azak and Busar continued to find ways to irritate each other, so the staff kept them separated, allowing only one outside at a time. Azak spent her life at the Fresno Chaffee Zoo, adjusting to its transformations. With her strong personality and many quirks, she gave us a peek into the intelligence of these fantastic apes.

Azak died on February 3, 2003, at 31 years old, but she ended her life content with friends, dirt, and lianas for swinging. Sharing her life with us taught us that orangutans are worth fighting for and keeping alive and well in the wild. Gary Shapiro, the researcher, formed a nonprofit for the protection of orangutans in Sumatra and Borneo. These apes—our closest relatives—are fighting extinction from poaching, the pet trade, and habitat destruction.

Busar had three offspring with Seibu and Sara, finally realizing Doc's dream of continuing the lineage of orangutan DNA. The orangutan exhibit was incorporated into the Asia habitat, bringing the primates closer to view through a glass window—a real nose-to-nose experience.

CHAPTER 28

The Bison-Tule Elk Exhibit

Paul Chaffee was a true visionary when it came to zoo design and layout. Never short of ideas, he was always willing to try something new. For example, Doc was one of the country's first zoo directors to try mixed-species exhibits. The two such habitats at the Fresno Zoo paired bison with prairie dogs and tule elk with kit foxes. The story of how these exhibits came to be is quite interesting.

In the 1950s, Paul and Peggy Chaffee drove their family of three boys—Dave, Dan, and Dick—from Chicago to California. On the way, they passed a small bison herd. These large, dark-furred, humpback mammals moseyed along the trail of grasses, enjoying their fill.

The boys pointed and shouted, "That's the animal that is in our cowboys and Indians movies." Fascinated, the family stopped the car to gawk at the animals seen only in movies.

In the mid-1800s, travelers on horseback and families aboard wagon trains traveled through the Great Plains to find new lands. They brought their cattle and sheep for meat, wool, and trade. On their way, the pioneers rode past the massive, short-horned bison, peacefully munching on the prairie. The plains bison were estimated to have numbered between 30 to 60 million animals. They were the widest-ranging mammal in North America.

Bill Cody starred as Buffalo Bill in movies highlighting his kills. Cody became obscenely prolific in killing bison, claiming to have shot 4,840 in just eighteen months. A British market for the bison hides brought out hundreds of hunters, which led to the horrific slaughter and near extinction of the species in just five years. On top of that, the government seized Native American land by encouraging the killing of the native buffalo (as bison are more commonly called in the United States), which led to Indian death by starvation.

Alongside the bulky buffalo, but out of sight underground, tiny two-to-four-pound prairie dogs were the glue that bound the prairie ecosystem together. They were a primary food source for other animals in the habitat web, attracting everything from coyotes to hawks to endangered black-footed ferrets. Even the smallest critters played a part in the ecosystem; without them, the system crumbled. The settlers, being new to the land, had no understanding of their importance and saw them only as a pest to destroy. The newcomers plowed up the ground that had sustained life for thousands of years; in its place, they planted wheat for their cattle and sheep. Ultimately, they destroyed the dynamic ecosystem and turned a once fertile land into a wind tunnel that swept away the topsoil and eventually drove the settlers to abandon the land.

Meanwhile, a similarly tragic story was taking place out West. In California's San Joaquin Valley, rivers flowed before dams slowed the water. The rivers created hospitable wet areas for the original 500,000 small tule elk that live there, named after the edible bulrushes, or tules, of the region. The Valley's terrain ranged from the grasslands and marshes of the central flatlands to the grassy hills on the coast. The Spaniards hunted the elk when they came to California; by 1870, the species was considered extinct. But in 1970, a small remnant herd was discovered in the tule marshes of Buena Vista Lake in the southern San Joaquin Valley. Efforts to help the species have been successful, and as of 2020, an estimated 5,700 tule elk were present in twenty-two herds spread across California. The elks are a welcome addition wherever they are found, as their grazing positively impacts the abundance and diversity of the state's native grassland species.

Also resident to the San Joaquin Valley were the six-pound San Joaquin kit foxes, which once thrived on the Valley's dry, barren lands during the summer. They played an essential role in controlling populations of small mammals, insects, birds, and reptiles. Their large, upright ears help lower their body temperature and give them exceptional hearing, while their black-tipped tail is used to communicate with others of their species. They can produce eight distinct sounds, shared through barks, screeches, yelps, squeals, howls, rattles, or hospitable chattering.

Farmers preparing their new land set out to eliminate all the strange critters, including San Joaquin kit foxes, in their farmlands. Unfortunately, after eradicating the kit foxes, the insects swarmed in and destroyed the farmers' crops, leaving the sharecroppers penniless.

"These little kit foxes support at least 136 other species through their various activities," said World Wildlife Foundation senior wildlife conservation biologist Kristy Bly. "They're the Chicken McNuggets of the grasslands." The farmers realized too late the damage caused by destroying the native species. It has taken decades for the kit fox to recover from near extinction.

Dr. Paul Chaffee was well aware of the plight of the above-mentioned species. In 1971, while serving as the first president of AZA Western District Zoo Veterinarians, he presided over a conference in Hawaii where he introduced the concept of a mixed-species exhibit. Excited to implement his new idea, which was a part of his 1970 Master Plan, he selected two sets of North American animals near extinction from the settlers inhabiting their regions. One major animal and one smaller species from the same habitat: bison and prairie dogs in one exhibit, and tule elk and kit fox in the other. In Doc's planning, every exhibit needed to convey an educational message, so he highlighted the early settlers' effect on the ecosystems.

But before he could implement his plan, Doc learned a lesson in city politics. The Parks Superintendent reprimanded him for enlarging the zoo without permission. His new plan incorporated ten acres from the City parking lot into his exhibit. Not discouraged, he scrambled to find another spot.

The bison-elk exhibit was an extended oval area divided in half. A barn separated the two sections. Each half had a pond and dry moat, sloping down the bottom edge so as not to obscure the view. The bison shared its space with seven male prairie dogs, much as they lived in the plains. The kit fox shared space with the antlered tule elk. The oval shape kept the smaller mammals from becoming cornered by a more dominant elk or bison.

Wooden poles sunk deep into the ground served as a fence, with plants and bushes strategically placed between the wall and the walkway, keeping the public from getting too close. The exhibit boasted an underground water and sewage system, and included lights to brighten the area during nighttime events. The completed bison-tule elk habitat was dedicated on June 15, 1976.

It soon became clear that the bison-tule elk exhibit needed shade for the animals and visitors. Nurseries donated large trees when they outgrew their tubs. Soon, Doc received enough trees to fill an acre. After borrowing a tractor, his friends showed up and turned it into a "planting party" day. Donned in jeans and a sweatshirt, Doc Chaffee grabbed a shovel and joined in on the project. He loved working the earth with his bare hands, always looking for an excuse for a tree-planting party. He had a way of making those days fun.

The new exhibits certainly contributed moments of interest to the zoo. A beautiful loquat tree stood in the bison-prairie dog section. One day, Doc found that a maintenance crew had removed the tree without permission. "Upset" would be just about the only printable word to describe his reaction. And one year, during the annual Safari Night event, word went out that an impending bison birth might occur. The partygoers were rewarded with a close-up view of the newborn.

The tule elk took to leaping out of his pen for a nightly walk around the grounds. The security had to arrange for an extra detail to scoot the wanderer back to his home. One evening, Doc got a call that the elk was stuck in the helpless South American capybara pen and couldn't get out. Grabbing his medical bag, he jumped up from the dinner table to deal with the wandering elk, whose antlers were now in full growth.

After sedating the animal, he sawed off the three-foot-long antlers to protect the rescuers. The now-undignified male was loaded into a pickup truck, ending that night's scouting expedition, and returned to his barn. For the next month, a docent volunteered for elk duty, sitting at the edge of the exhibit that had become the escape route. His job was to distract the antlered beast from his favorite leaping outlet. The docent devoted his time to reading and visiting with guests until the elk gave up his adventurous wanderings.

Doc had spent much of his early years convincing the maintenance staff that cement was too hard on the animals' feet and legs, something which he observed during his medical exams. He eventually replaced the dreaded cement with soil, despite complaints that cleaning would now entail more work. This time, his plan backfired. The prairie dogs dug a tunnel out of the exhibit and headed for parts unknown. Meanwhile, next door, the tule elk kept kicking the small San Joaquin kit foxes, who had no place to escape. Doc finally abandoned his plan for a mixed-species space after losing the prairie dogs and rescuing the kit foxes.

Over time, the Native Americans reintroduced bison to smaller grass areas. Researchers found that bringing the bison back to prairies doubled plant diversity and boosted the environment's resilience to extreme weather. Bison are central to the lives and traditions of many Native nations. They are also an umbrella species for many plants and animals sharing their habitat. Today there are about 15,000 free roaming bison in North America today. Another 400,000 are sold as livestock. The conflict between the American bison and cattle continues. Still, one cannot dismiss that the bison restored the grasslands for both species to survive.

As for the other three species, the prairie dogs are still endangered at 5 percent of their original population, and the kit fox remains on the endangered list. The Chaffee Zoo maintains an African Fennec fox, which displays the same bat-like ears and fluffy coat for heat protection. As mentioned above, extensive work is being done to help the tule elk population recover to a healthy number.

CHAPTER 29

The Birth of ZooLynx

Director Dr. Paul Chaffee was shocked when he read the City Parks Department's budget. It barely covered the zoo's operational expenses. He had to find new ways to increase his budget if he was going to improve the Roeding Park Zoo's conditions. Clearly, he had to take the matter into his own hands.

He hoped to encourage people to come out to visit the zoo by taking the zoo out to the people. So he set up his "Talk and Slideshow" program wherever he could get an invitation: schools, churches, organizations, and so on. In particular, he responded to older groups, sometimes driving an hour or more away, encouraging them to leave money for the zoo in their wills. He advertised the dates and locations for his meetings in the *Fresno Bee*. As word got out about Doc's presentations, more and more people attended them, eager to learn about the zoo.

During a typical presentation, Doc, dressed in his standard khaki shorts, short-sleeved shirt, and safari hat, set up the four-by-six-foot screen in the front of the room. He put the slide projector on a small table, plugged it in with a long extension cord, and adjusted it to the screen. At 7:00 p.m., he would open the door and wave in his audience, greeting them with his soft, gentle voice and twinkling blue eyes. He encouraged them to take a seat. His friends filled the room, anticipating an interesting evening.

Doc introduced the evening by regaling his audiences with shots of his Africa trips, showing the animals in their natural settings. He had a sly, mischievous sense of humor that had his audiences holding onto their sides, but it was his passion that captivated them. He shared his vision of improving the zoo and bringing in more animals—but it took money, he told them. The talks built a strong support base for the zoo, and the public was eager to respond when he put out the call.

Doc's unwavering goal as the director always included educating the public. He proposed forming a Ladies' Auxiliary during his first community meeting in January, 1971. Doc assigned Kay Miles as Education Director and put her in charge of planning and recruiting. Given her previous position as Zoo Society secretary, her background with wild-caught animals made her the perfect person to lead the group. The Zoo Society budgeted $1700 for the Ladies' Auxiliary start-up expenses. Their mission was to promote the Zoo Society through publicity, membership, and education.

A letter published in the *Fresno Bee* and the *Fresno Guide* invited women to the first Ladies' Auxiliary meeting on April 28, 1971. A dozen interested candidates showed up. They came with various backgrounds: teachers, homemakers, retirees, with various interests and skills. But they all had one thing in common: they shared a love of animals. The most significant decision of the day was creating their name. Looking for a way to link the Zoo Society Board and the animals, they decided upon ZooLynx, which nicely bridged the two. They used the zoo's lynx (bobcat) as its logo.

The Ladies Auxiliary's first project involved an event-filled week named Zoo Week, held June 7–14, 1971. The group's seamstress, Alice Carlton, created and sewed thick, green ZooLynx patches, which the ladies attached to their vests. The women organized activities for each event day, including daily tours for visitors. The week before, Kay led the novice guides on several practice tours to familiarize them with the zoo's various species and provided them with plenty of tidbits of information to impress the visitors.

Wednesday featured an afternoon outdoor fashion show in downtown Fulton Mall. Tables were set with animal shaped cookies, finger foods, and teapots. Dressed in zoo-themed outfits, the novice ZooLynx ladies served as models. To their delight, the event raised the most of any of that week's activities, with a profit of $102.50. An animal rental company brought an elephant and camel for public rides. The grand finale dinner and reception at the Tropicana featured Misty, a dancing elephant. The dinner netted $47.50 for the Zoo Society.

The success of Zoo Week set the future for ZooLynx. The ladies enjoyed working together, but two interests emerged. One group preferred to work with the animals they had fallen in love with as children visiting the zoo. A second group loved to put on parties as fundraisers. Their common goal to support the zoo made their combined efforts more effective.

Original ZooLynx member Helen Templeton shared how Doc inspired her: "Doc Chaffee shared his passion for conservation and education with the Ladies' Auxiliary. He told us that educating the public would have long-lasting significance. He had such a passion for his work, and I sat there riveted by him. I remember that feeling to this day."

The original animal tour group included Shirley Alexander, Roberta Beam, Rita Brake, Alice Carlton, Ginny Eville, Elizabeth Fillpot, Norene Hughes, Carol Jones, Ruth Kazmier, Pat Kirkegaard, Joyce Malone, "Packy" Markarian, Rae Myers, Phyllis Moore, Nancy Naylor, Robin Smith, Helen Templeton, Jane Van Zicklin, and Joanne Young.

The women were eager to start their formal tour guide training. Kay developed a six-week training session at her unincorporated home on Sierra and Fruit in July of 1971. Her unusual yard sported a private menagerie, including llamas, goats, a tortoise, and a sulfur-crested cockatoo. The ladies brushed, walked, lifted, and examined these pets in a true hands-on fashion, as they prepared to introduce them to the public.

Nine guides earned the right to be called charter tour guides. The docents were Kathy Clark, Fern Hicks, Carol Jones, Joyce Malone, Diane Martin, Phyllis Moore, Rae Myers, Mary Swanson, and Helen Templeton.

On October 13, the tour guides met their first group of six-year-olds. Guide Carol Jones stopped before every green sign to read off her "spiel." She had a precocious kid in her group, who insisted on running ahead to read the signage aloud to the group.

In November, the board adopted an official dress for the tour guides. Within ten days of "graduation," each tour guide needed to sew her uniform from the selected pattern and bolt of material. It consisted of a white blouse, yellow slacks or skirt, a matching long vest, and white shoes. In the winter, they wore thermal underwear to keep warm. After several attempts to hand-make the lynx logo patch, Kay ordered the patches professionally made for $1.50 each.

Meanwhile, the fundraising arm had many projects scheduled. After several fundraising luncheons, the kitty climbed to $35.70. For Christmas, the ladies created a cookbook. Each recipe had a cute animal twist to the names: Nosey's Forgotten Cookies, Tiger Striped Coffeecake, and Tortoise Toffee. The cookbooks were a big hit, selling for $1.00 each.

The Ladies' Auxiliary used its fundraising profits to buy itself a slide projector for the classroom presentations. They create slides of each zoo animal to prepare the children for their zoo tours. Each member donated their Green Stamp and Blue-Chip Stamp books for a punch bowl, silver tray, silver creamer, and sugar bowl for their preluncheon refreshments. One donor supplied dry sherry.

The noon meetings rotated among the members' homes, where they created bookmarks for the kids, planned fundraisers for needed wheelchairs, and built a lending library for research on the animals. Each month, a docent presented a program on one of the animals. They collected biofacts and acquired a boa and iguana for their classroom Zoo Mobile presentations. The guides drove their own vehicles to transport animals to the classrooms.

Doc Chaffee informed them of upcoming legislation that affected the environment. He had immersed himself in zoo legislation at the national level and encouraged the docents to form a legislative committee. Every meeting included a report and, often, letter-writing sessions.

The second class of eight trainees began in November 1971. This class lasted thirteen weeks, covering the material more extensively. Sometimes they met at the zoo, inviting Doc and zookeepers as instructors. The presence of the docents on the zoo grounds made a strong impression among the visitors. Soon, calls poured in for Zoo Mobile programs, classroom presentations, and tour guide-led groups.

The Ladies' Auxiliary had an impressive, productive first year. ZooLynx created bylaws, paid Zoo Society dues, and received a Zoo Society membership card. They instituted a tour guide training program, created a patch and a uniform, compiled research papers for an expanded zoo guide manual, and saw the need to develop a funding source for themselves.

In 1971, the first class of guides led 141 touring groups. During just the month of July, 1972, seventeen tour guides escorted 3,563 visitors through the zoo; the free and paid admissions totaled 51,116 visitors.

The first Ladies' Auxiliary group formed a unique bond. They enjoyed each other's company so much that they socialized outside the zoo. Their circle included the husbands, who found themselves increasingly involved in zoo functions. Their enthusiasm was boundless, pumped up by Doc Chaffee's expansive vision for the zoo's future.

Although it was only a six-acre zoo, he emphasized the importance of Fresno's Zoo in the world. "Doc encouraged us to look outward and not to put barriers in our creative thinking," said Helen Templeton.

CHAPTER 30

Kifli and Valentine Trade Zoos

On February 15, 1972, orangutan Suma gave birth to her fifth offspring, a healthy female. She was named Valentine to signify her birthdate and status as the zoo's newest sweetheart. The zoo had already planned to keep Suma's fourth offspring, the female Azak, as the gene carrier of the wild-caught orangutan couple Suma and Sumac, so Dr. Chaffee put out feelers to exchange a male for Valentine. When she turned fourteen months old, a well-matched male named Kifli became available in Brownsville, Texas. Doc agreed to deliver Valentine personally and bring back the male.

Orangutans are some of the most dedicated mothers in the animal kingdom. In the small exhibit, Valentine never strayed from Suma or Sumac. At her young age, she still clung to their hair when they strolled around their exhibit. In their native Sumatran rainforest, the young strengthen their grip by grabbing the mother's long fur while she climbs or swings through the trees.

In the wild, young orangutans will stay with their mothers for up to seven years, as they learn the skills they need to survive independently: where to find food, how to build nests, and how to raise young. Sumac continued to play a fatherly role in the upbringing of his offspring. Typically, male orangutans live a solitary life, coming together with the females only to breed. But Sumac adapted nicely to his captive life and enjoyed taking part in the raising of his offspring.

Doc had previous experiences trying to remove offspring from Suma and Sumac, and it usually did not go well. Often, the young were under three years old when the zoo decided to separate them; the babies clung as tightly as the parents. He predicted that Valentine would put up a loud struggle and create chaos in the enclosure.

First, Doc needed to put the four-foot Sumac with six-foot-six-inch arms into his night quarters before he could move Valentine. Someone could get hurt with an agitated Sumac's size and strength if he were not locked up. The 165-pound male checked out the approaching zookeepers with a suspicious eye. Sensing that something did not feel right, he turned his back, pretending they did not exist.

The keepers dug into their box of orangutan delicacies to distract the big male. His keepers had never misled him, so he casually followed his taste buds and headed toward the doorway. Sumac swung around just as the keeper pressed the button to close the gate and stuck his finger under it. He pried open a 150-pound door and lumbered back to protect Suma and Valentine. Everyone remained calm to assure Sumac not to worry about anything. Finally, after surveying the innocent-acting keepers, he strolled into the barn to enjoy his treats.

With Sumac out of the way, Doc tranquilized Suma with a dart gun. With her native instincts on full alert, she refused to go down. Doc medicated her a second time. Five minutes later, she crumpled into a sound sleep. Even asleep, she did not loosen her clutch on her baby, nor did Valentine release her death grip on Mom. With gentle determination, Doc eased a kicking and screaming Valentine from her mother. Zookeeper Perry Alexander wrapped Valentine in a blanket; he and his wife took her home for a couple of weeks to provide a gentle transition away from her familiar home.

Kifli was born at the Gladys Porter Zoo in Brownsville, Texas, a small zoo similar in size to the Fresno Roeding Park Zoo. Like in Fresno, the local community provided strong support. The public knew every animal and followed their life events with great interest.

The Gladys Porter Zoo had a long history with orangutans. In its fifty-two-year history, there have been twenty-five successful orangutan births. The zoo was the first on record to perform a caesarean section on a great ape. The historic procedure was performed in 1970 on an orangutan named Suzi by a local obstetrician and the late Don Farst, DVM, the zoo's previous veterinarian and director. And that newly delivered orangutan was the very same Kifli who was to swap places with Valentine.

Local Brownsville families kept a vigilant watch over the newborn and his mother. They hovered over every little quiver and tremor as he grew, pressing their noses against the partition glass in the nursery. Finally, the big day arrived to exchange Kifli for Fresno Zoo's Valentine, a day the Texas townsfolk dreaded. They had grown so attached to Kifli that it felt like losing a member of one of their own families.

In April 1973, Doc Chaffee and Peggy drove a crated one-year-old Valentine to the Gladys Porter Zoo. Finalizing the trade between Valentine and Kifli, who by then was one year old, the townspeople said their tearful goodbyes. With one last hug and the offering of a few more treats, Doc passed Valentine to her new zookeeper.

More than a sprinkle of tears brushed through Kifli's fans as they waited to wish one last farewell to him, and also to welcome a new sweetheart to their zoo. Doc focused on the future, hoping that Kifli would be a good mate for Azak, and that they would produce offspring together.

Doc and Peggy decided to make a little vacation out of the return trip. Traveling from California to Texas and back with a different orangutan in the car each way (Valentine going and Kifli coming back) required some creative stunts. Sometimes, they dressed the youngster in baby clothes to pass as a child while obtaining a motel room. Once, a mothering type tried to sneak a peek at the little bundle of sweetness. A closer look revealed an orange, hairy little creature with big round eyes staring back with equal surprise. After a wild night of Kifli screaming and banging on the crate, Doc and Peggy leaped out of bed, grabbed their things, and made a quick exit at dawn. They managed to keep one step ahead of child protective services!

Driving back through Arizona on an excellent April day with Kifli, they stopped for a short hike to view the Anasazi cliff dwellings. Doc parked in a shady spot, rolled down the window, then checked the crate to be sure he had properly secured the lock. Everything appeared safe and secure when they left for their walk.

As they returned to the car, a young boy ran up to them, yelling, "Hey, Mister! There is a monkey loose in your car!"

Fearing the worst for Kifli, they raced with hearts thumping in fear. A happy Kifli sat in the driver's seat, surveying the activity around him with a smirk. It took all of Doc's skill to entice Kifli back into his crate for the remaining (and thankfully uneventful) trip to Fresno.

Learning a valuable lesson the hard way, he never again forgot that orangutans are notorious for undoing bolts and crates. Kifli, aka Houdini, was particularly adept at removing doors. When zookeepers arrived at the zoo in the mornings, they were prepared for the unexpected. Kifli magically appeared in some unforeseen spots around the zoo, but he always returned to get his morning meal.

Kifli remained at the Fresno Zoo for fifteen years before transferring to Colorado Springs on April 29, 1987. Much to Doc's disappointment, Kifli and Azak did not produce any offspring.

CHAPTER 31

World's Best Reptile House

Death and danger are a unique draw, traits that make reptiles the most captivating of zoo animals. Dragging their parents through the nine-acre Fresno Zoo, the kids lead the way to the spine-tingling creatures that make one tremble with respect.

In the 1930s, a tortoise, turtles, and two five-foot-long spiny alligators occupied an outdoor space in the southeast corner of the zoo. The American alligator, the most popular of these scaled creatures, found its way to Fresno in a cigar box from Florida, where most alligators live in freshwater swamps. With only its eyes, nostrils, and ears visible, the gator sits like a motionless log in the sand, waiting to snatch its prey.

The alligator and saltwater crocodile share several similarities, including long snouts, powerful tails, short legs, and bony-plated backs. A quick way to tell the difference is to look at the jaws: the crocodile's jaw is elongated to a narrow point, while the alligator's razor-sharp upper teeth cover its lower U-shaped jaw. An alligator's powerful jaw muscles enable it to snap shut its jaws with power, but the specific muscles for opening their jaws are weak. As a result, an adult human can hold an alligator's jaws closed bare-handed. Animal handlers often use duct tape to prevent an alligator from opening its jaws when handled or transported. Luckily, alligators are timid toward humans and tend to walk or swim away if a person approaches.

Initially, the enclosure for the alligators at the zoo was a three-foot-high rock wall encircling a small pond, just low enough to reach over but high enough for little ones not to fall in. A walking bridge over the alligators' exhibit provided a quivering exhilaration for guests brave enough to stand right above the cold-blooded reptilians. It put "up close and personal" to the test. Unfortunately, the exhibit's open access made it too easy for guests to toss in coins, rocks, or any other small items to stir the motionless reptiles. It was a constant effort to keep the area raked clean. The necropsy of one alligator found his intestines filled with such small items.

During the winter months, the remaining alligator hibernated under a heat lamp out of sight. Finally, the zoo installed a heating pad in the pond for the gator so it could remain outdoors. As a testimony to the popularity of these lethargic creatures, people continued to ask where they were long after they were moved near the rainforest exhibit.

In 1974, Doc Chaffee decided the zoo needed an indoor reptile building to display the fascinating creepy-crawlers year-round. He told the herpetologist (reptile guy), Ron Tremper, "Put together a dream list to build a top-notch reptile house. Think big." Ron's inventive mind exploded with ways to imitate environments like the reptiles' various native homes. Given carte blanche, he made a list of an ideal display, including everything from individual chambers with temperature controls to programmable seasonal changes to match the reptiles' native environments. When he completed the assignment, he tiptoed into Doc's office with his long, expensive list, expecting Doc to show him the door. Instead, much to his delight, Doc was all in and bombarded him with questions about every issue he had addressed.

In 1974, Doc invited Dr. Charles Wright Jr., an Albuquerque, NM, scientist, to Fresno for a planning meeting. Wright was engaged in making highly specialized space-age detection equipment. Ron and Elso B. DiLuck, the architect selected to design the reptile house, joined the meeting with their list of questions about how they could incorporate Dr. Wright's inventions into their forward-looking plans. Scientists have recognized how sensitive cold-blooded creatures are to climatic conditions; thus, few zoos had any success with reptile breeding. With Dr. Wright's help, the zoo hoped to change all that with the revolutionary use of computers, before they were readily available to the public. Doc promised to make Fresno the "Snake Capital" of the country, although the Chamber of Commerce understandably hesitated to embrace that moniker.

"We are going to simulate nature in the exhibit areas, or the environmental chambers, as we call the modules," explained Dr. Wright. "Each chamber will be individually programmed to fit that reptile's needs. For example, a setting could indicate mornings at 5:30 a.m., with light rising and the temperature and humidity increasing as the day progresses." With a total budget of about $600,000, and an understanding of how to use Dr. Wright's technology, DiLuck began drawing up plans in 1976, communicating his progress during weekly meetings with Doc and Ron.

What emerged was unlike any other reptile building in the country. Incorporating the newly developed computer systems, each of the thirty-one individual chambers had its own controls. Keepers could set the day-night temperature needs, daylight hours, and seasonal changes for any reptile and amphibian species in the world. Fresno Zoo was the only one in the country, much less the world, that installed these computerized environmental modules.

The structure's design appeared as a stretched donut inside a takeaway box with a hole in the middle. Inside, one turned right to walk the one-way circuit through the building, viewing the exhibits housed in the structure's walls. The lighted display boxes were mounted at eye level, allowing guests a close-up look at these unique animals and their habitats. A walking ledge along the wall let the younger group step up for a better view of the house's forty species of snakes, turtles, and lizards that often lay camouflaged in their native greenery. The lack of windows to the outside was intentional so that the reptiles and amphibians would only follow the light-cycle programmed for their individual needs.

Keeping with the North American theme, the reptile building was placed next to the bison/tule elk exhibit. The locally found adobe bricks and wood structure blended well but appeared bland and dark. The mood was lifted by the installation of a bright ceramic work representing a tortoise and a snake by local artist Stan Bitters in front of the massive entrance doors, which added a whimsical fantasy element to the setting.

Ceramic sculptures at the Reptile House entrance, a gift from Jackie and Dick Duncan. *Courtesy of Jean Chaffee.*

On July 1, 1979, Roeding Park Zoo celebrated the grand opening of the Reptile House. Betty White, a Hollywood celebrity and animal patron, was a special guest of honor at the ceremony, serving as the official ribbon cutter, which brought out the press.

In addition to its numerous habitats, the facility also provided a work area for the staff, where the keepers raised their own food sources, like mice and crickets. Finally, with all the breeding expectations, a particular room was set aside for a nursery. Success came quickly, as some extremely rare reptiles successfully reproduced.

During Ron Tremper's tenure (1975–1983) as the zoo's first herpetologist, the American Association of Zoos, Parks, and Aquariums (AAZPA) awarded the zoo their first captive-breeding recognition for the rattleless rattlesnake and New Zealand gecko. Eventually, most of the species housed in the environmental chambers reproduced.

In 1983, the nationally recognized Honolulu Zoo reptile curator Sean McKeown joined the zoo staff. He was invited by the AAZPA to help capture and identify rare species on the island of Madagascar. As a result, the zoo received several exceedingly rare Madagascar reptiles. Fish and Game often contacted Chaffee Zoo when they seized an illegal shipment of reptiles. As expected, they arrived sick and weak, but after their thirty-day quarantine and receiving lots of special care, they recovered enough to go on exhibit.

In 2000, Mary Morgan became head reptile zookeeper, continuing the excellent reputation of the Reptile House. After thirty years in the zoo field, she had never received a bite from a venomous reptile. It takes skill, agility, and experience to master relocating a six-foot, potentially lethal viper to another space on cleaning day.

Today's visitors enjoy the habitats' painted background scenery and plants representing native habitats. Among the dangerous reptile residents are Gila monsters, green mambas, eyelash vipers, Gaboon vipers, and California rattlesnakes. On the other hand, blue-tongued skinks, eye-licking geckos, and chameleons blend into the leaves, along with the giant pythons, to the delight of the young visitors. Guests challenge each other to spot the well-camouflaged critters.

In 2010, a creative design team evaluated the Reptile House's layout and suggested combining certain module windows to make larger exhibits. Doing so created several combination exhibits:

- the California desert tortoise with the Gila monster
- a rainforest with colorful poison dart frogs and a hanging python
- an aquatic display with fish resembling sticks

- the Gaboon viper, an 18-pound venomous snake with two-inch fangs, representing Africa.

The Reptile House continues to grow and attract attention. It expanded its west wall for two new spaces, a king cobra and a Komodo dragon. The sides of Fresno City buses were painted with the cobra's flared head, advertising this latest arrival. The celebrated king cobra—one of the most venomous snakes on the planet—can literally "stand up" and look a full-grown adult in the eye. The king cobra had the larger room, while the equally fascinating Komodo dragon had a space the size of a walk-in closet. The cobra rarely flared his ready-to-strike neck, but did what snakes do best . . . which is not much.

Budak, a male Komodo, arrived in 2013 from Oglebay Good Zoo. He was hatched at the LA Zoo in 2010. Komodo dragons are the largest lizard in the world, growing up to ten feet in length. They use their long, forked tongue to smell and track prey, typically deer and pigs. Budak had little room to move in his small space, so he was fitted with a harness for a daily walk until he and the king cobra exchanged enclosures. His expected lifespan is nineteen years.

A four-year-old female Komodo, Saphira, arrived in 2018 from Jacksonville Zoo, with expectations for breeding. In the meantime, Budak was moved to a larger outdoor exhibit until the moon aligned for breeding. Putting male and female Komodos together is strictly monitored. The Komodo males can turn aggressive and harm the females. The pair now reside in the Kingdom of Asia exhibit.

Although not venomous in the strictest sense, the bite of a Komodo dragon is not only dangerous because of the physical damage it does, but also because it is heavily dosed with harmful bacteria. In the wild, prey who are lucky enough to escape from a Komodo dragon bite will nevertheless likely die from the bacterial infection. A Komodo dragon follows its escapee until this happens (usually within a week) and then consumes it.

Today, the Reptile House remains the most visited building in the zoo, fascinating to kids and adults alike. Despite the adults' occasional expressions of fear and disgust regarding the snakes and other slimy creatures, they still find themselves drawn through the large wood-carved doors of the reptile building. Proudly, the Chaffee Zoo Reptile House continues to receive recognition as The World's Best Reptile House.

The Reptile House's cobra enclosure. *Courtesy of Jean Chaffee.*

CHAPTER 32

Why Train Elephants in Captivity?

presented by Paul Barkman, 1981 AZAK conference, Fresno

There are three main reasons to train elephants in captivity. First, a trained elephant can be managed efficiently in captivity. For example, trained elephants can be treated medically without sedation. They can also be handled and moved at any time. This allows handlers to exercise the animals. And, since trained elephants are used to being handled, they can be given daily maintenance care, e.g., nail trims. Medical attention, daily care, and exercise are important in keeping the elephant physically healthy.

The mental attitude of an elephant is as important as his physical health. Training can keep the elephant's mind flexible. The give and take of training can help the elephant stay alert. Every being needs a reason for living, whether it's a simple task or a domestic duty. Training can fulfill this need in the captive elephants.

And finally, with handleable elephants, it becomes easier to breed them. A healthy, alert elephant is more likely to breed than an elephant in a "dull" environment. Since Asian elephants are rapidly disappearing in the wild, it is up to zoos and parks to breed these large land mammals.

The Cooperative Agreement Between Roeding Park and Marine World

The people at the Roeding Park Zoo recognize the need for breeding programs with Asiatic elephants. They acquired a young bull elephant, Thong'trii. Thong'trii is himself a captive-born Asian elephant. In fact, his grandfather was also in a captive breeding program at the Washington Park Zoo in Portland, Oregon. The Roeding Park Zoo hopes to continue the success of breeding in captivity with Thong'trii.

However, the people also realized that bull elephants are hard to maintain in captivity. So, they loaned Thong'trii to Marine World-Africa USA for training purposes. And, that's what this paper is about—the training of Thong'trii.

The Beginning . . .

Thong'trii had to learn many behaviors this past summer. Our goal was to prepare Thong to be a zoo elephant that was cared for by man. This meant he had to learn to listen to people. He needed to learn certain behaviors so the handlers could take care of him. He had to be accustomed to all the animals in a zoo. We wanted him to be able to walk past noisy delivery trucks and roaring tigers and not get scared.

So, the first thing we had to teach Thong'trii was to walk everywhere. In effect, we wanted to take away the fear of the unknown by exposing him to as much as possible. In order to do this, we had to establish a "safe" area for Thong'trii. A safe area is an area where the animal is comfortable and contented. If an elephant is released into a safe area, he will stay because he feels secure.

When Thong first arrived at Marine World, we kept him in a pen. He was walked around the pen with four people; one person on each side of him, one person in front, and another in back of him. The person in the rear held a chain attached to Thong's back leg. As Thong gradually got used to the area, and to the people, we used less people to walk him.

When he felt comfortable in the pen, we started walking him out of the gate and then quickly brought him back in. We gave him a food reward for going out of the pen. We kept increasing the distance and time out of the pen. When he walked with us, we fed him. If he tried to run away, the back person held the chain tight and the front person would stop him from running forward by using the elephant hook.

Thong learned fast. By the third day, he could be walked anywhere in the park. After a week, we could walk him with just one person.

My Philosophy of Training

Even though Thong'trii could be walked with one person within a week, it wasn't until the fifth week that we could really

Paul Barkman and Troy Celis tend to Nosey and Kara. *Courtesy of Betty Barkman.*

trust him with one person. Trust is something you need when working with elephants. At first, the elephant will work from fear. When we first walked Thong, he obeyed because we would discipline him if he didn't. But as he learned, we'd trust him a little. And, he started trusting us. When he trusted us, he started working with us instead of doing everything out of fear.

Once a trusting relationship is established, it's easier to teach new behaviors. When Thong'trii was learning the initial behaviors like "stretch out down," "lay on side," "back up," and "foot up," we would reward him with food. As he learned these behaviors, we withheld food. Once we knew he'd learned a behavior, we didn't give him food rewards anymore. We had to trust him to do it. And, because we trusted him and because we knew he'd learned the behavior, he'd do it.

The training is based on this trust, but of course just trust in not enough. Training is basically communicating with the animal. The trainer lets the animal know what he wants.

In Asia, where *mahouts* have been training elephants for generations, they let the young elephants watch the older elephants working. That way when an elephant is beginning his training, he already has an idea of what he's supposed to do. In a sense, the big elephants were teaching the younger ones without them knowing it.

At Marine World, we adapted this technique when training Thong'trii. Thong was always kept near three female elephants and everything they did, he watched. Then, he'd try to do what they did.

When the big elephants were walked across the park to go to work, Thong was right there in line, tailed up. We never taught Thong his place in line, he just learned it from the big elephants.

At the end of the day, when the elephants were taken to the lagoon for their daily swim, Thong was in the water with them. It's pretty hard for a man to show elephants how to swim. But since I could control the older elephants, I could encourage Thong by sitting on an older elephant that already knew how to swim.

Swimming doesn't come naturally to an elephant in a captive environment. Most captive elephants don't utilize the water in their exhibits because they have never been taught how. Without another elephant, it is pretty difficult to get the idea across. And, it's too bad that a lot of elephants never learn. They seem to enjoy it so much. Swimming gives them time to relax, gives them time to do what they want to do.

The purpose of training is not to completely dominate the animal. A trained elephant should trust his trainer, do the behaviors when commanded, but still maintain his own spirit. You never want to let him lose his own personality. Always, he should retain his own individuality.

Keeping this in mind, I try to get to know an elephant while training him. When I know an elephant's weaknesses and strengths, I can plan an individualized training strategy. Not all elephants are alike and you can't train them the same way.

In Thong's case, he was so eager to learn that I didn't have to use drastic measures. Sometimes, trainers find it necessary to use block and tackle and ropes to drag an elephant into a position. We never had to use ropes on Thong. He adapted very well to training.

Even though Thong was easy to train, we still had to discipline him in the beginning. We did use an elephant hook on him. But now, we don't need to strike him. An elephant should progress beyond the point of physical control by the handler. There comes a time when the verbal command "steady" should be enough to calm an elephant and make him behave. An elephant and his handler should establish a communication so that the elephant is not afraid. The calmer an elephant is, the more natural a state the elephant is in and this results in an easier trained animal.

I want to stress the importance of training elephants by professionals. Asian elephants are so rare and endangered that we can't afford to lose any, especially the bull elephants. Not only is there a need for professionally trained elephants, there is also a need for professionally trained keepers. An elephant can survive by himself, untrained and unhandled, in a zoo, but think of what he could've been.

CHAPTER 33

Sumac Loses His Mate

On November 29, 1973, keepers arrived at work to discover that the twenty-three-year-old orangutan Suma had delivered her sixth offspring. It was a surprise, as she had not shown any typical signs during pregnancy. She had proven herself an excellent mother with her previous five babies, so the staff relaxed, expecting no problems. Doc basked in the highly prized birth. Every birth of an endangered species aids in recovering the species, a primary goal of zookeeping.

Zookeepers checked on the three-pound newborn, Geoffrey, his eyes and smile encircled by white, looking at his new world. Staff inspected him several times an hour, looking for healthy signs, such as hanging on to his mother, nursing, and alertness. All characteristics looked good, but the real test would come in one week, if Sumar had enough milk to nourish a baby; if not, the baby weakens and falls off its mother around the seventh day. Fortunately, that milestone passed uneventfully. Suma wrapped her long arms around her newborn and cuddled him as he gripped her fur as she moved. These were all good signs.

Everything progressed smoothly . . . until the third week. That's when signs of change in Suma's normal behavior became a cause for concern. She appeared tired and listless and did not respond typically to her keepers. She had not eaten her usual amount in recent days. Keepers tempted her with her favorite foods, but she ignored them.

These red flags caused the concerned staff to monitor her closely. Doc began antibiotic treatment, thinking she might suffer from a flu-like virus. The newborn's health was also a worry. A twenty-four-hour watch was set up.

The first sign of serious trouble came when Geoffrey no longer clung to his mother. He lay on the floor next to Suma, whimpering and seeking her attention. Later that morning, Suma lay unmoving on the cement floor. The staff roped off the area to keep zoo visitors away from the scene.

Typically, orangutans live solitary, elusive lives. The veteran keepers watched in amazement as Sumac, the enormous male ape, interacted with his thirteen-year mate.

Sumac sensed that something was wrong with his companion. He kicked Suma's hairy leg to rouse her, but she did not respond. Her mate grew agitated and kicked her again. Same reaction. He hoisted her with his massive arms and tried to shake her awake. Baffled at her lack of response, he dropped her. The 165-pound male, with his dark cheek pads and narrow eyes, paced around the enclosure, totally frustrated, gluing his eyes on her lifeless body.

Meanwhile, the fragile infant gripped his mother's long, orange fur. The exasperated male picked up the limp Suma again, trying to awaken her. The attached infant hung on, shivering and crying; he needed rescuing immediately. This time, the frustrated Sumac dropped his lifeless companion next to the chain-link fence, where the staff stood watching helplessly.

With that, Doc began issuing orders. Sally grabbed a pile of warm towels from the nursery while Linda prepared the isolette (a warm enclosure for baby animals). Phil dashed off for a pair of bolt cutters to open a hole in the fence. Doc stretched his arm through the hole Phil made and extended his fingers toward the infant, sliding him closer to the fence. He gently pried the tiny fingers off Mom's chest and carefully moved the infant through the hole and away from danger. Wrapped in towels, baby Geoffrey was rushed to the nursery for IVs and fluids. The distraught Sumac paced in the opposite corner, ignoring the rescue effort. All the keepers' focus shifted to the survival of the female's last offspring.

The loss of Suma hung over the zoo like a dark cloud. Walking through the grounds, Phil reported hearing a loud, mournful wail. He had never heard a sound anything like it; it reverberated within him. The resonating calls sent chills down the spine. For weeks, Sumac's cries for his partner permeated the zoo grounds. Phil imagined the massive male scanning the forest treetops for his lost soul mate. It left an unforgettable mark that touched all those who witnessed his reaction.

Animals are viewed by some as lacking emotions, but these two, Suma and Sumac, challenged that opinion, although one must be careful not to interpret animal behaviors by human standards. However, the frequent public displays of affection between Suma and Sumac had won the public's hearts. One often saw them with their arms around each other. It was easy to feel the tenderness when they sat face to face, exchanging kisses with their long lips.

Suma's loss prompted a ripple of concern. Doc wondered if he had missed apparent symptoms. Did she die of a contagious disease? If so, could other primates catch it? Could it be transmitted to humans? University of California, Davis, pathologists and microbiologists performed a necropsy on Suma. The report indicated she died from an acute Valley Fever infection. Suma created history by being the first primate diagnosed with a disease endemic to the San Joaquin Valley.

The staff steam-cleaned the orangutans' apartment to kill any possible Valley Fever fungus. Valley Fever is not a virus and, thus, not transmitted from one person to another. It spreads through contamination of the premises, feeding utensils, or dirt. Once the spore gets outside the animal, it can live on its hair and spread to other animals. The diagnosis opened the door for UC Davis to offer trial testing of Valley Fever vaccines on the zoo's primate population.

After the trauma of losing his mother, nursery aides welcomed the orange ball of fur, Geoffrey, with lavish hugs and attention. His irresistible round, soft eyes captured many a heart. After one and a half years, Doc began searching for a companion for Geoffrey. He found the perfect match at Portland Zoo, a young orangutan named Julie, and made preparations to bring her to Fresno. Like traditional arranged marriages, the respective Portland and Fresno Zoo "families" of Julie, age nine months, and Geoffrey made plans for their introduction. Raising the two youngsters together increased the possibility that they would get along and produce offspring.

After three months of red tape haggling, plans were made for the two young orangutans to meet. Before completing the transfer, the US Department of Fish and Game attempted to block the move. The Department insisted that the transfer violated the 1973 Endangered Species Act, claiming it was a commercial sale. Julie became a "cause celebre" as both zoos disputed the decision. They stated that this move would enhance the species, not endanger it further. Government officials finally agreed, and Doc chartered a plane to bring Julie to Fresno.

Doc and two nursery attendants, Sally Smith Becker and Linda Cover, flew to Portland airport, where they met Portland's zoo director, Dr. Ogilvie, and the primate keeper. Doc welcomed Julie, who appeared frail and small for her size. He gave her a quick checkup and inquired about her health history. The time came for Julie's farewell hugs and kisses as she entered the travel crate for the flight. But first, Portland director Dr. Ogilvie gently removed her for one last hug. When he handed her to Dr. Chaffee, she stretched across to Dr. Ogilvie and kissed his cheek. She then tenderly bussed Doc's cheek. With that, she left her familiar surroundings for the move to Fresno.

A young, ginger-shaded orangutan, Hephzibah, also joined the group for the trip to Fresno. Hephzibah's final home was to be the Oakland Zoo, after spending a month in Fresno's quarantine facility. Because of all the to-do surrounding Julie's sale to Fresno, the Oregon press was on hand at the airport to write the story's final chapter. Julie, the shier of the two, clung to attendant

Linda, her head pressed against her chest. She peeked out, then quickly ducked her head back in. On the other hand, Sally had her hands full with Hephzibah, who was very outgoing and entertained the press corps. Using her hook-like hands and long fingers, she clapped and danced, grinning from ear to ear. Sally clung to her charge, desperate to keep control.

Hand-raised, the orangutans traveled in the passenger part of the airplane, just like other toddlers. Once on the plane, it became a challenge to keep the lively Hephzibah in her seat. Sally gave Linda a look of envy as she cast her eyes across the aisle at the calm, fuzzy-headed Julie, asleep on Linda's lap.

Sally offered to pass the acrobatic ape up to Doc, who was sitting with the pilot. He declined; Sally was doing just fine, he said. However, when the plane landed in Fresno and the press met them with cameras clicking, Doc reached for the calmer ape for the press release. Doc and Linda emerged ready for the cameras, showing off their new additions. Sally, on the other hand, hid her disheveled head while desperately hanging on to the bouncy one so she wouldn't escape.

All animals that are transferred between zoos go through a month of quarantine. Once they arrived, Julie and Hephzibah spent time in quarantine to ensure no viruses would be introduced. Sadly, the fragile Julie did not live past the quarantine period. A necropsy on Julie did not reveal any contagious viruses. Hephzibah went on to the Oakland Zoo.

Sumac received another mate from China, who was named Linda. They had two offspring. The genes of Fresno's two native-born orangutans, Suma and Sumac, as well as Linda's, are found in many zoos throughout the United States. The AZA tracks the DNA of every animal registered in an accredited zoo and determines which animals are best suited for breeding to keep the genetics pure.

CHAPTER 34

Geoffrey

Suma died while the two-week-old Geoffrey clung to her. After a traumatic rescue, Doc wrapped him in a warm, moist towel and rushed to the nursery. All hands were needed to keep the tiny two-pound baby alive. Doc immediately consulted Dr. John Conrad, a pediatrician at Valley Children's Hospital. He prescribed the same treatment for Geoffrey that one of the preemie babies in his Neonatal Intensive Care Unit would receive. Doc injected vital electrolyte fluids and dextrose, and he inserted a stomach tube for continuous infusion.

Offers poured into the zoo as concerned local citizens monitored developments through the news. Two women called in to offer their human milk, Children's Hospital extended a helping hand, and pediatricians around town offered to be on call as needed. Many recall it as their most memorable patient; the genuine concern of the citizens made the tense situation easier to bear.

Zookeeper Sally Smith watched Doc care for little Geoffrey with skill and compassion; he inserted the needles into the tiniest of veins with adeptness and gentleness. Stories about his concern for the sick and injured had preceded him, but she now witnessed it for herself. He had a magical touch to cure the seemingly incurable.

Geoffrey needed round-the-clock professional care, so Doc prepared an incubator and took the infant to his own home, where his family pitched in for frequent feedings. Geoffrey sipped one-half to one-and-a-half ounces of milk every two hours. Within a few days, he went off the extra fluids and then gradually adjusted to a standard Enfamil formula. It was hard work, but lovingly applied and considered a privilege by all who were involved.

Susan McCracken accepted responsibility as a foster mother when Geoffrey became strong enough to move into her house. She fell into parenting the little orangutan with gusto. Often one could see a little orange head peeking through the car window as he accompanied "Mom" on her errands. She and her husband, Jeff, took turns going out for groceries.

At three months, Geoffrey ate a teaspoon of oatmeal with each three-ounce bottle. His growth, monitored weekly, gave the zoo valuable information. If anyone ever asks, a three-month-old orangutan's head circumference is 11 inches. Friends donated a travel bed. Zoolynx volunteers pitched in their trading stamp books for a nylon playpen. At six months, Geoffrey had grown six times his birth weight

Baby Geoffrey and his mom.

to 12 pounds. He now took his bottle every three hours, had two teeth, and started eating a jar of strained baby food each day. He could sit up on his own and crawl across the room.

Doc never missed a chance to show off his animals. He persuaded Susan to bring Geoffrey with her to a fashion show at the Hilton Inn, where she modeled safari clothes. Doc felt she needed Geoffrey's presence to best show off the African outfits. After being stuck in the house all day with him, she jumped at the chance to mix with humans. Susan later reflected, "Young and with no children, I had no idea what to expect when we went out in public. When I got in the elevator, several men joined me. I wrapped Geoffrey a little tighter." One of the gentlemen wanted to see the baby, so she let his head peek out. "What a cute baby," they oohed. "Oh my, what orange hair he has!"

At ten months, Geoffrey started caring for himself. He ate solid food on his own. He used the McCracken furniture to practice forest movements, climbing up the curtains, leaping to the table, then jumping onto the couch. Susan had mixed emotions when the day came to return him to the zoo nursery.

Geoffrey needed some primate company to learn proper ape behavior. The Oakland Zoo agreed to send Kalanyo, a young chimpanzee, to Fresno for a short sojourn. Both primates, having been hand-raised away from other animals, cowered and clung to the keepers when they first saw each other. The introductions began with a "right chop" to the jaw and a foot in the mouth. Within a few days, however, they calmed down to play and wrestle like normal apes.

Keepers learned to brace themselves for unexpected leaps into their comforting arms. After a quick hug, they dashed back for more play.

When Kalanyo returned to Oakland, Geoffrey missed his friend and became lethargic. Primates are social animals that require lots of companionship. Without it, they become depressed and listless, and even death can result. Human companionship plays a role, but has its limits. With exclusively human companionship, primates may eventually reject their primate counterparts and refuse to interact at all, including breeding. They become isolated from their species. It was a tricky juggling act raising an orphaned primate.

CHAPTER 35

Fred's Bumpy Road to a Family

F red, now an adult, had developed into a majestic, powerful lowland male gorilla. He watched over his territory with piercing black eyes and flared nostrils. Fred had all the stud markers, with good looks and an easy temperament, an extremely thick, muscular chest, and a protruding abdomen. His skin and hair were both black. Adult gorillas have long, muscular arms, which are 15 to 20 percent longer than their stocky legs. The males can weigh up to 500 pounds, twice as heavy as the females, and stand about five and one-half feet.

Fred's wild-caught genes made him essential to the captive breeding program. The massive male had yet to prove himself, not that he hadn't tried. With the loss of his childhood mate, Nina, the lonely Fred needed a new companion. So in 1975, Doc arranged with the San Diego Zoo to provide a female on a breeding loan.

Betsi, a full-grown, fifteen-year-old female half his size, originated from the same lowlands of Cameroon as Fred. As an orphaned youngster, she had first gone to Frankfurt Zoo, where the staff raised her; motherless, her quirky habits had endeared her to the team. After a smooth courtship, she warmed up to Fred, allowing him to breed her. But no babies resulted.

Two-and-a-half years later, worrisome changes began to occur in Betsi. The active ape became listless and lost her appetite. Doc prepared her for a complete physical, borrowing a portable X-ray unit from Fresno Sierra Hospital. Her scans and blood tests showed nothing unusual. As a last resort, he called the UC Davis veterinary school for further help. Doc took Betsi to Davis, but tragically, she died within the week of Valley Fever.

Betsi was the third Fresno primate to fall prey to Valley Fever in five years. The loss came as a shock. Doc had worked hard to create a healthy environment, only to have his charges be struck down by an unpreventable disease. He told reporters, "Gorillas are rare in zoos, but we will attempt to find another female to continue the propagation of the species."

San Diego Zoo responded with thirteen-year-old Alvila, the daughter of two lowland gorillas from Cameroon. The San Diego Zoo had hand-raised Alvila when her mother could not nurse. For great apes, parenting is a learned behavior, and so Doc worried that without any previous nurturing experiences, she might reject her potential babies with Fred. According to the breeding loan, San Diego would get the first offspring, Fresno would keep the second one, and so on.

Introductions between two large animals carry a risk of injury. The two gorillas were first situated next to each other in their bedroom enclosures. Gentle grunts and cooing gorilla sounds were coming from both apes. Doc called the media to alert them to the face-to-face meeting that was soon to happen.

Alvila went out first to explore the common area. Once she appeared comfortable and set in her place, the doors opened for Fred to meet and impress his bride. Running upright on two feet (bipedally) across the floor, he beat his chest, grunting loudly while racing back and forth. Then, making a sharp turn, he ended by swinging around a center pole. This display exhibited the male's dominance over his domain. Accepting this, Alvila maintained a respectable distance when he took off on his sprints. However, regarding more important encounters, Alvila held her own, nodding to Fred when he had that "look" in his eyes.

After lovemaking between Fred and his new bride, Bruce, her caretaker, circled an expected due date for the birth. Ideally, Alvila would accept her role as a mother. However, she might reject or even injure her newborn, not knowing what to do. Doc prepared a backup plan for the staff to step in to remove the newborn for hand-raising. But the timing would be critical.

On March 21, 1979, Alvila delivered a healthy infant. A team of keepers began a twenty-four-hour watch. Every activity of Alvila and the infant, Alberta, was entered into a notebook: Alvila nursed the baby within six hours, showed some tender affection, patted Alberta on the back, and kissed her. The staff felt good, and things progressed normally until the critical seventh day. Then, unexpectedly, little Alberta loosened her tight grip. With that, Alvila put the weakened newborn down and walked away.

Doc realized the mother didn't have enough milk to nourish Alberta. The minute the female saw the keepers enter the back, she knew what was coming and picked up the infant by the foot. Then, when Doc aimed the dart gun at her, she dropped the little one and ran to the far side of the quarters. Feigning disinterest, the keeper calmly enticed the suspicious female into the barn with her favorite treats. Quietly sidling up to the door switch, he closed it, separating the mother from her baby.

Once Mom went behind the closed doors, they swept in to retrieve her infant. Alberta was rushed to the nursery, where Doc started intravenous fluids. The veins of an infant gorilla are smaller than a human preemie, so needle insertion calls for an experienced, steady hand. Doc's friends, pediatricians Dr. John Lattin and Dr. Larry Miller, agreed to accept the tiny ape and prepared a separate room at their hospital. After wrapping up the infant in warm blankets, they drove to Valley Children's Hospital on Shields and Millbrook, where the doctors immediately hooked up the necessary fluids and antibiotics. Some personnel and patients caught sight of the hairy bundle, which led to a lot of whispering and staring.

Doc packed an incubator and took her home for round-the-clock care while keeping San Diego Zoo informed of her situation. Neonatal specialist Dr. Visheswara, from Valley Children's Hospital, joined the "on call" team. Bottles tangled from the lamp over the incubator with tubes leading to the tiny infant's veins. Every two to four hours, the Chaffees alternated getting up to give medications, adjust flow rates, change diapers, and collect specimens. Alberta's condition gradually improved, and soon her formula feedings stretched past two hours.

No event in the zoo's history created more interest or compassion than Alberta's. During her thirty-day stay in Fresno, Alberta became a celebrity. The local stations kept a running commentary about her every movement. The San Francisco radio station KGO called daily, the national wire services called often, and the *Fresno Bee* covered the story's every twitch and turn. The phone never stopped ringing.

Considering Alberta's delicate condition and the ongoing need for intensive care, Doc decided she needed to go to the San Diego Wild Animal Park's well-equipped nursery. The zoo staff said farewell to the adored Alberta with mixed emotions. Doc set a time for Alberta to be placed by a nursery window for a final public viewing; a long line of visitors wound through the zoo to catch a glimpse of this renowned and beloved fragile ape.

Fifteen months later, on July 26, 1980, Alvila and Fred produced a second infant. His name, Jitu, meant "giant" in Swahili. Hopefully, Jitu would inherit Fred's genes and grow into a handsome, giant ape. According to the loan agreement, he would remain in Fresno as the second-born. The staff placed sawdust all over the exhibit in case Alvila dropped her infant to the floor again.

At the critical seven-day mark, the infant's eyes glassed over as he hung loosely unto Mom's fur. When Jitu finally released his hold, his mother dropped him in the sawdust. Doc had his gun ready to tranquilize Alvila to retrieve the infant. However, the new mother had gained extra weight during her pregnancy and did not go down. Despite her lack of maternal instincts, Alvila had no intention of giving away another offspring. Instead, she grabbed her newborn by one leg and dragged him, face down, across the sawdust-covered floor. The staff grabbed a hose and aimed the full force of water at her before dashing in to rescue little Jitu.

Checking him thoroughly, the zoo vet feared Jitu might have an unseen injury from his traumatic ordeal. Doc took the infant to Valley Children's Hospital emergency room. Fortunately, there were no apparent injuries beyond the initial trauma. The size of a normal human infant, he weighed in at six pounds nine ounces, and measured 19 inches long.

Alvila and baby Jitu.

However, one can only imagine the stories that circulated about the town. A bearded gentleman wearing a khaki shirt with a zoo logo and tie hustled through the hospital, carrying a bundled package with a fuzzy black head sticking out, featuring wide-eyed coal orbs and yellow pinpoints. The man looked vaguely familiar.

As he had with Alberta, Doc took Jitu home for several days of personalized care. The newborn then returned to the zoo nursery, where he was doted on by his eight devoted "mothers." Within a month, he learned to smile and discovered his tongue. He also learned how to reach out and touch those eight familiar faces. Gorillas have opposable thumbs like humans; and like humans, he stuck his hand in his mouth to suck his fingers and thumb. He also had a crib, disposable diapers, and toys to entertain him. During the second month, he began to make gorilla noises. His round black eyes focused on the two-pound, bright-eyed marmosets, their long tails swaying; they passed the time making faces at each other.

During the two years that Jitu stayed in the nursery, his father, Fred, died of heart failure, and his mother, Alvila, returned to San Diego. As a result, Doc had to make some hard decisions. The time had come for the young ape to go out on exhibit, but he was too young to be alone. Finally, in Jitu's best interest, he left Fresno for San Diego's gorilla troop, where he lived as a family member, rejoining his mother and sister.

San Diego Zoo has always acknowledged Fresno Zoo's key role in creating a family of lowland gorillas to perpetuate the species.

CHAPTER 36

Moja Goes to the Dentist

In 1980, Doc Chaffee received a call from the Los Angeles Fish and Game Department that a nine-week-old lion cub needed placement in a zoo. A wealthy LA family had been keeping him in their home as a pet, probably the offspring of a circus animal—but it was now time to place him in a better home. At birth, the cub weighed just three pounds, but by now he had grown to 15 pounds, the size of a small to midsized dog. Brown camouflage polka dots peeked through his sandy-brown fur coat. Cute and lovable like his tamed cousin, the kitten, one couldn't resist embracing him with hugs. The little lion cub had gained some local notoriety, and before his departure from Los Angeles, talk show host Johnny Carson invited the celebrated feline on his show as an honored guest.

Doc was familiar with Fish and Game, as they frequently contacted him for assistance in finding homes for illegally shipped animals. He was happy to help out the young lion, and drove to LA to pick him up. Knowing the cub was hand-raised, Doc let him ride in the front seat of the car with a nursery aide, meowing in her lap.

The mellow cub came with the name Moses, but his keeper, Mary Swanson, suggested calling him Moja (mō-jha), because it sounded stronger. The name means "number one" in Swahili, as in King of the Jungle.

The young, tawny-furred cub went directly to the zoo nursery, where the hired Fresno State College biology students immediately smothered him with attention. At three months old, he would normally transition between milk and regurgitated meat from his mother. Because he was raised in a home, Doc prescribed extra milk and gave him ground meat.

The hand-raised carnivore displayed gentle tendencies, encouraging some of the animal keepers to buddy up to him. They arranged their days to fit in a visit to the zoo's newest purring occupant. This irresistible little bundle of fur worked his charm on every animal lover who crossed his path. His most ardent devotee, reptile keeper Dana, always managed to sneak in a roughhousing session during the day. Although Moja was growing out of his caged enclosure in the nursery, his calm personality did not present any red flags.

When Moja turned five months and was nearly an adult, Doc finally acknowledged he had outgrown the nursery. His sharp nails and canines could prove deadly if he decided to turn on his helpers. The nursery staff gave Moja one last hug and waved goodbye as he moved to the outdoor feline barn. Chopper and Alice, the zoo's two resident adult lions, were in the run next to him to watch over him. Visitors flocked to meet this young, aspiring lion king, who had finally been let outside to join the other exotic cats. His playful pawing and soft snarling more resembled that of a domestic cat than a feared predator, drawing plenty of admirers from the public.

Dana continued to play and wrestle with him, even after Moja moved to the more oversized pen. Despite being hand-raised and having a good temperament, Moja was 100 pounds of firm muscle. But Dana, a strong, burly man, loved frolicking with the playful cub and ignored the reality that each play session was, in fact, a potentially life-threatening situation. One day, the fun skidded to a halt. During one of their wrestling sessions, Moja drew blood when he playfully nipped Dana on the arm. Fortunately, it was just a scratch. Dana attempted to hide the injury, but it bled more than he expected. He discreetly opened the first aid cupboard for a Band-Aid, but the blood drew Supervisor Mary Swanson's attention, and she insisted that Dana give up his man-beast playtimes.

She had turned a blind eye to his ongoing interactions with the growing feline, but her dream zoo job could be at risk if either one got injured. With regret, Dana had to settle for petting the young lion through the cage bars. Moja missed the daily contact with his friend; he learned how to sidle up to the bars to encourage a rubbing fix from Dana.

When Moja turned ten months old, his behavior changed almost overnight. Now, the easygoing feline barely moved or reacted to his buddy, Dana. Rather than rolling around and pawing his sharp claws at the gawking humans, he laid his head on his feet and rubbed his mouth.

Concerned, the keeper reported this abnormal behavior to Doc. While making his regular rounds, the vet took time to observe Moja lying on the ground. The lion stroked his jaw with his paw and wrapped his big mouth around the bars, rubbing up and down. He showed all the signs of being in pain.

Most unlike his typical self, Moja refused to eat. When offered a bone over his head, the lethargic animal ignored it, not opening his mouth. Doc reached through the bars and lifted Moja's lip for a better view. Peering inside, he spotted a dark baby canine, which explained the cat's pain. Having neither training nor dental tools to work in a lion's mouth, Doc needed to contact a dentist.

An active zoo docent, Katherine, offered the services of her husband, Dr. John Grieco. After talking by phone, the two men decided that Moja had to come to the office. He needed X-rays, and Grieco could not modify his X-ray machine to make it portable. Having a lion as a patient also required the dentist to adjust his office, as none of his other patients arrived sound asleep, tied down, or covered in fur. The dentist cleared his calendar, and the zoo staff prepared Moja for his visit.

Moja received a heavy dose of tranquilizer while at the zoo. Working in a lion's mouth is no laughing matter. Once asleep, the keepers wrapped Moja in a cargo net and loaded him into a van. It took four keepers to move the 137-pound carnivore. One staff

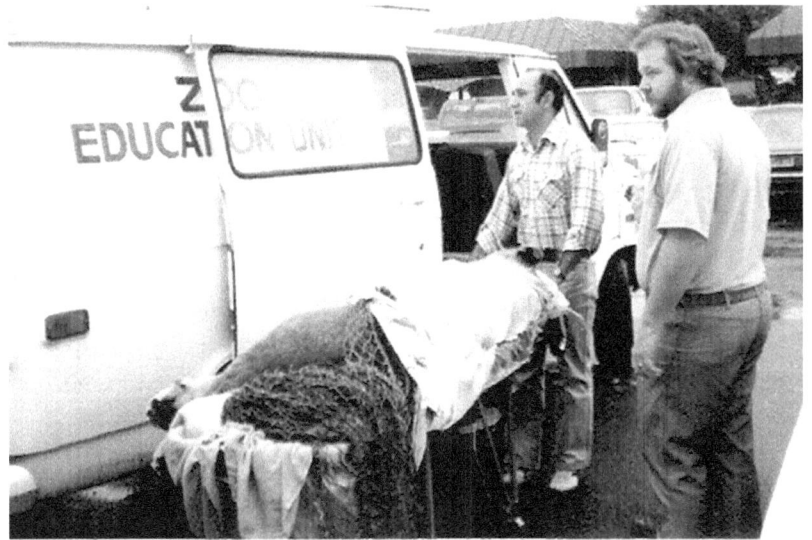

An unconscious Moja on his way to see the dentist.

member sat in the back with him, ready to give another injection if he appeared to rouse. They drove the van across town, avoiding sharp turns or quick stops. They arrived at the dentist's office on First Street between Shields and Ashlan without complications.

The troupe carried the sleeping Moja in from the parking lot, which took him past several medical offices. People stared out of the office buildings, confused by what they saw. The date, October 31, Halloween Day, stirred the imaginative minds of those who watched this odd parade passing by. It felt like a scene out of *The Wizard of Oz*. "Mommy, Mommy, there's a lion out there." "Oh no, it must be someone dressed in a lion's costume." "I don't know, it looks like a lion."

Having no table to lay Moja on, the zookeepers placed him on the floor, wrapped in the cargo net. The net would keep him immobile for a few minutes if he woke up, giving them time to inject another sedative shot. Dr. Grieco took several X-rays of the tooth, hoping he could save the front canine. After reading the X-rays, he realized the cracked baby tooth had caused an infection and couldn't be saved.

A return visit was scheduled for two weeks later. During the interim, Dr. Grieco gathered up the proper lion-sized tools for extracting the painful canine. Borrowing a gurney from a nearby mortuary, the dentist met the zookeepers in his office's parking lot. They picked up the sleeping lion, laid him on the gurney, and rolled him into the office. His eyes were covered with a towel, as the eyelids do not close when an animal is anesthetized.

Dr. Grieco slid the gurney under the X-ray machine. A fellow dentist, his wife, and various associates joined in on this memorable day, all crammed into the small room. The keepers gathered just outside the door in case of trouble. Once, Moja raised his head and gave it a shake. Dr. Grieco and the witnesses dashed out of the room as the keepers ran in. The photographer could not move to escape, so she kept taking photos.

Moja yawned and laid back down, unaware of the panic he had just caused. The zoo staff assured everyone he was still asleep, and Dr. Grieco returned to finish up the extraction. Moja returned to the zoo with a missing canine but as a much happier young lion. Fortunately, an adult tooth grew to fill the empty spot.

CHAPTER 37

Chopper, Alice, and Moja

After the stunning yellow-and-black-striped Bengal tigers Sheba and Rajah passed away in 1978, they were replaced with two adult lions, Alice and Chopper. Mary, the feline keeper, favored Chopper and boasted about his handsome appearance. Chopper's sleek body oozed fierceness, with his bright yellow eyes staring one down. Alice's smooth, lean body, minus the mane, complemented Chopper. In the accompanying exhibit, young Moja's growing mane gave evidence that he was maturing into an adult lion. In addition, his camouflage baby spots were disappearing beneath his emerging yellowish-brown fur.

Moja, still young and energetic, challenged the staff to find ways to keep him occupied. He tirelessly swung the hanging rubber tire or tossed his bowling ball with a resounding bang. Chopper and Moja passed many an afternoon spraying and respraying to scent mark their territory. Keepers amused themselves judging the length of the potent jet streams. Alice's spray won with a length of 17 feet. The zoo needed a sign that warned, "Visitors, Beware of Spray," or "Stand close at your own risk."

Domestic and wild cats are notorious for their odiferous showers; both sexes of tigers and lions are frequent squirters. Once, an over-enthusiastic photographer learned the hard way as he climbed over the outside public rail of the tiger exhibit to get a better picture. His wife kept yelling at him to get away. Before keepers Mary and Lisa could warn him, the female tiger backed up to the edge of the exhibit and drenched his lens! All had a good laugh——except the photographer.

Finally, through natural attrition, the zoo was down to two tigers and three lions. Doc could now start his in-house project to renovate the cat barn. The big cats were locked in their bedrooms while the crew worked outside of the barn. The barred windows brought fresh air inside and let them enjoy the action. Moja's paw reached through the gap at the top of his door, as he supervised the construction. Standing on his tippy toes, he stretched his paw to play "tag" with the workers. Mary reminded the crew not to pet the clawed carnivore. All zoo animals were *not* tame, and it could lead to a disaster.

The dividers between the three runs were removed, giving Alice and Chopper twice as much space. The cement floor was replaced with two feet of dirt and then topped with a foot of soil. Doc planted his favorite bamboo, giving the enclosure a natural look. With the hard work finished, the exhausted staff lined up to watch the animal's reactions when they stepped out. Would they be tentative? Would they spray everything? How would they react to having dirt under their feet for the first time?

Instead, the lioness walked straight to the bamboo and, with one swipe, obliterated the plants. The two tore up the dirt and destroyed months of work in minutes, turning it into an expensive enrichment activity.

An outside contractor took over the total renovation of the tiger and lion outside areas. The three lions had the wider south side of the barn; the two tigers were on the north side. This time, the plants lined the outside of the exhibit, away from Alice's paws. Large land-scaping rocks and small ponds created privacy areas for the cats, hidden from the public. For four additional months, the felines settled in their bedrooms while the work went on outside their doors.

Moja loved to throw his bowling ball, which provided a much-needed diversion; he became quite adept with his two front arms. He threw the ball so hard it created grooves in the lower bricks of his bedroom. The sound of the ball on the cement reverberated throughout the barn. The ball eventually went into the toy box for an extended timeout, but the grooves remain evidence of his vigorous play style!

When the exhibit reopened, Moja rotated going outside with Alice and Chopper, as the two males were not permitted to be together. After Chopper died in 1983, Moja and Alice were put together for company. Although Moja was now larger than the female, she intimidated him, so that he cowered in the corner. This full-grown adult male slunk around the female like he had stolen her dinner. Moja did not realize his size and strength, so he kept himself on the opposite side of the exhibit, where he felt safe.

Alice bonded easily with humans. Her sweet personality endeared her to keepers, who knew that the big cat loved having her ears scratched. The lioness plastered herself against the metal mesh, receiving her daily massages. Alice became edgy without her full measure of meat whenever she was placed on a diet. To appease her, the keepers created a routine, fooling her into thinking she got extra food. The female received a reduced portion of her ration before Moja got his dinner. Afterward, she inhaled the remainder. Then, she strutted away as if she had one-upped Moja with an extra treat. Moja and Alice maintained a cordial relationship until her death nine years later, leaving Moja alone during his remaining years.

Staff tried different ways to enrich the lone feline's days with unique toys. He carried a two-foot-long piece of heavy, rough log in his mouth. His "indestructible" Boomer Ball was promptly punctured with his powerful fangs.

Moja had the best spot in the zoo. It bordered a special event location, which was situated on a busy pathway leading from one side to the other. To amuse himself as innocent passersby walked by, he backed up to the bars and took aim. As the visitor let out a scream, Moja shook his head and, without so much as a glance backward, walked away, watching for his next victim.

Chopper.

A total party animal, he recognized the signs of event preparation and settled in to enjoy the evening. The party tables were placed at least 20 feet away to protect the guests from Moja's unexpected sprays. During such gatherings, he ignored the call to go in at night. Moja resisted their temptations of favorite special treats and instead turned his backside to the barn while keeping his eyes on the activity. The frustrated keeper had no choice but to clean his enclosure after the party.

The tawny-brown-maned male had a perfect view of the hoofstock yard, which the giraffes and various antelope shared. At first, the zebras shared the area, but they played by different rules. Without horns to protect themselves, they resorted to biting and kicking to defend their space and were soon removed to a separate area.

When a hormonal scent wafted in the air, it alerted Moja to keep a steady eye on the neighboring activity, zeroing in on the female giraffe giving birth. He went on high alert as he paced around his enclosure, imagining fresh meat on his plate. Low rumbles warned the long-necked beasts that danger was close. The giraffe adults closed around the newborn to protect it from the predator. Hoofstock on the open plain must be able to stand, walk, and run within the first hour of birth to escape the lurking killers, but this newborn was slow to stand up. Sensing the predator's presence, an adult gently kicked the infant to urge him onto his feet. Finally, the anxious adults were removed to give the newborn space to stand up.

Moja's relationship with his keepers extended his life by a few years. During his senior years, he needed meds injected through IVs. Staff developed a plan based on his normal behaviors to avoid having to sedate him. Moja loved to have his back scratched. Mary fed him a steady dose of treats as he edged up against his wire cage to be in position. At the same time, Dr. Lynch inserted a needle while Moja remained still, mesmerized by the massages. He died in June 2000 at age 20, long past the life expectancy for lions in the wild and even among zoos.

Those living in nearby neighborhoods recall hearing the moans of the cats piercing the night air as if reaching out for their distant relatives. It is still felt deep in their soul.

CHAPTER 38

Trees of Life (a Piece of the Tropical Rainforest)

In the early 1980s, Doc traveled to Peru and Ecuador to see the rainforest and its reputed devastation firsthand. Aboard a boat meandering down the Rio Negro, an Amazon tributary, he studied the water's edge. He was captivated by the beauty of the forest's multiple shades of green. The chirping and singing of birds, all dressed in an array of colors, filled the moist air. When exploring on foot, the guide used his machete to hack a path through the overgrowth. Doc traded in his customary shorts for long pants and socks for protection.

Where does one look first? Do you look overhead for tree-hanging snakes or down to avoid raised roots, sharp spines, or camouflaged reptiles slinking through the grass? Whooping monkeys swung through the trees, while the iridescent blue morpho butterflies sucked up juices from dead animals. The trees nurtured life for hundreds of species, each finding their niche in the complex ecosystem.

Next to this lushness, a swath of barren land exposed the mountainside. The effects of soil erosion went beyond the loss of fertile land. It interrupted migration paths that animals had followed for thousands of years. It created flooding, which sent the rich topsoil downward. Tropical forests are crucial to the world's climate. They transpire during daylight hours, releasing copious amounts of moisture and oxygen into the atmosphere. The South American rainforest helps drive Earth's atmospheric circulation cycles, which move oxygen and freshwater around the planet.

Earth's future depends on the health of the rainforests, and what the environmentalist in Doc Chaffee saw alarmed him. A thousand images of Doc's trip buzzed around in his head during his flight home. The rainforests support an abundance of life seen nowhere else in the world, but unfortunately, man's destructive practices put it in danger. Doc pondered the question, "How can I communicate a tropical rainforest concept to Central Valley residents living in a desert-like area?"

By the time Doc stepped off the plane, a plan had formed in his head. He wanted to build a Fresno-version rainforest, as similar as possible to what he had experienced in South America. Not wasting any time, he called on his friends for help. A pilot friend flew a small team to the San Diego Zoo to meet with its rainforest exhibit builders for suggestions. Donning his Peruvian tropical shirt and wide-brimmed hat, Doc met with the Fresno Zoo Society Board. He shared his vision of a walk-through exhibit where more than fifty species and a like number of people could share the space.

"Imagine an uncaged, natural feel of a rainforest with no barriers," he told them. "Birds, reptiles, and mammals moving freely in the enclosed structure, just as in a South American rainforest." Excited to share his vision, he took the board members on a walk to the exhibit's potential home, an empty lot located in the southwest part of the zoo. He spread his arms toward the deserted area, describing what he saw in his head. All they saw was a lonely valley oak tree, where he imagined lush greenery, nesting birds, and wandering visitors. However, over time the board members had learned to trust Chaffee's vision, and so they vowed to support his project. Doc always pushed the boundaries with his unusual dreams. Some worked, and some didn't, but he was not one to give up pushing the norms for a better facility.

Fundraising for the walk-through rainforest exhibit began in 1984, with an expected construction cost in mind. Josephine Maddis's estate donated $350,000, which kicked off the campaign. As is common with construction estimates, the costs escalated, capping out at $2.2 million. Fresno area builders Mauldin-Dorfmeier began construction in 1987. Every day, Doc walked by to watch the progress and make suggestions.

A fine mesh screen, suspended from 70-foot-tall straight poles sourced from Oregon, enclosed the 22,000-square-foot exhibit. A cascading waterfall fed a stream that flowed the length of the exhibit. Thatched roofs on the two entrances and the natural-looking concrete boulders that formed the waterfall and stream helped set the South American look and feel of the place. A suspension bridge over the waterfall provided a mesmerizing view of the pond, where turtles lazed on the rocks. Inca terns, with their distinctive red, curled mustaches, raised their babies in crevices found in the cracks of the waterfall.

A suspension bridge crosses the rainforest exhibit's waterfall.

The water wandered in a shallow stream through the exhibit, was recycled underneath, and then pumped back to the waterfall. Innocent visitors, usually young males, used the waterfall to cool themselves off on hot summer days by tossing a handful of water over their faces. Observant docents often felt torn between telling the face-washers that ducks swam in that water or pretending to ignore it, letting the boys remain innocent. To date, no one has reported any harmful effects.

The skywalk near the waterfall took one up to a platform that wrapped around the valley oak tree for a bird's-eye view of the tropical rainforest. To achieve the full sensory experience of being in the middle of a rainforest, a spray-mist system pumped moisture into the air. The system kept plants soaking wet, as in a real jungle, and helped keep the exhibit cooler in summer and warmer in winter. Aquatic birds of all sorts—such as scarlet ibis, egrets, and spoonbills—found their fill of fish in the bowls placed next to the stream.

The aquatic birds took to the trees over the water to build their nests. Selecting foot-long sticks, egrets laid them one on top of another as a nest to lay their eggs. The flimsy structures swayed at the top of the trees as the observer held his breath, fearing the eggs would fall to the ground. Peeping sounds let Mom know her chicks were hungry. Flapping their wings on the edge of a limb, the chicks built up their strength to finally take flight, as Mom encouraged them at one end and Dad welcomed them from a distant tree. For many visitors, watching the birds cycle through a year of mating, building nests, and raising their young sparked a lifelong interest in birds.

The symphony of bird calls alerted one to the multiple species hidden in the trees. The squawking, yellow troop of sun conures enhanced the sense of being in a tropical rainforest. One must carefully seek out the blue-crowned mot-mot, the gray-necked wood rail, the sun bittern, and the red-crested cardinal, all quietly tucked away in the thick branches. These timid birds were among the most beautiful and well worth the search.

"The biggest animal management challenge was selecting compatible species," stated Doc. "We had to determine what species would get along and what the right population density would be." Four thousand dollars was budgeted to acquire exotic birds; altogether, more than fifty species of birds, mammals, lizards, and turtles were brought into the exhibit. Keepers monitored each species for aggression and set up feeding stations to minimize competition for food.

The exhibit's rainforest logo featured the distinctive toco toucan, with its large, curved, yellow-orange beak. The distinctive beak appears heavy, but under the covering, its sponge-like bone is surprisingly light and is well-adapted for fruit eating. The black spot on the tip shows toco toucan chicks where to go for food. The toucan's squawking informs everyone that they are the kings of the forest. Doc favored the splendid toucans, that is until the pair began stealing other birds' chicks as a meal source for their own chicks. Thus the unique pair lost their regal status and were relegated to a birdcage off to the side.

The golden lion macaques were the most spectacular residents of the tropical rainforest, but they were plagued by illnesses. These small, doll-like primates with a soft, yellow collar framing their head, lost their fear of people and approached guests (with a bit of coaxing), took food, or jumped on them, which guests either loved or else caused them to throw up their hands in quick retreat. It became necessary to remove the monkeys for their own safety. A small, dug out, pitted area with a shallow pool was allotted for the anteaters, rounding out the South American species. Unfortunately, it didn't work out for the anteaters, who were replace by spectacular blue and yellow macaws, with their long hooked beaks.

During the warmer months, reptiles would make their appearance. The side-necked turtle and iguanas found their niches, which sent kids on a search to find them. The iguana always stopped traffic as it moved from one part of the rainforest to another. The reactions to the iguana were culture related, ranging from fear to curiosity to treating it as a pet.

"Wildlife should provide endless hours of viewing pleasure for visitors," said Doc. His mission was to inspire Fresnans by giving them a taste of a tropical rainforest. Unlike traditional zoo displays, Doc eliminated barriers that separated animals and people. Instead, he wanted them to become guests in someone's home. "Stop, Look, and Listen" was the protocol for the tropical rainforest exhibit. Benches were scattered around to encourage people to sit, listen, and absorb. The birds built their nests and raised babies as though visitors hardly existed.

A volunteer Rainforest Rangers program was formed to better appreciate and protect the tropical rainforest. Paths on both sides of the stream gave a view of the plants and wildlife from different angles. The rangers guided guests through the exhibit, with reminders to be respectful of the occupants and to stay on the paths and let the animals pass quietly. Most people look down to watch where they step, but here they were encouraged to look up into the trees. At the same time, the rangers were always careful to remind visitors to close their mouths when under the trees.

In addition, the rangers also taught hordes of schoolchildren zoo etiquette for walk-through exhibits, which they then passed on when accompanying their families. The rangers promoted the aforementioned "Stop, Look, and Listen" protocol during quiet times. The rangers studied the birds as they went through the seasons and watched young hatchlings grow until they fledged out of the nest, stepping out on wobbly tree limbs to view their new world.

The adjacent Maddis House, with its humid, temperature-controlled environment, provided a protected space for those animals more sensitive to the Valley's weather changes. Initially, it housed various hummingbirds, but as they are very territorial, the population was always being reduced to one remaining "tough guy." Then, it became a butterfly haven, which became too expensive and time-intensive to manage. Later, a slow-moving sloth could be seen working his way from one side of the exhibit to the other, while iguanas lazed on a tree limb next to the walkway. Although the Maddis House give visitors an up-close-and-personal view, it has been a difficult place to keep in balance. At one point, a pack of rats took over, which forced a five-year closure.

During his illness in 1990, Dr. Chaffee frequently sought out the rainforest as a place that brought him peace and comfort. Once, when he entered the separate, closed-door Maddis House, hummingbirds fluttered around his head. One insisted on plucking hair from his gray beard to line its nest. It was the highlight of the day.

Doc's vision to inspire Fresnans by giving them a taste of a tropical rainforest became a reality. Recently, the rainforest's inhabitants have struggled during bouts of avian flu, which necessitated closing the exhibit to guests for periods of time. Nevertheless, the Chaffee Zoo Tropical Rainforest remains a jewel in the zoo.

CHAPTER 39

Nosey Needs Ya

Nosey the elephant lived not only at the Roeding Park Zoo but also in the hearts of the people who knew and loved her. At almost 32 years old, Nosey had lived all but three years in the tiny barn she had entered upon her arrival that warm September day in 1949. Strong steel poles enclosed her 17 x 50-foot concrete world, where she greeted her adoring fans. Her tiny night barn measured 14 x 20 feet. When she arrived as a 2,000-pound three-year-old, no one seemed bothered by such limited spaces. But by the late 1970s, it became apparent she had long outgrown them.

Doc often expressed his concerns over his beloved Asian elephant's living conditions: "If you see Nosey, it's heartbreaking. She sleeps on concrete floors and hasn't had a bath in thirty years. Her feet need a pedicure from standing on cement. It is painful to watch her shuffle around in that tiny closet of a space, bored to tears, with her ears down. When excited, she trumpets, runs a few steps, and then runs out of room. She deserves better than this."

A decent elephant living space became the number one project on Doc Chaffee's list. He hated the hard surface that ruined the pachyderm's feet and the mini-bedroom where she could barely turn around. The zookeepers did their best to make Nosey happy, putting their hearts into caring for her by finding ways to enrich and enliven her days. She followed the keepers as they cleaned her pen, her trunk gently brushing their arms as they worked. Occasionally, Nosey found a well-placed treat in their pockets.

The elephant knew precisely when the zoo gates opened each morning. Standing on her bars, she reached her trunk toward the zoo entrance. She looked forward to the swarm of visitors who had fallen in love with her. They were a substitute for the herd she missed. She sniffed around for goodies or reached out her trunk for a loving pat. Sometimes, she snagged a sweater or hat, threw it into the air, stomped on it, and then ate it. Her favorite trick was scooping up a lady's purse, filled with so many items to investigate with the fingers on the tip of her trunk. The guests giggled and laughed over her antics.

Nosey had her animal friends, too. She and Clyde, the camel next door, exchanged their daily over-the-fence greeting; Nosey's trunk reached out to Clyde's extended lips. One day, Doc sedated Clyde in his pen to remove a lump in his neck. A concerned Nosey stretched out her trunk as she observed every movement. Something did not feel right to her. She stepped up on the next bar for a better view and screamed until the operation ended. When Clyde

Nosey greeting her fans.

192

stood up, Nosey finally relaxed, knowing her friend was safe, and she could rest.

The visitors loved being with Nosey but complained when they neared her pen; the odoriferous stink permeated the air surrounding her. Keeper Sally got approval to add an elephant bath to her daily responsibilities. A bucket of water with a spoon full of Clorox and a push broom got rid of the stench. This ritual soon became Sally and Nosey's favorite part of the day.

The community, troubled about Nosey's welfare, began to make its voice heard. Letters to the editor expressed their concerns. They felt Nosey deserved an upgrade from her cramped exhibit. Nothing about the small space suited her needs, and she had been in it long enough. Finally, in 1974, fundraising efforts began for a new exhibit, expected to cost about $150,000, but the attempt failed for various reasons.

For his renewed effort to improve Nosey's living space, Doc dared to dream big. Elephants are social animals and work as a team, raising the babies and keeping a safe circle around the vulnerable members of the herd. Here, Nosey had only herself.

His plans called for a large elephant exhibit with room for companion elephants, and he wanted one suitable for breeding. Always the idealist, he realized the prestige of housing a breeding facility for elephants would put Roeding Park Zoo on the map and bring visitors to the city. But the upgraded design would cost hundreds of thousands of dollars more. Doc Chaffee estimated that the two-and-a-half-acre exhibit, with its planned waterfall, artificial rocks, plants, and 12-foot-deep swimming pool, would cost about $950,000. The City of Fresno would only consider budgeting a fraction of that cost. The Zoo Society annually funded renovation projects and small new exhibits, but did not have the capacity to underwrite Doc Chaffee's dream exhibit.

In an attempt to drive public participation in realizing Doc's dream, the *Fresno Bee* ran an article featuring a picture of an isolated Nosey peeking out her tiny barn window. The heart-wrenching photo grabbed the community's attention. The "NOSEY NEEDS YA" fundraising slogan tapped into the public's love and care for her. Long-time zoo members reminisced about the original 1949 campaign to purchase her. Back then, the children brought their dimes and nickels in glass jars, participating along with the grown-ups in bringing an elephant to Fresno. This new campaign targeted the same people who had supported her arrival. Now, like Nosey, they were in their thirties and forties. This time, they came forward with tens, hundreds, and thousands of dollars instead of dimes and nickels.

And so once again, the community rallied around Nosey, this time to build a much more suitable home for the town's mascot. As before, kids joined the fundraising effort for Nosey. Two 14-year-old boys started making 100 elephant refrigerator magnets from dough art. Then, they went door to door, selling their magnets for fifty cents apiece. When the State Board of Equalization found out about these enterprising boys, they required them to add a tax to each elephant magnet.

Fundraising events, such as bake sales, raffles, tournaments, private parties, and car washes, swept through the community. The traveling Circus Vargas brought one of their elephants for a refreshing bath at a car wash. Businesses in the area also contributed to the efforts. A spaghetti cook-off at Cedar Lanes Shopping Center bolstered the campaign. The most creative donation came from a local Texaco gas station. They donated 35 percent of one day's profits, attracting attention by displaying a great white shark tank in a side trailer. These donations brought much-needed attention to Nosey's needs, but were financially only the tip of the iceberg. In the first ten months, the campaign raised $250,000. Within two years, construction began with available funds of $878,977.77.

Groundbreaking ceremonies took place on December 8, 1981. Nosey did not know it, but her life was about to turn for the better, changing in ways she never dreamed possible.

CHAPTER 40

Nosey's Million Dollar Asian Elephant Home

The Zoo Society committed to a three-year plan to raise nearly one million dollars for the construction of Nosey's new home, with the goal to have her move in by 1982. It was the largest local fundraiser ever in Fresno. The community joined forces to support it, and with the combination of small door-to-door collections and large donations, the goal was met.

Creating an elephant breeding facility meant installing additional safety features. Stout cement walls separated the three bedrooms, with the bull in the middle, squeezed in between two females on either side. Special care went into the design of the bull's middle room. A critical feature was the sturdy hydraulic doors to the room, controlled from a separate workspace. Each female had access to an outside door, but the male had to wait until his keeper opened his doors. An escape opening from the bull's room was built into the design. It was barely wide enough for a human to slip through but too narrow for the elephant. The L-shaped opening turned into a narrow, eight-foot hallway toward the workroom. Although the male's long trunk could reach around the corner, he couldn't grab the escapee.

The architectural firm Shoenwald, Norwood, House, and Oba went to the Portland Zoo to study the only Asian elephant breeding exhibit in the United States. Doc knew what he wanted in the plan: it needed a natural setting with water, while also being educationally appealing. He wanted the public to get to know and love Nosey the way he did, and the best way to do that was by creating an exhibit that made it easy for people to observe her.

Elephants love water and bathe frequently. After three decades of no baths, Doc was determined to give Nosey everything she had missed. The pool required an area shallow enough for the elephant's trunk yet deep enough so she could immerse herself in the water. Sandy, the architect, got creative in designing the elephant pool, as this was a first for her. She started with a clay model to practice with slopes, heights, and contours. Using an elephant toy from her grandmother's collection to provide a sense of scale in the model, she calculated the depths and dimensions of the pool. Doc oversaw each project stage, impressing the design team with his clear vision; he continued to emphasize both the animal's needs and curb appeal.

Creating the effect of a natural waterfall was a significant challenge. Using natural rocks created potential problems, because an elephant's powerful trunk and strength could move them around. Another consideration was that the exhibit's waterfall was designed to hide the barn's cement wall, but the heaviness of the rocks leaning against the wall compromised its structural integrity. Fortunately, a Southern California rockwork company was able to create artificial rockwork that was strong enough to handle an elephant's weight but light enough for the wall.

Four levels of platforms around the exhibit would allow people to view the elephants from different perspectives. However, the most critical issue was maintaining Nosey's close relationship with her public, something all had cherished for the past thirty-three years. Most people understood how much she had suffered and were willing to sacrifice their desires for Nosey's well-deserved decent housing.

Construction began on December 8, 1981. The project was divided into three phases, so that donors could more quickly see the fruits of their fundraising efforts.

Phase 1 was the barn. It comprised three large, concrete, sky-lit rooms, maintained at a constant temperature. The rooms also had individual heating and cooling ducts. Cool air came from the semi-underground barn in the summer months and circulated through the rooms.

The second phase, the rockwork, cost about $250,000. The fake rocks added a natural feel to the enclosure, while the waterfall helped cool the temperature in the compound. The roar of the water alone made it feel at least ten degrees cooler. "It's elephant-proof," said Doc. "The inch-thick synthetic rock filled with fiberglass and cement can resist the temper of an angry male elephant. They should last forever."

The third phase involved the yard and walls. The area was designed to be elephant-friendly, giving them lots of solid, rough walls against which to rub their skin. Trees were commonly used for massaging, but the downside was that elephants liked to push them over! The solution was to install steel poles around the lone tree to protect it.

The final touches included landscaping and lighting. The leading concern was keeping certain things out of the long reach of Nosey's trunk. Her name described her well—*Nose*-y. She would pull, tear, feel, and eat anything within her grasp. After measuring her trunk length, Doc warned about the plants they wanted to install beside her gate. "I'm sorry, but the plans call for plants here," they said, "so we have to put them here." It took her all of ten minutes to wipe them out.

The height of the tower viewing area was another issue. Doc warned that Nosey could reach up there. Again, the response was, "Sorry, the plans call for this height." As a result, the first guests to visit the new exhibit reached out to feed Nosey peanuts, just like they had done for years in the old enclosure. Her trunk swayed too close toward the guests, looking for her daily dose of treats. This activity resulted in the area being fenced off.

Every day during construction, Doc and the elephant keeper, Paul Barkman, checked on the progress. Doc watched the pool with skepticism, wondering if the side angle was too steep to allow elephants to walk back out. After workers had dug the eight-foot-deep hole for the pool, the men worried. Could the animals get in and out without a problem? "Bring the young Thongtrii over for a trial run!" Doc told Barkman. Thongtrii had just arrived a few weeks earlier with Barkman to help prepare Nosey for the move (see chapter 42. Nosey Meets Thongtrii).

Fred Rawly, the construction boss, built a dirt ramp, just in case Thongtrii couldn't get out. Thongtrii walked down with ease, but once he got there, he panicked. Looking around, he couldn't find a way out. Time, patience, and tempting treats finally got him back up the ramp. Barkman had to walk the nervous male around the zoo to calm him down. Thanks to Thongtrii's trial run, the pool was redesigned to include steps.

Fred was proud of his achievement. He stood at the overlook, observing every little detail, and marveled at how Doc's vision had come to fruition. For all the challenges in the design, it turned out beyond expectation. Prior to the grand opening, he chose it for his wedding, with the serene, majestic waterfall in the background. The elephant bedrooms were transformed into the bridal party's dressing rooms. The bride and groom entered from both sides and met at the altar, where 150 guests greeted them with a shower of peanuts instead of the traditionally thrown rice.

As construction supervisor, Fred worked closely with Doc, and he grew to respect him greatly. Fred said that working with Doc at the zoo was the most satisfying project of his career. He had supervised the Splash Mountain project at Disneyland, but his biggest challenge was working with animals who couldn't tell him their needs. Watching Doc relate to the animals and seeing his deep level of caring affected his own attitude toward wild creatures. He recognized they weren't so dumb, but had intelligence and unique needs and ways of communicating.

Nosey's move-in day was scheduled for September 10, 1982, which would be the thirty-third anniversary of her first day in the original pen, September 10, 1949.

Years later, in 1990, the Discovery Channel brought their crew to Fresno to feature the elephant barn. Homebound at that time, suffering from melanoma cancer, Doc watched it on television. Up to his last months, his head continued to be filled with plans. He had put off building a proper vet hospital; instead, he focused on better enclosures for the animals. With a short time remaining, board members came to the house to hear his final wishes. Seven years later, an animal clinic was completed, with X-rays, surgery equipment, and a quarantine area for treatment recovery and for incoming animals. Doc would have been proud.

Nosey finally gets to swim!

CHAPTER 41

Nosey Meets Thongtrii

Doc Chaffee's plans for his new Asian elephant exhibit included an interior room for a bull to fulfill his dream of having elephant offspring. Portland Zoo advertised the birth of a male elephant named Thongtrii (pronounced Tong tree, meaning boss). He was born on October 5, 1979, and sired by the largest bull in the country. Doc had a week to come up with $12,000. He contacted twelve of his wealthy friends, who happily gave him $1,000 each. Portland agreed to keep the newborn for as long as possible, an arrangement which served both parties. Paul Barkman was still working at Marine World USA in Vallejo but had accepted the position as lead elephant keeper at the Fresno Zoo. He looked forward to working with the young elephant.

In 1980, at 19 months, Thongtrii had outgrown Portland's facility. He took after his father with his fast growth. Smaller than their African counterparts, Asians are the most commonly found elephants in circuses and zoos. They originally hail from Thailand, where they have been domesticated for centuries. Their smaller size is well-adapted for walking through dense rain forests, and their smaller flat feet keep them from slipping on muddy slopes. Although their wrinkled skin looks old, it is quite pliable and houses up to 60,000 muscles and corresponding nerve centers. The trunk is what gets the most attention, as it weaves in and out with great flexibility. Elephants' trunks are truly amazing, all-around tools. They use their trunks for breathing, watering, feeding, touching, dusting, sound production and communication, washing, pinching, grasping, defense, and offense.

Paul Barkman agreed to take Thongtrii under his wing and train him at Marine World until the completion of Fresno's new barn. Doc felt comfortable knowing that the young male would get the best of training from Paul. Barkman drove his truck to Portland to transport Thongtrii back to Vallejo, where he worked the youngster with four females. Training bull elephants is no small task. Bulls kill more keepers per year than any other zoo animal; they are unpredictable, and their moods change quickly. But Paul drew on his experience working with circus bull elephants. He shunned whipping them into submission, but instead used the positive reward approach. He felt confident Thongtrii would see his trainer as a friend and not turn against him.

In June 1981, Doc contacted Barkman, asking if he could bring Thongtrii to Fresno for a surprise visit during a Safari Night event. His donors had begun questioning whether their expensive elephant really existed. Barkman loaded Thongtrii into a travel trailer and arrived just as the event opened. He led the celebrated mammal to a green area, where guests reached out to touch and feel the elephant's rough skin. While chatting with the guests, Mayor Karen Humphrey found the trunk wrapped around her wine glass, sipping a taste. She did not know whether to scream, run, or pat his trunk.

When the party wound down, Barkman loaded up the superstar for the six-hour trip home. It was near midnight when he reached the outskirts of Los Banos. Barkman slowed down going over the railroad tracks, so as not to upset the sleepy animal with jiggling and bumping, but his trailer got stuck on the tracks. Barkman attempted to drive forward, then backward. He pushed and pulled, but the wheels would not budge with their heavy load. He peered down the tracks and spotted a train's swirling light moving in his direction.

Panic began to pound in his heart when, by chance, a policeman came up behind him. "What's the matter here?" he asked. Barkman pointed down the track as the train moved closer and closer. The policeman got into his vehicle, moved up slowly against the back of the trailer, and gave a slight push. The wheels wobbled against the rails. With one eye on the approaching train, the officer continued to push the trailer until it was across the tracks to safety—to Barkman's great relief.

Doc Chaffee had planned every detail in building the elephant enclosure; he met with his keepers for a year, contacted other zoo directors, and even met with circus trainers when they were in town. The plans for the elephant enclosure were moving along on schedule. Barkman was a critical person in the whole process. In March of 1982, the time had come for Barkman and Thongtrii to move to Fresno.

Barkman came a week ahead to set up temporary quarters for Thongtrii. The hay barn adjacent to Nosey's pen was the perfect spot, as it would allow the two eyeball time before their first physical meeting. After completing his work, Barkman returned home to pack up his things and get Thongtrii. Shocked, he found a defeated, bruised youngster. The female elephants had beaten him, leaving open wounds and cuts, like the losing boxer in the ring. The cantankerous and irritating Thong had been left alone to face the exasperated females, who took advantage of his keeper's absence.

Barkman loaded the battered and beaten pachyderm into his trailer and moved to Fresno. They arrived late in the day, after the others had gone home. Doc and Nosey's keeper, Sally, greeted Barkman and directed the driver to unload Thongtrii. The pathetic young elephant stepped out of the trailer, head hanging down, sad eyes peering out, remnants of dried blood still visible on his trunk. The females' kicks had left him limping with a battered knee. Doc shuddered as he watched the piteous elephant shuffle down the truck ramp. Although Barkman had warned Doc of Thong's sad condition, it still brought tears to Doc's eyes. Thong's knee had received the worst abuse, and it took months of treatment before he healed.

Barkman painted a yellow line around the hay barn as a warning for staff to stay away from the newcomer, and Doc prepared a bed of hay. He also set up a cot for Barkman, so that the young pachyderm would not be alone that first night. Barkman stayed up all night, soothing Thongtrii's fears. As the days passed, he cut back on the time he spent with Thong each night, retreating to his cot for longer naps. Paul kept up this schedule of staying through the night and leaving during the day to sleep until Thongtrii felt comfortable in his new surroundings. Before he left in the mornings, he fed the male and cleaned the quarters before staff arrived for work.

Zookeepers snooped around, peeking through a crack in the wooden shed, until curiosity overcame them. What did this Thongtrii kid look like? How big was he? So finally, the bravest one stepped over the yellow line and took a few steps for a glance at the new guy. The cute little elephant had an ornery streak that garnered respect from the very beginning. Thongtrii immediately charged, reminding them of their boundaries. They did not reveal their transgression to Barkman, who had given strict orders not to step over the line.

Barkman had six months to develop a bond between Nosey and Thongtrii before the big moving day into the new exhibit. When Nosey first saw Barkman and Thongtrii, she recognized the trainer but screamed at the stranger. She backed up to the farthest point in her exhibit—about 40 feet! Her ears stuck straight out to give a bigger impression, her eyes bulging, her trunk up in the air—she was ready for fight or flight. Nosey had not been out of her iron bars for thirty years, nor had she seen another of her kind in all that time. She was terrified!

During the upcoming move, Nosey would need to walk outside the zoo's fenced grounds along the frontage road of Belmont. She had not experienced the sounds of nearby passing cars. She needed to acclimate to a host of new sounds, sights, and smells. The exhibit would be finished in six months, and the isolated Nosey would need every bit of that time to prepare for moving to her brand-new quarters; otherwise, the transfer would be potentially dangerous and frightening.

Barkman walked Thongtrii around the zoo, as he had done every day at Marine World. They stood next to Nosey's bars as the two elephants got acquainted. The first few days, Nosey kept her distance. It took days, and many peanuts, before Nosey edged over to meet her new companion. Nosey stretched out her trunk to touch Thongtrii. This marked a turning point, and Barkman now felt it was safe to put the two together. He gave them baths and fed them peanuts. Nosey seemed to enjoy having a friend for the first time. On occasion, Thongtrii tried to push Nosey around, but Nosey shoved him right back, asserting her authority. Barkman was excited to realize that Nosey, indeed, had an innate matriarchal instinct, while Thongtrii's memories of the Marine World beatings were still fresh for him.

Thongtrii enjoys his new home.

During their daily walks, Barkman took the youngster down to the new elephant construction site to become comfortable in the new surroundings. Barkman and the building crew became good friends. One day, Barkman offered to let Fred, the construction supervisor, hop onto the young male and take a ride. Fred gladly accepted, assuming that it would be like riding a horse. He sat naturally on the elephant's shoulders and tried to clasp his knees around the barrel-like middle, where the prickly hairs on the elephant's back surprised him. However, to ride an elephant, one sits astride the short neck, just behind the head, where it is easier to clutch the knees. Thongtrii, like most youngsters, did not like to walk anywhere; he preferred to trot. And so poor Fred hung on for dear life, grabbing onto a tuft of hair between Thong's ears. It was the ride of a lifetime, something he never forgot. "Nothing like riding a horse," he declared.

The day fast approached for completion of the exhibit, and the many preparations for the big move were well underway. Nosey and Thong had developed an excellent bond, much to Barkman's delight. She had gotten over her fear of seeing another elephant and enjoyed spending the days with Thong. His ornery nature kept her alert and on her toes, waiting for his next antic. Their friendship would take on a deeper meaning during the move.

Paul Barkman and Sally Smith Becker
with Thongtrii.

CHAPTER 42

Nosey's Big Move

Friday, September 10th, 1982, brought shorter days and cooler weather. The trees were beginning to turn. The Fresno State football season was in full stride. The Ringling Bros. and Barnum & Bailey Circus had returned to Fresno, holding a downtown parade led by Targa, the lead elephant. Doc, as he did most every year, opened the season as the circus's ringmaster. Excitement was in the air.

Over at the zoo, Friday, September 10th, meant a new beginning for the town's beloved mascot. Or it could end in disaster. Nerves were on edge.

The sun was barely up when people began to quietly arrive. The animals noticed the change and began to stir. Keepers gathered to review their procedures. Reporters checked their cameras. Staff and onlookers climbed fences for the best view.

Doc checked all the boxes in preparation for the big move. He had not slept for days as he rehearsed every step of Nosey's transit from her old barn to her new home. He did his best to anticipate any pitfall that might spook her on her walk. As the crow flies, the new quarters were only about 200 yards away, but the anxious leader scratched that shortcut option because there were too many narrow lanes for the entourage. Circus elephant trainer Axel Gautier accompanied Doc to preview the route and note potential trouble spots. The best route would take her outside the zoo grounds along the Belmont frontage road, passing Playland, and entering through the

back delivery land-
ing of the new
exhibit.

Few slept that
night, the move
spinning through
their heads as they
prepared for a day
of celebration, or
worse, a tragedy. At
6 a.m., the team

Doc and Nosey share a moment together.

assembled, numbering nearly one hundred. Fresno Bee reporters
and cameramen were sworn to secrecy: the more people, the more
likely the distraction, which could cause a loss of life and, in turn,
the director's job. Doc stated that there would be no press releases
until after the move. A recently hired employee, Scott Barton, got
the least desirable task. He carried the loaded, high-powered rifle—
"just in case." Everyone took their assigned places and prepared for
the most white-knuckled, nerve-wracking day of their lives.

Doc Chaffee gave Nosey a dose of Rompin, a sedative. In her
thirty-three years, she had needed little medical attention, and it
was uncertain how she would react. The solitary mammal noticed
that this day was different: new faces, whispered sounds, tractors,
people everywhere. Her head was raised high, her trunk sweeping
the air to catch strange smells, her ears flapping in concern. She
sniffed uneasiness in the air. The first dose of sedative didn't slow
her beating heart. After the second dose of Rompin, Nosey's head
relaxed and her breathing slowed.

A day earlier, in preparation, Doc had removed both the outer
bars and the chain-link fence surrounding the small exhibit. He
left one bar in place to keep her secure. Barkman put the specially
forged, cloth-covered bracelets on Nosey's ankles.

At 6:15, Axel pulled up in a donated shiny big rig from which
Targa, the lead circus elephant, emerged. Mouths flew open in

stunned disbelief at his massive size. It was one thing to see him in a circus setting, but quite another to be feet away. Targa wore a leg chain, specially forged for this day, to lead Nosey and provide reassurance. She would function as an anchor for the procession.

When Nosey saw the huge pachyderm back up into her spot, she trumpeted fear and rage in a tone never heard before. Barkman sidled up to his charge, whispering in sweet tones to calm her nerves. Petting her side and rubbing her leg, he took his time, making sure she relaxed with his touch. Slowly and carefully, he connected the chain from Targa's back leg to Nosey's front leg.

Doc, saying a silent prayer, raised his hand to signal the beginning of the momentous walk. "Remove the last bar," he ordered. Then Axel gave Targa the command, and Nosey felt a tug on her leg chains. The massive animal inched forward until the smaller one could no longer hold out against him and reluctantly began to move.

Once out of her pen, Nosey's rear leg chains were attached to a backhoe. The driver, Robert Borrego, was to function as the third elephant in the procession, keeping Nosey in the middle. A second tractor drove alongside to provide a second anchor if she chanced to bolt. Barkman and her keeper, Troy Celis, each held a set of chains to guide her, gently talking as the parade proceeded down the path. Nosey's trunk weaved side to side, desperately grabbing at the handrails of the exhibits and overhanging tree limbs as they passed by. The whites of her eyes shone in panic mode.

They continued past the Bird of Prey exhibit and toward the zoo's south maintenance gate, sometimes creeping, other times trotting. Doc walked backward, just ahead of them, keeping an eye on everything while giving instructions, ready to make an adjustment or change the plan on an instant's notice. Scott kept pace, ready with his gun. He prayed that he would not be remembered as the one who took down the town's most beloved zoo animal.

Recalling the day, Paul Barkman said, "We were nervous because we barely had her under control. She lurched and weaved all over the road, and we were never quite sure where she might be going. We kept her channeled into a semblance of a straight path. She would go just so far and then put on the brakes." Every time she did that, the other elephant tensed up. Targa did not pull her but gently tightened the chain. The frightened Nosey grabbed onto tree branches to halt the march.

Nosey makes her way to her new home.

As they progressed to the maintenance gate, Robert misjudged the width of the gate and got stuck. The procession halted while he disentangled his backhoe. "We turned onto Belmont frontage road," Barkman related, "beating the early morning traffic. The parade continued outside the zoo grounds to where the rainforest is today. That is about where she finally got the hang of it. Things were going smoothly for the time being."

As the parade rounded the corner near Rotary Playland and headed toward the back gate of the new exhibit, the pace picked up. The followers had to run to keep up with Nosey. Then the two elephants began to run. The men jumped out of the way to avoid the swaying chains. At one point, Nosey's momentum propelled her into the lead in front of Targa and the tractor. Her keepers finally got her under control, and Targa regained the lead.

Barkman relates: "One of the hairiest moments came when we rounded the corner into the back entrance. There is a slope where the trucks drive in for deliveries. When the entry gate opened, she refused to move. The backhoe tractor could not coordinate with Nosey to make the turn. Targa went one way and the tractor went another way. Nosey ended up split-legged and twisted in the chains. When she did that, she turned and faced the wrong way. Confused, she pulled back on the tractor. She spread her legs out and refused to budge. Her eyes popped out, her ears splayed back, and she screamed."

Frustrated, she head-butted the tractor to get it out of the way. It lifted off the ground, as Robert desperately hung on, fearing for his life while staring up at the enraged elephant. Finally, the men were able to disconnect the chains attached to the tractor. Robert, a Fresno Parks employee, later said that when he volunteered to operate the tractor, he had no idea he would face one ginormous elephant and one enraged elephant.

The parade finally made it to the last hurdle of the walk. Targa eased Nosey onto the landing, the tractor following as the circus animal moved into position at the entrance to the tunnel. The next part had the potential to be the most dangerous section of the entire procedure. Nosey hesitated at the entrance of the long dark hole which stood between her and her new home of comforting dirt, friends, and water. Setting her feet, she shook and rumbled in terror. It was a death walk for anyone to accompany her, so Targa had one last job, to lead the frightened Nosey through the tunnel into the yard.

Axel walked Targa through the tunnel. Once set, he gave orders to pull. The big elephant gave a hard pull and Nosey had little choice but to proceed. Then, from somewhere deep inside her, she gathered her resolve and raced through the tunnel, chains flying through the air. One chain whipped around Barkman's legs. He fell on his back, kicking his feet free to avoid being dragged.

With the sounds of cheers echoing in her ears, Nosey arrived in her new home. Barkman removed the chains linking her to Targa. Once inside, they quickly closed the gate, and Nosey settled down. Barkman looked over at Doc. He was "ecstatic, beaming as broad as the Grand Canyon," recounted Barkman. Many months of planning and talking with experts in the field had ended with Nosey the elephant safely in her new home.

Relieved, Doc walked with Axel and Targa back through the tunnel and gave the circus elephant an affectionate pat on the rump. As Axel left, he yelled, "Don't you worry about her falling in the pool. That Nosey don't go nowhere she doesn't want to go!"

Doc had ordered champagne for everyone to celebrate Nosey's successful transfer from her old home to her new. He popped the cork with a grand flourish, filling everyone's glass as they joined in raising their arms. "Hear, hear. Mission accomplished."

Doc said to Barkman, "If you remember anything in your life, remember this day. It is the most significant accomplishment you will ever have. Moving that elephant was the hardest thing we have ever done."

Doc tethered Nosey to the poles enclosing the large shade tree in the yard. He did not want her wandering around in her groggy state and falling into the pool. Later that day, Barkman brought Thongtrii over from his barn to join her. Thongtrii stayed by her side, never moving, and provided what only another elephant could; he understood his job, to make her feel safe and comfortable. For three days, he stood beside her. At night, he went into the barn. Then, in the morning, he returned to stand next to her. Finally, gathering her courage, Nosey moved around to investigate her new surroundings.

Barkman put out little treats for Nosey that led up to her bedroom. She went just to the edge, then stopped as if she spied an invisible barrier in front of her door. Finally, on the third day, she stepped over the little ledge. Barkman commented, "I don't know what happened, but it was like a cork popped out of her." She put her big foot over the ledge, looked around, and quickly ran inside. Then she turned, trumpeted, and swung her trunk at the door, as if to say, "Ha, ha, I did it." Still, she paced around her barn, clearly missing something. The keepers scratched their heads and wondered until someone recalled her friend the rooster from the old barn. He fetched the rooster, brought him over, and Nosey quieted down right away. She showed no fear after that.

The old girl settled into her new life, immensely enjoying the wonderful amenities her old exhibit lacked. The staff wore a path in front of the exhibit to watch her toss dirt over her body and roll on her back. She dipped her trunk in the pool, testing the water. Many tears flowed from big men who had waited decades for this day. Finally, she was in a place where she could be a real elephant, doing real elephant things.

The move overcame many obstacles to become a reality. Even with all the unpredictable events, the transfer to Nosey's new dream home happened. Many hands came together to bring a better life for their beloved Nosey.

CHAPTER 43

Stuck in the Door

At last, the two elephants, Thongtrii and Nosey, had a chance to establish their relationship, as they settled into their new home. For Nosey, everything was new. The six-ton adult with the 3,000-pound kid, the male versus female dynamic, and the mother figure and youngster relationship were new experiences for the thirty-three year old.

For Nosey, even dirt was something new. The matron cautiously walked on the unusual surface, feeling it with her toes. Her feet hadn't felt dirt her entire time in Fresno. She practiced how to pick it up with her trunk. She tossed it over her body, laid down on it, and rolled in it. She had fun in her new habitat, in large part because her new home had a deep swimming pool where she could bathe and cool off, once she got brave enough to step in it.

Nosey's years of living alone made her protective of her own space. Not used to having anyone around, Nosey ate and slept alone in her new bedroom behind closed doors. Doc at first worried she might push her new friend into the pool if he irritated her; she had the bulk to shove Thongtrii away if she wanted to. Fortunately, overall the two adjusted very well to their new surroundings and each other.

Two weeks after recovering from the big move, Doc received an invitation to bring the young male to a Republican campaign event for George Deukmejian. Happy to accommodate the politicians with their party symbol, he fantasized about piles of money coming into his zoo. The Giffen Ranch hosted the party on the beautiful Kings River, which could easily accommodate an elephant visit, with plenty of space for him to enjoy himself.

Those in attendance included the twelve who donated toward the purchase of the male. They were excited to see him again after his previous year's Safari Night appearance. Few could forget the hair-raising drive home when the truck got stuck on the railroad tracks near Los Banos. Now that he was located in Fresno, the campaign organizers invited their political mascot as a perfect draw to their event.

Doc lined up a moving truck to transport the youngster. Dressed in his standard khaki shirt, pants, and safari vest, he went ahead to the Giffen Ranch to arrange the safest place for the trunked guest to meet the eagerly awaiting people.

Paul Barkman, dressed in jeans, a long-sleeved shirt, and leather shoes, went to get the elephant to load him into the truck. Thongtrii did not mind the trips; he seemed to enjoy going places. But this evening, the large Asian mammal could not be found. Panic! How could he get out of his room? After calling his name and walking around his space, the keeper discovered his pencil-thin tail wagging a plea for help. He was stuck in the people's escape door. He had apparently been checking out his new quarters and took one step too many. The opening made a tight, L-shaped turn into a narrow hallway leading to the keeper's workspace. Thongtrii had managed to get his head through the door, but his hips were stuck in the corner turn, a space barely wide enough for a keeper to walk, much less a 3,000-pound elephant. Much as the trainer wanted to laugh at the youngster's circumstances, he had an appointment at a big fundraising event calling him.

Paul, a 160-pound man, tried maneuvering this huge animal through the door. He wrapped a rope around Thongtrii's big head to pull him forward, but achieved nothing. Then he got behind him and pushed. Again, nothing. Neither approach moved him more than an inch.

The trainer began to get desperate, knowing that Doc and his influential friends were waiting for him. Panicking, he went through the cupboards and found mineral oil. Grabbing a towel, he rushed back to rub the oil all over the beast's body. With the rope still wrapped around the head, Paul tried again to pull the mammoth animal through the doorway. Taking a deep breath, and with a silent prayer, he jerked on the rope, and—*pop!*—Thongtrii slid out. The work area was large enough for the elephant to walk through, but one more people door stood in the way of getting outside. Paul rubbed the trunked animal all over with mineral oil one more time. Then he took the rope wrapped around Thong's head and wrapped it around his strongest arm. Confident he could pull Thongtrii through the door, he set his feet, counted to three, and pulled as hard as he could. The elephant slipped through the door and, suddenly, they were outside the barn.

Paul led Thongtrii up the ramp and into the waiting truck. At last, they were on the way to the party, some thirty to forty minutes away. In this time before the convenience of cell phones, the two men could not contact each other. They had to trust that each followed the schedule and would appear sooner or later.

When the truck backed up to the party event, a frantic Doc and his anxious host rushed to greet them as they grinned with relief. Barkman had them laughing with his description of the oily, slippery antics needed to get their mascot out the door and into the truck. The happy trio led their mischievous guest around the grounds, letting the partygoers pat the trunk and laugh at the stories. Locating a grassy area for Thongtrii to perform, the elephant made up for his tardiness by giving the party group a first-class production. He went through his entire repertoire of twenty stances. Standing with all four feet on the tub, he stretched out his trunk and tail to its full length. Next, he balanced on two feet, with one foot stretched out front and one leg stretched to the back. He turned around on all four feet before stepping down.

Doc stood in the background lapping up the cheers and the *ooohs* and *aaahs* from this exclusive gathering, confident it would translate into long-term zoo support.

For the grand finale, Paul sat on Thongtrii's knee as he lifted it while turning around on three feet. The audience showered the pair with applause and praise. The popular young entertainer ended the night with a cool swim in the Kings River.

However, the pushback came fast and furious for Doc. The zoo, unfortunately, did not have a donkey to appease the other political side, so he vowed to stay neutral by never indulging in politics again.

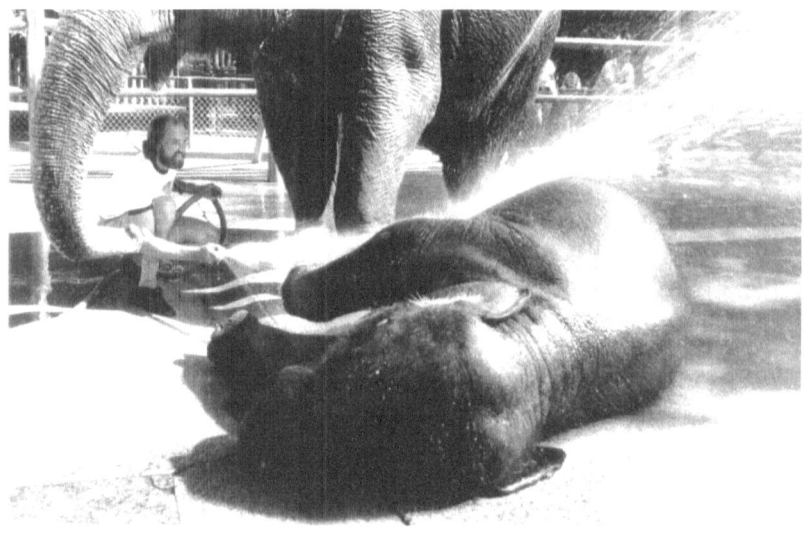

Paul Barkman gives Nosey and Thongtrii a refreshing shower.

CHAPTER 44

Thongtrii Attacks

By October 1982, a month after Nosey's hair-raising move, the two elephants had settled into their new lodgings. With the move behind them, Paul Barkman created a daily routine for his two still-shaky elephants. Both keepers and animals throughout the zoo felt the move's unsettling effects; each department focused on a prescribed daily routine to settle everyone down.

Finally comfortable, Nosey swayed around the yard, using her trunk to examine every crack and crevice along the wall. She scooped up dirt and tossed it on her back. She rolled over like a cat, massaging her back. She touched the pool's edge with her toes but hadn't yet dipped her trunk into the water. Excited, she raised her trumpet, letting out a call that telegraphed her friends back home about her new address.

Most zoos don't handle male elephants because they are unpredictable and dangerous. But with the Fresno Zoo's desire to become a breeding facility, Doc prioritized security. Each bedroom space was the size of a mid-to-large living room, with foot-thick cement walls on all sides. The outdoor waterfall that filled the swimming pool lay on the north wall, keeping the inside temperature steady and comfortable. The flowing stream muted unpleasant noises with soothing sounds. Thoughtful architectural design had produced an appealing, functional, secure, and safe environment for the two massively popular animals.

Thongtrii's room was sandwiched between Nosey's outside room on one side and an unoccupied room designed for another female on the other side. The two outer rooms led directly to the outside. The idea was that after the females were out of the barn and comfortable in their outdoor space, the keeper would open the male's electronically operated door from his separate workspace. The male's path led him through a female's door to the outside. With this arrangement, keepers had no intervention with Thongtrii. In the event of an emergency, the male's room had a human-sized, L-shaped escape doorway that led into a narrow eight-foot hallway, just wide enough for an average-size keeper to slip through to safety.

Barkman spent his days working with both trunked mammals. Nosey started almost from scratch, having received little to no training during her thirty-three years at the zoo prior to Barkman's arrival in Fresno six months before the move. The need to train the three-year-old, one-and-a-half-ton, stubborn Thongtrii was imperative, before he became more troublesome. His massive father's genes hinted at potential danger unless Thong could be kept under tight control. Nevertheless, Barkman's years of working with circus elephants gave him the confidence to walk into their exhibit for hands-on training, moving in and around the enormous mammals.

Barkman treated the youngster's footpads, sore from just six months of standing on Nosey's old cement-floor exhibit. He appreciated the older elephant's silent pain after being restricted to the unforgiving surface for so long. Hay was thrown on the new exhibit's indoor cement areas to soften the beds, so the elephants had a comfortable place to lay down. Then, using physical therapy techniques, Paul put the male on a swaying specialty board, easing his foot pain.

As he did his daily physical check, Paul noticed a minor cut on the side of Thongtrii's head. Doc gave him a tube of Scarlet Oil Wound Dressing to use on it. Still, something felt wrong. After all his years working with elephants, Barkman had a sixth sense when something wasn't right. He warned his helper, Bruce, that Thongtrii seemed restless, and he felt uneasy about the male's odd behavior: his head was bobbing and his eyes had a wild, bizarre look, almost forewarning trouble. Bruce told him not to worry; Asian elephant males usually mature around fourteen, and Thong was only three.

Like females, males have a cycle, a condition associated with establishing dominance and mating. The condition, called musth, produces increased aggression and creates certain physical side effects. These include severe migraine headaches that affect vision and the oozing of a dark, greenish liquid from an opening near the temporal (modified sweat) glands under the eyes. The liquid serves as a warning sign to stay clear of the male. Thongtrii was years away from reaching his teen years, and there were no signs of the green discharge on his temples. Barkman usually felt comfortable around the young male, who he had been working with since the elephant was twenty months old. But not that day. That day felt different.

Barkman related, "I noticed a little cut on his head, so I checked it out, picking at it. Unfortunately, I hit a sore spot. When he swung his head to get away from my hand, he knocked me down, promptly sending him into a rage. The bulls are like that. Then he picked me up [with his trunk] and threw me across the room."

When an opponent appears weak, a male elephant cannot control himself and goes for the kill. Fortunately, Thongtrii still had his legs attached to the sway board. After the first hit, he stepped back, allowing his keeper to regroup. Barkman saw him wavering and quietly sidled toward the human escape opening. That's when he heard the chains ripping off the board and saw the monster charge him.

For the next twenty minutes, the raging male head-butted him, picked him up in his trunk, and tossed him around. Paul knew the beast was trying to pull him apart, limb by limb. When he heard his bones cracking, he realized he was in desperate trouble.

"The attack lasted nonstop for what seemed like an eternity," Paul continued. "It was hard to tell because I kept passing out.

Finally, the monster threw me in the direction of the exit. I didn't have the energy, but I saw the opening and told myself I must try. I am dying. If I don't get out of here, I am as good as dead. I could not get my breath. I was in shock. I could not believe it, but somehow, I stood up and walked out of the room. I don't know what made me do it, but I stood up, went through the opening, and escaped death."

The beast did not give up, however. Instead, his trunk searched for Paul around the L-shaped opening. "He got hold of my foot, but he slipped, and I pulled free."

As the injured man staggered to the end of the wall, he inadvertently knocked a telephone off the hook, a telephone Doc, by some wondrous coincidence, had had installed just the day before. He grabbed it and started punching numbers. Fortunately, Barkman's wife, Betty, who was getting ready to step into the shower, stopped to answer the phone. She heard gurgling sounds—*uh, uh, uh*—and nearly hung up. Then she detected the sounds of an elephant roaring in the background and a whispered "elephant barn." Confident that he had reached help, Barkman lay back on the floor and elevated his feet, realizing he would likely go into shock.

Betty knew she had to act fast to save her husband's life. She called the zoo office, and Doc answered on the first ring. After explaining Paul's plight, she threw on her clothes and took off. After a quick 911 call, Doc raced to the barn, fearing the worst.

Barkman described his injuries: "I woke up and saw all this blood on the floor. Why should I elevate my feet when I have a head injury? I felt the warm feeling coming over my body again, and I could not reach the phone for a follow-up call. I started thinking that here I am. I escaped the mad elephant's room alive, and now I won't make it.

"I blinked and looked up, and Doc's two eyes peered into me. He assured me that the paramedics were on the way. I could not talk, but he kept talking to me. I felt the warmness coming over me again. When I woke up, I found myself in the hospital, and there I saw Doc's two eyes, staring down at me. My boss followed

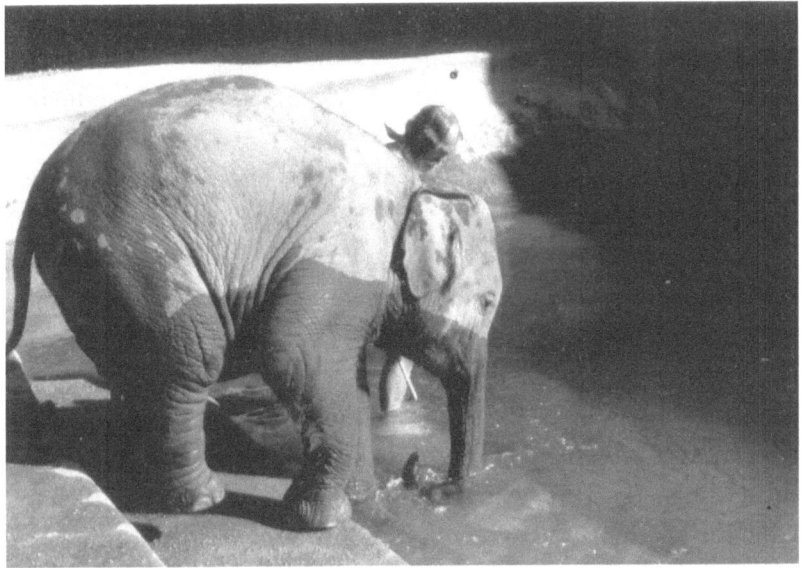

Paul Barkman and Thongtrii in happier times.

the ambulance to the hospital. He needed to see that his elephant trainer had survived the attack." Barkman had ten broken ribs, a compound arm fracture, a punctured lung, more cuts than one could count, and numerous contusions. His body was smothered in a pool of blood.

A *Fresno Bee* reporter asked, "What did it feel like getting attacked by a 3,000-pound male elephant?"

"Kind of like an atom bomb going off," replied Paul. "I thought I would die. It felt like being caught in a washing machine and unable to get out."

No one realized that Thongtrii had a congenital bone disorder that caused him great pain. His mother had something similar. Her bones broke down, and she died early. Thongtrii's father, at 10' 6", ranked as the largest elephant at any zoo. Yet the bigger he grew, the weaker his bone structure became and the more pain he suffered. Thongtrii put on a lot of weight as a youngster, but his body could not manage it.

Like father, like son, Thongtrii endured pain all his life, which is why he was so cranky, mean, and mad all the time. When other elephant people saw a picture of him, they could tell from his bunched eyes that he was in excruciating pain.

Elephants are statistically the most dangerous animals to keep in captivity. Interactions with captive elephants are responsible for more zookeeper deaths than any other captive animal. As a result, the Association of Zoos and Aquariums recommended training only be conducted with protective bars between the keepers and elephants.

In 1988, Doc was invited to the elephant keepers' annual conference as a presenter, giving him the difficult task of addressing the elephant keepers' concerns about the AZA's new guidelines. Convincing this stubborn audience into accepting the protective guidelines required a particular person who had their respect; their lives depended on it. Dr. Paul Chaffee was the most qualified. He spoke to them calmly, and they listened. Although elephant trainers fought it, many zoos and zookeepers agreed with the protective arrangement. It has saved lives, although some elephant keepers—the toughest people in the zookeeping trade—still fight the rules and sneak in for personal contact.

Born Free USA's Exotic Animal Incident Database has documented 168 dangerous incidents of escapes, injuries, and deaths in North America directly involving elephants from 1990 to 2017. Over half of these incidents (101, or 60 percent) occurred at zoos. Of the total, 53 resulted in a human injury, 17 resulted in a human death, 19 resulted in an animal injury, and 12 resulted in an animal death.

CHAPTER 45

Forgiveness

Paul Barkman peeked through a swollen eyelid into a cold, sterile room, wondering where he was. Every part of his body was on fire. Even his fingertips hurt. His wife, Betty, was at his side, holding his hand. Slowly twisting his head around the room, he stared through the foggy atmosphere, vaguely recognizing the bearded man hanging over him, staring into his eyes.

Doc had followed the ambulance to the hospital. He waited at his bedside, pleading with God to save the injured man's life. "I needed to see for myself that you were still alive," he told his elephant keeper, peering into his eyes. It was hit or miss for hours, but elephant keepers are tough.

The flimsy, half-body, blue hospital gown Barkman wore could not disguise the full extent of the damage caused by the three-year-old maniacal elephant. Every part of his body was beaten, battered, bruised, broken, and bleeding; his arms were bandaged from wrist to shoulder and set in slings.

The damaged man spent six months in the hospital, healing ten broken ribs, two broken arms, and numerous internal injuries inflicted by the elephant attack. Doc visited the hospital regularly. He painfully concluded that he would have to replace Barkman as an elephant keeper. After finally finding his ideal elephant man, somebody who shared his vision, he would now lose him. Doc gasped in astonishment when Barkman announced he wanted to come back.

A steady stream of attorneys paraded through the elephant keeper's hospital room, ready to take on his case suing the City of Fresno. But Barkman's mind was in a very different place. He kept thinking he had just started this job and had not even had a chance to prove himself. He felt like he had messed up and wanted to return to do it right. So, he waved the attorneys away, telling them he had no intention of filing a claim.

"This is what I do," explained Barkman. "I work with elephants, and I know the risks."

With the city's disability money, he took a three-week leave and flew to Thailand. He was determined to connect with Nosey's home base and learn more about handling male elephants. Barkman easily connected with Thongtrii's former Thai elephant keepers. He swapped stories with the *mahouts* who lived with their animals twenty-four hours a day. They made him tell his story repeatedly, finding it easy to relate to his terrifying encounter with the male. If Paul left out a detail in the retelling, they quickly filled it in; they knew his story by memory.

He towered in their eyes because he had survived an attack and lived to tell the story. It rarely happened. Whenever Barkman showed a picture of Thongtrii to the Thai trainers, they said, "Uh-oh, devil eyes." They noticed something else that spelled trouble; he had a crooked tail. Working alongside these experts, Barkman studied the do's and don'ts of managing male elephants.

When he returned home, Barkman, fresh from his training with the *mahouts*, knew he had to start all over with Thongtrii. The Thai keepers emphasized that he had to reestablish control over the elephant. Engaging in physical discipline, they said, would demonstrate that he was the alpha leader. Although Paul opposed using the whip, he realized it would be the difference between life or death in this situation.

From then on, Paul made sure that he always worked Thongtrii with another elephant around. He kept one elephant between him and the male when he was out in the yard . . . with one exception.

Near the end of 1983, Thongtrii got a nail in his foot. He had been digging in the yard and unearthed a spike nail left from the exhibit's construction. He limped on three feet as the nail penetrated his heavily padded foot. His limp worsened daily, indicating the problem wasn't going to resolve itself. Doc and Barkman agreed they could no longer put off dealing with him. But how?

They studied the situation, trying to decide what to do. Doc hesitated about darting Thong with a tranquilizer, because he might fall into the pool. The trainer stood on the observation deck, close enough to check out Thongtrii. This time, he saw fear in the elephant's eyes.

Barkman decided he would be safe going into the yard, given the male's painful limp. Steel poles surrounded the only shade tree in the yard to keep the elephants from knocking it down. He saw that he would be safe if he could squeeze between the steel poles. The elephant couldn't reach far enough in to grab him.

Doc reluctantly approved the plan, saying, "OK, I trust your judgment, but I'm standing close by with the gun." He wouldn't hesitate to use the stun gun if Thongtrii made any aggressive moves toward Barkman.

"I'm OK. My plan should work," Paul answered. "The animal is in agony and desperate for relief."

Even though Barkman had been gone for nearly nine months, he and the elephant had been together since Thongtrii was two years old. Together, they had been through several moves and, despite the devastating attack, had created a close bond. An animal will acknowledge his trainer as the one who provides direction, food, and affection, and Barkman felt confident relying on their history. Barkman could see the pain, but a hurt animal can be unpredictable. Still, he couldn't ignore the suffering Thongtrii. It was his responsibility to remove the nail, and so he set out a plan.

With his eyes on the pained mammal, he slipped into the yard and eased his way to the tree, maneuvering his slender body inside the poles. Then he called Thongtrii to him. The injured male hobbled over with slow, painful steps, the distress showing in his eyes. He avoided touching down on the foot with the spike in it.

Once he reached the tree, Barkman gave the command, "Lift." Standing on three feet, the elephant raised his injured foot. Barkman put his hand under the ankle and lifted it to the pole, where he had a better hold. Examining the area where the spike went through the skin, he saw it was red, indicating it may be infected. Paul gave it a tender touch and Thong's foot flinched. Flashbacks of the attack popped into his memory—same animal, now double the pain. But he realized that he had no choice. It was his job to remove the spike.

He gently wrapped his hand around the spike's head and pulled. It barely moved. A second time, he braced his foot against the bars and, taking a firmer hold on the spike's head, he pulled, giving it a strong jerk. The spike finally slid out.

At that point, the keeper decided it was safe to walk the male back to his room while Doc stood ready with his gun. He eased himself between the iron bars and stepped into the open ground. The injured male didn't move; he hesitated until his trainer called his name.

"Thongtrii, come." Thongtrii started to follow but continued to hobble on three legs, unaware that the spike was out.

As they walked back to the barn, Doc rolled a bottle of betadine, a soothing antiseptic, to Barkman. Standing in the barn, the elephant keeper again ordered, "Lift." Paul reached under the raised foot to spray the wound. Then when Thongtrii put his foot down, he felt relief and realized it didn't hurt anymore. At that moment, his eyes changed from fear to his everyday dangerous look.

Suddenly, Paul realized the male was between him and the escape door; he had a sense of déjà vu. His heart started to race, his breathing shortened, and he felt his neck turning red.

Oh, no, here we go again. No! he told himself. Stay calm. You can't let him sense fear in you.

Then, the most amazing thing happened. Thongtrii looked at his keeper, then at the door. He stepped back, as if to say, "I'll give you this one."

Paul realized the male had allowed him to leave, but that was probably the last time. Taking no chances, he vowed never to be caught in the maturing male's room alone again.

Much later, when I asked Barkman about his relationship with Doc Chaffee, his eyes teared up, and he spoke with great fondness. "Doc was always in the right place at the right time. When things went wrong, he was there. I never made him mad. I knew what to do and what not to do. I never did anything without checking with him first, but Doc gave me plenty of leeway."

Barkman's primary purpose was to relieve Doc from worrying about the elephant barn. He trusted his keeper to watch over everything. "Doc gave me confidence in myself. He had high expectations. He did not tell you, but one felt it."

"Sometimes, I would see him after I had done something that worked. I'd be all proud, and Doc would say, 'Well, that's good. I'm glad you did that.' He would nod, you know, as if he expected it. That was typical of him."

When Barkman's dad died, he had so much he wanted to tell him, and he didn't get to say it. "When Doc died, I wanted to tell the man, 'You know, you gave me my start, my career, made me what I am.'"

Barkman thought of himself as just an elephant trainer, but then Doc found him, and his whole life changed. Before long, Barkman had a whole breeding herd and would lecture at conventions, because Doc encouraged him to become more than "just" an elephant trainer.

"Years ago, Doc told me, 'We have a million-dollar barn and expensive elephants. We need to have an experienced handler, and that is why I chose you. You can make this program work.' Doc gave me my life memories. He made my dreams come true. I am so proud of our work together."

CHAPTER 46

Nosey Meets Girlfriends Shaunzi and Kara

It was an exciting time around the zoo. Doc's decades-long dream to build a decent home for the beloved Nosey became a reality in 1982. She finally had plenty of space, a pool, and other amenities. For her, it had been thirty-three years of patient waiting for the simplest basics in decent housing. And in addition, she had Thongtrii, who stood by her side for three days while she adjusted to her new home. He provided the comfort and companionship she needed.

Doc had obtained his young bull elephant to fulfill his breeding zoo ambition, but now he had reason to worry about his decision after Barkman's attack. Thongtrii, as a three-year-old, had already exhibited erratic, threatening behaviors, in addition to nearly killing his trainer. Paul Barkman reassured Doc that he could handle the male. He would make sure that another elephant was always between him and the unpredictable one. The plan was in operation and the team was ready.

His dream to establish a breeding zoo led him to bring in a younger female. As soon as he got word that the Cristiani Brothers Circus in Florida was closing and had announced the sale of four female elephants, he flew into action.

Doc approached the Fresno City Council to approve funds needed to purchase not one, but two elephants from Cristiani. The total cost was $75,000, plus $4,500 for shipping. The *Fresno*

Bee sponsored a contest called "Name the Elephant," which raised $14,500. The prospect of having a baby elephant at the zoo captured everyone's imagination, and hopes ran high for breeding success.

Dr. Chaffee sent Barkman to Florida to select the best two of the four. Barkman still had a cast on one arm from Thongtrii's attack. The circus trainers pointed at him and shouted, "This is the man who works the bulls." Fussing over Barkman as a hero, they threw him a beach party.

Paul studied the circus elephants. Which two would fit in with Thongtrii and Nosey? At the farm, what he found upset him. The elephants were chained together in a line. Keepers threw grain to the line, but the largest elephant, Sheba, apparently took most of it, leaving little for the rest, their trunks reaching out for any scraps left over from the lead female. All four were in terrible shape and barely moving, with ribs outlining their sides and heads hanging in misery. Paul strained to select the best two of the pathetic four. He ultimately decided on Kara and Shaunzi.

Kara had been orphaned at three days old in 1975, when she was barely walking. Her herd had raided a banana plantation, where her mother had been shot. The other elephants ran off and abandoned the baby. Fortunately, a family bought her from the local elephant orphanage. She was about 400 pounds at the time, making her still a very young calf. She was bottle-raised for two years and then taken to Florida to join Cristiani's circus.

Shaunzi's records are vague, indicating only that she was born in a Thailand logging camp in 1970. Since her herd instincts were strong, she most likely grew up in a more normal setting than Kara's. After about a year, she was captured and sent to the United States for circus work until 1983.

Barkman boarded the two on the truck for the five-day trip across the country. Doc had alerted the press of their arrival. They were gathered around the transport truck when it backed up to the elephant barn ramp. The *Bee* photographer stood poised with his camera. He was anxious to make the next day's front page.

Shaunzi and Kara enjoying their new home.

Kara stepped out of the truck first. Doc gasped in shock at her fragile state. Her bones outlined her body, and her head hung in weakness. Paul quickly led the two to their rooms for time to recuperate. They needed to feel comfortable in their new space and know where to find food and water.

Doc kept bugging Paul to bring the two new females out for photos. "Are you ready yet, Paul? Isn't it time to bring them out?" The lead keeper relented for a short photo op, but their need to rest came first.

Paul planned the introductions between the two veteran animals and the two newcomers. First, Kara and Shaunzi went out on the yard by themselves. The next day, he cracked Nosey's door to let them interact with the matron. Then, they talked to each other through a slit in the door. Finally, the day arrived when they met in person, with just the big bar between them that separated the barn from the yard. Since there were no problems between the girls, they all went out on the yard together.

The next step was the male. Paul took the introduction slower with Thongtrii. His steel door was opened a crack to allow him to sniff the strangers. Each day the door opened a little more, until his trunk was able to examine the females' faces and bodies. After a week with no aggressive signs, they finally went out together.

Shaunzi and Kara had no access to a pool during their circus days. It had taken Nosey several weeks to build up the courage to get into the water. How long would it take the new girls? They watched Thongtrii and Nosey get in the water to swim every day and soon followed them in, as the four enormous mammals enjoyed themselves

Doc marveled at the changes in Nosey's life. She could finally throw dirt on her back, lie down, and take a swim. She had girlfriends to share her day. It was an exciting time at the zoo.

Doc's vision for an elephant breeding facility was never fulfilled. He observed breeding, but no babies were ever conceived. Doc received word that a German veterinarian specializing in elephant infertility was at the Washington Park Zoo in Portland, Oregon. He invited him to Fresno to test the elephants. In preparation, volunteers were recruited to desensitize Nosey to having people near her back quarters. Standing on a stool just behind her back leg, she was patted and rubbed. This was something of a stressful experience, as even a simple twitch of the foot could send one flying.

The specialist vet had a long instrument with a camera attached that he wove through Nosey's vagina. What he discovered was that Nosey was full of tumors, leaving no room for the sperm to travel. Apparently, instead of sloughing off her eggs during estrous, they attached and remained inside her. Doc's dream for baby elephants was dashed when it was subsequently discovered that none of the females could conceive.

It was a major disappointment for Doc that his vision for a breeding facility did not materialize. Still, he found satisfaction in knowing he created a space where the public could see and understand the relationship between the elephants, along with other species hosted at the zoo. By observing them, people could relate to their emotions of fear, protection, friendship, and loneliness, and realize that animals, like humans, can build intraspecies relationships. Anyone who has a pet recognizes that they are emotional beings. They respond to positive reinforcement and withdraw from abusive treatment, much as children.

The purpose of zoos is to bring the wilderness habitat into the civilized world, for people to learn about it and appreciate what we don't see. Each species has a purpose and an important niche in making the world function. Unfortunately, it is people who interfere with nature's complex web of relationships, and who then claim confusion when the flora and fauna react adversely.

CHAPTER 47

The Last of the Asian Elephants

Thongtrii had suffered most of his life from migraine headaches and an untreatable problem in his right front leg elbow. As a youngster, he had stepped on a nail buried in the dirt during construction. It became infected and continued to fester. He had been fitted with a special sock and an elephant-sized sandal to keep the foot clean. Following the attack on Barkman, the two had worked out a manageable relationship, but he continued to lead a troubled life. He inherited his father's genes of overgrowth, which led to his early death.

At age 13, weighing 9,000 pounds, he fell and could not get up. The consensus had been to euthanize him when he could no longer stand on his own. Thongtrii was put down in February of 1993.

The most noticeable changes occurred in Kara, who had arrived in Fresno in poor condition. Her keeper, Amber Talley, reminisced about her. "Kara was this funny little elephant who definitely had her own ideas and opinions about everything. She taught me that it's not the size of the elephant in the room, but the size of the attitude in the elephant. I don't know if it was because we were born in the same year, or that we both shared a stubborn side, but getting to know Kara for all that she was, was one of the greatest gifts I've ever experienced." Part of Kara's "attitude" was keeping the peace. She knew her role was to protect Barkman by creating a barrier between him and Thongtrii.

Good friends Nosey and Thongtrii.

Kara was euthanized in 2017. She had been receiving care and attention for osteoarthritis issues, including physical therapy, laser therapy, and anti-inflammatory medication. Elephants understand death and have their own grieving processes and rituals surrounding it, so Shaunzi was sent in to say goodbye to Shaunzi, her last remaining friend. Following Kara's death, Shaunzi was transferred to the Los Angeles Zoo to be in their herd.

But it was Nosey, who for decades was the heart of the zoo and mascot for the town, who stilled the hearts of thousands when word went out of her death. The air grew silent as each person grieved, remembering their memories and what she meant to them. Nosey died in November of 1993, three years and one month after Doc Chaffee. Like Thongtrii and Kara, Nosey's knees finally gave out on her. She is buried in an undisclosed spot on the grounds. The strong, resilient elephant keeper team confessed to tears flowing as they worked on her that day.

The Fresno Chaffee Zoo and Nosey were synonymous, and Doc and Nosey were intimately connected. He had ached for her, given her poor living conditions, and fought the City of Fresno for years for the funds to improve her habitat. That fight finally came to successful fruition in 1982, and she was able to enjoy the last ten years of her life in comfort. During Doc's last days, he expressed satisfaction that he changed the conditions for Nosey, which had been one of his primary goal as zoo director.

He reminisced about two major highlights with the beloved animal. First, was the day Nosey laid down on the ground of her new exhibit for a nap after years of standing on cement. Every day for the next ten years, she laid down for a nap on the soft dirt.

The other highlight was how, somewhat enviously, Doc had watched Barkman ride the female elephants, never dreaming he would ever have the chance. One day, Barkman waved Doc over to where he was working with Nosey. He commanded her to go down on a knee, then helped Doc step up and swing his leg over her neck. His eyes bulged in wonder as he said, "This is nothing like riding a horse." It was a long held dream come true.

Doc Chaffee riding Nosey.

CHAPTER 48

The Legacy of Dr. Paul Stanley Chaffee (1928-1990)

After coming to California from Michigan, Doc Chaffee operated the McKinley Pet Clinic for ten years. When his landlord invited him to assist at the zoo, he immediately jumped at the chance. From 1960–1965 he served as a consultant to the zoo.

The zoo's collection of wildlife challenged him to open his books and pursue his studies beyond domestic pets. There were problems he needed to address. The zoo animals were not breeding and died as babies, or later from poor health. When he discovered the zoo maintained no files, he brought in every animal to create health and dietary records. They received vaccinations and diet changes, which resulted in immediate improvements. Adding shaded areas during Fresno's hot summers and heat lamps during cold, foggy winters made their lives more comfortable.

In 1965, Doc became the Fresno Zoo's Director/Veterinarian, which at last gave him the authority to make critical changes. As leader, he had to deal with personnel issues, which he found difficult. But receiving the City's bare-bones budget sent him into shock. The budget covered basic food and care, but left little for improvements. He hoped for no unexpected emergencies. However, always the protagonist, he looked outward for funding and engaged the Fresno Zoological Society to develop a workforce of volunteers and raise funds. He went anywhere and everywhere to share his vision in an effort to build a loyal base of financial support. He had a reputation for stretching a dollar a mile.

In 1970, Doc's master plan emphasized quality over quantity in exhibits. The public's complaints about the cages, small enclosures, and inhumane conditions were addressed. He exchanged cages for open-air exhibits and replaced cement for dirt. Climbing apparatus and playground equipment were added for activity options. Keepers created ways for the animals to search for food that imitated the wild. He established an education program for training volunteers as guides. Introducing Brucie the Chimp to school children and stirring up Rotary meetings was his escape for fun.

The first Zoo Docent graduates were ready to lead tours and give classroom talks the following year. As Doc got busier, he turned the Zoo Mobile program over to the trained docents. Residents at senior facilities and school children loved the opportunity to touch reptiles, birds, and insects. The personal interactions with the animals and the docents also produced strong community support for the zoo.

Voter approval of the 1978 Proposition 13 forced the zoo to reshape its thinking. Doc realized he had to recruit more volunteers to fill the shortages in funding. He scheduled community meetings with slide shows at school cafeterias, and he gave guided tours and lectures educating the public on the importance of proper care and suitable exhibits. His sly, off-the-cuff wit had his audiences engaged and laughing. He had a way of making everything fun, and people clamored to be with him.

Dr. Chaffee was a popular local, national, and international lecture circuit speaker. Every year, at least one elephant zookeeper in the US was injured, maimed, or killed by one of their charges. Safety procedures were required to protect lives. The AZA selected Doc to address an openly hostile elephant zookeeper conference to promote the AZA's new safety guidelines. His calm, soft-mannered approach emphasized the need to implement noncontact

Doctor Paul Chaffee.

handling of their elephants. He reminded them that lawsuits could halt all elephant handling. He managed to ease the resistance and won many of them over to the changes.

Locally, Doc didn't hesitate to speak up for the protection of the world's vanishing wildlife. He spoke against the practice of toxic agricultural sprays, including DDT, which had tremendously reduced bald eagle and condor populations. He didn't make friends in the farming community, but his concern for animal protection led him to speak out where he saw a need.

Many Fresnans took advantage of his numerous safaris to Africa. They caught his passion and returned as dedicated supporters of the Zoo Society's efforts. The staff, on the other hand, learned to take vacations while he was on safari, knowing that he would come home with new plans and projects for them.

Doc believed that experiencing wildlife led to a better understanding of the wonder of nature. His first major exhibit was a walk-through aviary that brought man and birds together. In 1978, the first of its kind reptile house was designed using computers, before computers were commonly used. Each compartment was programmed for seasonal changes, temperature, and daylight. As a result, rare and endangered reptiles were born in captivity. It received an AZA Outstanding Exhibit of the Year award and still ranks as a top reptile exhibit.

Doc's travels to the South American rainforest and the destruction he saw there led him to replicate a Fresno version. The resulting mixed-species walk-through exhibit, designed around an existing Shamel ash tree, included an iguana, an alligator, and a golden lion tamarin, in addition to a host of beautiful birds.

Perhaps Doc's most ambitious goal was to develop a captive elephant breeding program. Worldwide, both Asian and African elephants are threatened by poachers, who are after their tusks. Poaching had reduced elephant numbers by nearly half in recent decades. Having seen the magnificent animals in Africa, Chaffee's heart felt compelled to do something.

His vision for Nosey's new enclosure included a breeding herd. "A person can't appreciate something he doesn't know anything about," said Doc. Although the zoo had three females and one male, breeding efforts produced no offspring. Unfortunately, the exhibit was too small, and only the bigger zoos had bulls. Nonetheless, the foresighted elephant breeding program drew the interest of the Discovery Channel, which filmed a program highlighting his work. Too sick at the time to join the crew, he watched their program from home.

Doc's commitment to serving the public came in many forms. In 1980, Dr. Chaffee became President of the American Association of Zoos and Aquariums, a 3,000-member national association dedicated to improving animal habitats and the survival of wildlife. Leading up to that office, Doc served on every AZA committee as chairman. As soon as he joined in 1965, he realized the need to meet with other zoo veterinarians in the state. He formed and served as the first president of California Zoo Directors, CA Zoo Veterinarians, and the national Zoo Veterinarians. He accepted a coveted invitation to join the World AZA organization. In 1989, the AZA dedicated its highest award, The Marlin Perkins Award, to Paul Chaffee for his years of dedicated service. A vacancy opened for vice-president of AZA. Doc was voted to replace the outgoing vice-president, setting him up to be president for the second time in 1991.

Under the guiding eye of Dr. Paul Chaffee, the Fresno Chaffee Zoo was transformed from an undeveloped, minimal facility to one of national and international acclaim. It took twenty-five years for Doc to accomplish this. Sadly, his life was cut short by melanoma cancer at age 62. Yet, he left behind a legacy that created the foundation for

Doc on safari.

Fresno Chaffee Zoo's exemplary wildlife spaces that we enjoy today.

He passed away on October 20, 1990, but not before the City of Fresno, the Rotary Club, and the Zoo Society honored him by renaming his beloved zoo the Fresno Chaffee Zoological Gardens. His friends flew in from across the United States to share in the recognition.

We will always cherish our fond memories of this amazing person. A common midmorning sight was the white-bearded man in his familiar khaki safari shirt and pants strolling through the zoo to check on his friends. Nosey the elephant reached her trunk out to search for his hidden snacks as he gave her a loving pat. Mudder and Fodder strolled toward the fence for their morning rhino head rub. The largest open-mouth greetings came from Bubbles and Bulgy. Doc reached in to rub the bare jaw between the hippos' molars and canines. He often tossed in a head of lettuce as an extra treat.

The topper was the ostrich's hula dance mating greeting. Swinging, swaying, and shaking, the flightless bird showed his love for his caretaker.

He never failed to check on his human crew, as well, always inquiring about their families by name. What struck his staff was Doc's sincerity; he didn't offer passing comments but real interest.

Doc Chaffee was held in the highest esteem for his kindness and generosity. His goal was to leave the world a better place than he found it. All who knew him acknowledged he achieved his goal.

CHAPTER 49

And then there Were Two Births

Some consider the Fresno Chaffee Zoo's African elephant breeding program to be its crown jewel. But the road to get there was long and arduous.

"Dear *Fresno Bee*, my name is Angel and I am nine," wrote Angel Arellano in her letter to the newspaper. "I heard that the Chaffee Zoo is having money problems. I am very worried for the animals. I think if everybody in Fresno gave $1 to the Chaffee Zoo it would help a lot. Here's my dollar."

The *Fresno Bee* published the letter, written on Thanksgiving Day, 2003, by a girl with a soft spot for stray cats. After listening to three generations of elders bemoan the decline in funding for the zoo, Angel grabbed her aunt's stationery, which, appropriately, was bordered in animals, and scrawled a letter that changed the future of the city's much-loved zoo.

After years of unsuccessful efforts to fundraise for the zoo, Angel stirred the hearts of the residents. As a result, Pelco (a large, Fresno-based concern) manager David McDonald volunteered his staff to lead the fundraising efforts for Measure Z, which would institute a one-tenth of one percent sales tax in Fresno County to fund the zoo. McDonald and the many other Measure Z supporters were successful in getting the measure on the ballot, and voters enthusiastically passed it by a 73 to 27 percent margin. It's passage set a new trajectory for the zoo.

A private nonprofit entity, the Chaffee Zoo Corporation was formed on January 1, 2006, and was given full control of zoo operations. No longer constrained by city bureaucracy, the zoo could now be run more efficiently. A separate Zoo Authority Board oversaw Measure Z spending to ensure it met the legal requirements of the Measure Z sales tax. Plans long stockpiled in many people's mental storerooms were at last brought out to the light. Board meetings bubbled with excitement over the possibilities.

Scott Barton was hired as zoo director in 2009. His first order of business was to complete the Sea Lion Cove exhibit before Measure Z went up for vote renewal in five years. The citizens needed living proof that the taxes collected by the measure was worth it. All doubt was cast aside when the award-winning Sea Lion Cove exhibit opened in 2012 to raving reviews. Record attendance followed, as people flooded through the front gate to see the playful sea lions.

Angel Arellano, now a 20-year-old college student, supported the renewal of Measure Z in 2014 by pointing to the Sea Lion Cove exhibit. "This is the kind of stuff that would happen if we passed the second Measure Z, these big exhibits that are being built," she said.

Angel couldn't have been more correct, as construction on the massive African Adventure exhibit was well underway. Toronto elephant keepers Vernon and Nicole Presley accepted Fresno's invitation to join the Chaffee Zoo staff. Toronto Zoo had sent all their elephants to a sanctuary and left Vernon searching for a new position. The couple packed their two kids and worldly goods into the car and waved goodbye to family and friends in Canada as they headed off for an exciting new adventure. The Measure Z-funded African elephant exhibit, then under construction, excited them, and they looked forward to working at a well-funded, forward-moving zoo.

On October 15, 2015, Columbus Zoo director and safari leader Jack Hanna flew to Fresno to celebrate the opening of the highly anticipated African Adventure. He came to honor the memory of his AZA friend and former colleague Dr. Paul Chaffee on the fruition of his longtime dream to provide a home for African elephants. It took twenty-five years, but it had become a reality.

African elephants are uncommon in zoos. They are the largest animals walking the Earth. What's amazing is to come upon a herd of these 14,000-pound, gray-brown mammals emerging from the forest without a sound. Their large, Africa-continent-shaped ears fan the air to sweep away the heat or to give fair warning to the enemy. Their long trunk is an amazing multi-use tool. It smells, eats, sucks water, sends messages, takes peanuts, and tears out trees. Don't get in the way of their well-worn path! This 14-foot-tall block of muscle is impenetrable. The mammoth can push anything out of its way, including a safari touring jeep filled with excited, camera-touting tourists. The African elephant can easily tip over this vehicle using his long, ivory tusks, upending its passengers.

But Vernon felt up to the assignment. The first two African elephants, Amy and Betts, had arrived together in May of 2015, prior to the exhibit's opening, from Riddle's Elephant and Wildlife Sanctuary. Betts, ten years old, was born in the sanctuary. Amy, 30, was imported from Africa when she was rescued from a culling. The safari leader contacted a Colorado rancher friend, asking him to adopt the elephant until he could find a permanent placement. Cowboy Bob, also famous as the Marlboro man, agreed to adopt the animal, unaware it was an elephant until the truck arrived. He fell in love with Amy and treated her like one of his horses, until she outgrew his ever-expanding trailers. From there she went to a circus, until it folded from bankruptcy, followed by Riddle's sanctuary. Amy received daily physical therapy to ease joint issues. Cowboy Bob continued to follow Amy and sneaked in several Chaffee Zoo visits before she was euthanized in December, 2017.

The Chaffee Zoo's African elephant male, Vus'Musi, was born at the San Diego Zoo and came soon after the females. He was 13 years old, but, unfortunately, no offspring came from the trio. Excitement grew with news that two new females would soon arrive, bringing hope that offspring could be in the future. A mother-daughter pair from the Dallas Zoo came in October 2018. Dallas Zoo had been part of an elephant rescue operation in Swaziland in southern Africa. Their native-born elephant genes were valuable for preserving the endangered species, and breeding was encouraged by the AZA. Mother Nolwazi was approximately 24 years old and her daughter, Amahle, was nine.

Nolwazi's bossy personality intimidated Vus'Musi and no breeding with her occurred. He bred with Amahle once, but nothing else was observed. After four years and no further activity, Vus'Musi was returned to San Diego Zoo.

A male named Mabu came from Reid Park Zoo in Tucson, Arizona. Amahle, now 15, was ready for breeding. He arrived and wasted no time getting the mother-daughter pair pregnant, breeding with both within two weeks. He had lots of experience, having sired a dozen or more previous calves. Then the twenty-two-month calendar countdown began.

Vernon and the elephant team began intense preparations for the double births. Training for the females was increased. They prepared for all potential problems during the birthing. As the time drew closer, daily testing of the pregnant females' progesterone levels was conducted. A drop would indicate a pending birth. Because the levels showed no change, the staff waited to set up the 24/7 watch.

Feeling comfortable that Nolwazi's time was not imminent, Vernon flew to Milwaukee for an elephant conference. Once there, he got antsy after she showed a slight drop in progesterone. He had waited twenty years to experience the birth of an elephant and he did not intend to miss this one, so he flew home early.

On Thursday evening before he went to bed, he checked the elephant barn's remote camera on his phone. Nothing showed. At midnight, he checked the camera again. This time there appeared to be some activity, dust stirring from movement. Jumping out of bed, he dashed to the zoo to be greeted by a newborn just standing up. Baby number one, a male, was born on August 16, 2024, at 12:34 a.m., according to the camera. Nolwazi walked around her newborn, then used her foot to gently help it stand up on all four feet.

Baby Thando.

The baby immediately tried to nurse but was a little too short. His trunk could not reach her nipple. The staff shoveled in extra sand until he was high enough to suckle. An embedded scale indicated he weighed 200 pounds.

Amahle gave birth to a second male on August 26 at 9:28 in the morning, when the staff was on duty and able to observe the historic occasion. This was Amahle's first birth. Her mother, Nolwazi, and her halfbrother stayed close by, lending support, but did not interfere with her. The birth canal route is complicated. The fetus has to travel about five feet from the uterus, then up over the hip bones and out the vagina, falling to the ground.

Mother cleaned up the grayish newborn and then let him rest. Slowly, she got down on her elbows and scooted toward the calf. She placed her tusks and head under his body, helping him to stand. He was a little bigger than his halfbrother, weighing in at 173 pounds. He began to nurse right away. His Dumbo-size ears flapped as he gained strength in his legs, twirling around.

The entire community was on alert. The elation was palpable. Word spread through the air like a whirlwind, picking up steam until one and all were wound up with joy. They couldn't get enough of the treasured pictures coming out of the elephant barn. Not one but two African elephant births. A miracle.

The Fresno Chaffee Zoo, during its ninety-five years, has been recognized for breeding rare reptiles and adding to the populations of endangered species such as the white rhinoceros. But the births of two African elephant males within two weeks was one for the history books.

It is a credit to visionaries who are not afraid to break through tradition and reach for the stars. Doc Chaffee had viewed the future through different-colored glasses. He may have been laughed at to think that a San Joaquin Valley farming community zoo would ever breed elephants, much less the rarer African elephants. But that's how dreams come true.

A nine-year-old girl with the perfect name, Angel, and her letter to the *Bee*, were the catalyst that finally made it happen.

Thando and Davu frolicking on the grass.

APPENDIX

Burleigh Lockwood, the Bat Lady

Burleigh Lockwood's life has been dedicated to learning and teaching. As a respected expert in her field and a gifted communicator, equally at ease with adults as with preschoolers, she has been an invited lecturer at national conferences and zoos throughout the United States.

Many words can be used to describe Burleigh Lockwood: scientist, naturalist, biofacts collector, environmentalist, mentor, teacher, researcher, writer, speaker, inspiration. There are too many dimensions to her to narrow it down to one outstanding attribute. However, "Bat Lady" is the name she responds to most often. There is a long history as to why. As the Fresno Chaffee Zoo's biologist prepares to retire after forty-three years, she was invited to share her story in her own words.

§ § § § §[1]

I became a wildlife biologist when I was three years old. I started going out into the yard and watching. I got down on my belly and watched ants build their roads. I learned to mess with their little brains as I drew a finger across one of their roads and watched the confusion that happened. I took caterpillars and worms inside to my mom for identification. She was squeamish and could not help me much. I began cataloging life as I saw it, remembering what I had seen before and what was new.

---

1. The text that follows was provided courtesy of Burleigh Lockwood.

When I began to read, I began to collect animal stories and wildlife books. I received a three-volume set, *Mammals of the World*, and had it memorized by the end of fourth grade. I won an award in the fourth grade for teaching my fellow schoolmates about rattlesnakes and the look-alike gopher snakes. I had picked up my first snake, a kingsnake, on the way to my second-grade class and was well acquainted with snakes. I got in trouble for having a large gopher snake in my desk in sixth grade.

My dad being in the Navy, we moved a lot, and I learned a lot about different habitats during our travels. It was natural for me to go into biology as I entered college. I attended Cal Poly, San Luis Obispo, during the late 60s and early 70s, with a major in ecology and a minor in chemistry. I had to work to pay my way and had a seasonal job with California Fish and Game, doing the first field study of the Blunt-Nosed Leopard Lizard (*Gambelia silus*) on the Carrizo Plain, in preparation for that grassland habitat to become a national monument. The study lasted two seasons, and included capturing, measuring, sexing, and mapping each lizard encountered. I also took field notes on any giant Kangaroo Rats (*Dipodomys ingens*) and Kit Foxes (*Vulpes macrotis*) I sighted.

As I approached graduation, I had to decide on a senior project. Cal Poly's motto is "Learn by Doing," so, in order to graduate, a student had to complete a yearlong research project and paper in the manner of a master's thesis. I sorted through potential subjects and settled on bats because I like to study things that other people do not like. At that time, no one liked bats. Even my advisor questioned my selection.

After consideration, my advisor suggested a possible study site, the old adobe on Turri Ranch. Every weekend for a year I went to Turri Ranch, about ten miles from San Luis Obispo, to study the Pallid Bat (*Antrozous pallidus*), one of the few species of bats in the world that can take off from the ground . . . with prey. The roost site was in an upstairs bedroom of the adobe farmhouse that had been built in 1850. The downstairs had been relegated to the storage of cattle feed, fertilizer, and equipment for the ranch after Mr. Turri built a new ranch house for his new bride. The adobe was amazingly well insulated, the walls being about two feet thick, so the upstairs roost site (one of the two bedrooms) kept a consistent plus or minus 60° Fahrenheit.

I had been twice into the adobe's upstairs, during the day, to locate the bats and make a plan. There was no doubt that bats were in residence, for under the center beam was a pile of bat guano the size of an eight-foot table. I looked up and saw their cute little-dog faces peering down with large black eyes at this intruder. I could also smell them, one of the two bat species I can now identify by smell. When disturbed and nervous, the pallid bats emit (from a gland across the muzzle) the odor of skunk. I quietly looked around, formulated a plan, and took my leave, planning to return at night. This study turned out to be my introduction to how truly *un*scary bats are. The only time one ever offered to bite was when I picked it up.

At the time of the Turri Ranch study, there was no way to find or follow bats as they flew. The roost site had to be known. It was serendipity to find a roost site. Luckily, the fidelity of a bat species to a given roost site is high, mostly because there are so few sites that offer their very demanding specifications for temperature and humidity. Bat detector equipment was not to become readily available for over a decade. Human hearing can seldom detect sounds as high as 20 kilohertz (kHz), but bat detectors address this problem. The Pettersson Ultrasound Detector is a rather simple machine that converts the ultrasonic echolocation calls of the bats to a frequency audible to the human ear (as high as 150 kHz down to our average high of 15 kHz). Bat detector units now are highly sophisticated, computerized sonogram and bat species identifiers.

At Cal Poly, I became well known on campus as the Bat Lady, sharing my findings with fellow students. Bats do not usually come to mind when one is thinking of cute, cuddly animals. In the sky, they look like weird birds, but they are the only truly flying mammals.

Although millions of bats might live together, most species have no leader and little obvious social structure. They zip around at night, doing their insectivorous or frugivorous or pollinating thing, and spend the day sleeping upside down. Seventy-five percent of the world's 1300-plus bat species are insectivores, including all of the bats in North America. Fruit bats *must* live in tropical and subtropical forests, where there is ripe fruit somewhere every day. The only time that any bats in North America are not insectivorous is when the cactus, agave, and other succulents of Arizona and New Mexico are in bloom. Several species of nectar-feeding bats move north from Mexico for the flowering season. After the flower show, the bats return to Mexico.

Many bat species have outsized ears and funny projections on their noses, features that help to exaggerate their alien reputations. These are, however, adaptations that facilitate the echolocation calls on which their navigation and prey-finding abilities depend. Regardless, the world's bats are animals on which we humans truly depend, as they—depending on the species—eat tons of insect pests (including millions of the mosquitoes that plague us), pollinate a great many plants, and disperse the seeds of many tropical trees and shrubs.

Leaving San Luis Obispo, I matriculated to California State University, Fresno, to begin working on a master's degree in wildlife biology, again studying bats. This time, the plan was to investigate the distribution of the twenty bat species across Fresno and Madera counties. While attending Fresno State, I met fellow student Susan Anderson, who was working on a double major in business and biology, with a view of stepping into the new Education Department at Fresno Chaffee Zoo (then called The Fresno Zoo, and Roeding Park Zoo prior to that). Susan was having difficulty with her Mammals lab, and I began helping her learn the "cheap tricks" for remembering the identities of various skulls and such. We became good friends.

In 1981, the zoo director, Dr. Paul Chaffee, hired Susan as the first full-time Zoo Educator. She was to establish summer camp programs, among other education ideas. In the meantime, I was working for the US Forest Service as a wildlife biologist. In early 1982, the zoo's plans were in full swing for summer camp. These were to be week-long camps for elementary-aged children from the greater Fresno area. In spring of 1982, the lady who was helping Susan with curricula development and processing early registrations suddenly plunked her binders and other materials onto Susan's desk and said, "I quit." In desperation, Susan called me, pleading for a helping hand.

I was in the midst of a five-year field study on the California Spotted Owl (*Strix occidentalis*), working four ten-hour days per week for the Forest Service, but I thought I could work out a schedule. Susan and I began to build an education program that was to become a very successful endeavor. At the end of my owl study, I quit the Forest Service and hired on at the zoo, with stipends from the Fresno Zoo Society. Our two-decade working relationship was mutually beneficial. I was officially hired by Fresno Chaffee Zoo as a biologist and full-time educator in 1993. I was considered as rehired in 2006, when the zoo became Fresno Chaffee Zoo, Incorporated.

During the later years with Susan, the zoo started a teacher training program for Fresno, Madera, and Central Unified teachers. I and a fellow biologist taught teachers how to teach science in an exciting and engaging way. At the behest of their districts, teachers would come for an intensive day of professional development.

As the department naturalist, I honed my story-telling techniques and began doing speaking engagements in school classrooms by invitation of the teachers. Having done extensive studies of lizards, kangaroo rats, and the fish of the San Joaquin River Basin for Fish and Game, and fish habitat surveys and the spotted owl study for the Forest Service, owls and bats became my most frequently requested topics of presentation, but plenty of other topics were often selected.

Burleigh Lockwood captivating her young audience.

During my presentations about owls, I focused on the Spotted Owl, but addressed all nine of the owl species found in the Sierra Nevada at that time. The Forest Service study assignment had been, "Find out how many breeding pairs of spotted owls there were in the Sierra National Forest." That meant covering the entire mixed conifer and fir forest areas, with calling stations set up half a mile apart. Ultimately, the study's range extended into the lower elevation oak woodland areas as well. Studying owls is a challenge. There was no readily available GPS system at the time, but even so, GPS only tells you where *you* are. It will not track the owls. The study used topography maps and compass triangulation. I had to learn to mimic all nine owl contact calls (their hoots) and can still mimic most of them. I love to teach my audience to hoot, but nothing makes me laugh more than the stunned response I get in reaction to my very loud rendition of the Barn Owl's screech.

To answer a lingering question, yes, we found them all. With night drives and hikes to call-stations, mapping by flashlight, and

rigorous day-time follow-ups to find nesting sites, we found thir-
ty-six breeding pairs and their nests. I have become the Chaffee
Zoo's Owl Lady as well as Fresno's Bat Lady.

Through the Zoo's growing Education Department, I advertised presentations on "Any Natural History Topic to Any Age,
Preschool to Adult." Donning subject-themed T-shirts and mis-
matched earrings, I matched my various Zoo Talks to sundry audiences, which soon included docent groups at other zoos as well as
docent training for Fresno Chaffee Zoo. For the docents, and any
zoo staff that was interested, I have written fact sheets on all of the
animals that have been in the zoo collection since I started, back
in 1982, as well as information pages on many related subjects. I
have designed quizzes for self-education among the docents and
education staff. I have also been responsible for the curation of what
is called our Biofacts (**biological artifacts**) Collection, such as skulls
and other skeletal material, taxidermy mounts, skins, feathers, nests,
scat (that's "poop" in elementary school lingo) and any other form
of animal sign that helps students visualize and understand the animal world. Curation involves collecting and preparing specimens,
caring for them, and repairing them as necessary. Animals do not
live forever, even if we want them to, so when a zoo animal died, we
did not "throw it away." I would prepare the skulls and what other
material the Education Department could use. After their deaths,
those animals continued teaching.

Hopefully, the staff, docents, and teachers have benefited from
my knowledge of ecology, environmental science, and the inter-
twining lifeways within the world's many habitats. I have always
told my various audiences that, if they ask me a question that I cannot answer, I love it, because it makes me go and learn something
new. Even though I am retiring (at age 80) from my forty-three-
year tenure in Chaffee Zoo's Education Department, I shall not
end my quest for continued learning and sharing a love of science.

Acknowledgments

I want to acknowledge the people who shared their stories and knowledge of the Fresno Chaffee Zoo's history with me in the research for this book. Lorraine LoStracco and I worked together for five years reading, researching, interviewing, and writing these stories. Thanks to Mary Swanson, Kim Cook, Betty Barkman, Paul Barkman, Joan Newcomb, Linda Cover, Denise Chaffee, Nicole Presley, Vernon Presley, Alysia Martinelli, Sally Becker, Andra Christianson, Lisa Condoian, Marcia Dobbs, C. A. Sharp, Joan Pratt, and Gary Shapiro for their insights behind the scenes. There are many others, too many to name, but their support and encouragement was appreciated.

This community is proud of their contributions to the history of the zoo. It is *their* zoo. They have supported it, not big money corporations. Long-time supporters shared their memories for Nosey the elephant, often shedding tears. She was personal to them. The responses to my stories in the zoo docent's newsletters encouraged me to keep writing. Many groups have sat through my PowerPoint presentations and shared more information. The seven children's books I wrote—illustrated by Ernie Hergenroeder—allowed me to meet fans of the old zoo. With it came more stories of apes throwing "stuff" at them or Nosey stealing a sweater, twirling it before stomping and tossing it into the air, finishing off the performance by swallowing it.

Primarily, the purpose behind the writing of this book was to maintain Doctor Paul Chaffee's legacy. He was a visionary who inherited cement floors and cages and turned them into natural habitats that reflected how the animals lived in the wild. He wanted the public to share his love for God's creatures. Although gone too soon, he left behind his conceptual blueprints for future growth. Doc would be bursting with pride over the two baby elephants, a dream come true.

A special thank you goes to my editor, Kent Sorsky, who patiently walked me through the process of editing and completing the stories. It never would have happened without him.

The flamingo habitat, first established in the 1950s, is one of Fresno Chaffee Zoo's oldest exhibits.

About the Author

Jean Chaffee and friend Chisulo. *Photo courtesy of Jean Chaffee.*

Long-time Fresno resident **Jean Chaffee** spent her early years on a dairy farm in Madera surrounded by animals. Following graduation from Fresno State and Pacific College, Jean spent twenty-six years as a teacher and school principal.

Jean has two children and four grandchildren, with whom she has shared many traveling adventures, from camping in Yosemite to African safaris. Dr. Paul Chaffee introduced her to the world of wildlife. She trained as a Rainforest Ranger for the opening of the Chaffee Zoo Rainforest in 1988. Her love of the zoo has continued with the culmination of seven children's books based on the animals at the zoo: *Nosey the Elephant; Moja the Lion; Azak Learns to Read; Bulgy, Bubbles and Babies; Longo the Giraffe; Nosey's Big Move;* and *Bosco the Wild One.*

In 1997, she retired from education to research and compile a one-hundred-year history of Fresno Chaffee Zoo, from the Roedings to the African Savannah to the Kingdoms of Asia. Now a Zoo Docent Emeritus, she enjoys sharing her passion for the zoo.